# Communicating the UX Vision

## 13 Anti-Patterns That Block Good Ideas

# Communicating the UX Vision

## 13 Anti-Patterns That Block Good Ideas

MARTINA HODGES-SCHELL
JAMES O'BRIEN

AMSTERDAM • BOSTON • HEIDELBERG • LONDON
NEW YORK • OXFORD • PARIS • SAN DIEGO
SAN FRANCISCO • SINGAPORE • SYDNEY • TOKYO

Morgan Kaufmann is an imprint of Elsevier

**Acquiring Editor:** Todd Green
**Editorial Project Manager:** Lindsay Lawrence
**Project Manager:** Stalin Viswanathan
**Designer:** Matthew Limbert

Morgan Kaufmann is an imprint of Elsevier
225 Wyman Street, Waltham, MA 02451, USA

**British Library Cataloguing-in-Publication Data**
A catalogue record for this book is available from the British Library

**Library of Congress Cataloging-in-Publication Data**
A catalog record for this book is available from the Library of Congress

ISBN: 978-0-12-420197-2

For information on all Morgan Kaufmann publications
visit our website at www.mkp.com

For Ed and my parents. You are my inspiration.

For Melissa, and for Mum and Dad.

# CONTENTS

Foreword  xxiii

Acknowledgments  xxv

Introduction  xxvii

## 1 SPEAKING DIFFERENT LANGUAGES  3

Summary  9

The "Speaking Different Languages"
  anti-pattern  9

You know you're in it when...  10

Patterns  10

  Stakeholder safari  11

  The meeting before the meeting and the
    meeting after the meeting  12

  The meeting before the meeting  13

  The meeting after the meeting  14

  Lowering the wall  14

  Step back  16

  Play it back  16

If others inflict this anti-pattern
on you  17

Terminology explained  18

Takeaways  21

## 2  HAVING DIFFERENT KPIs  23

How organizations measure success  24

Intrinsic motivation  25

When KPIs clash  26

Summary  28

The "Having Different KPIs" anti-pattern  28

You know you're in it when ...  29

Patterns  29

Diligent discovery  29

Tu casa es mi casa  30

Don't butt heads  30

If others inflict this anti-pattern
on you  31

Don't try to handle organizational change
singlehanded  31

Terminology explained  36

Reference  36

Takeaways  37

## 3  NOT EMBRACING EVERYONE'S GOALS  39

Onto the right path  40

The sore thumb paradox  42

Summary  43

The "Not Embracing Everyone's Goals"
  anti-pattern 43

You know you're in it when... 43

Patterns 44

  Be the canonical source of why 44

  Active agreement 44

  Consciously internalize 45

  Stakeholders are people, too 46

  Present in context 46

  Co-design 46

If others inflict this anti-pattern
  on you 48

Terminology explained 49

References 49

Takeaways 50

## 4 PRESENTING WITHOUT CONTEXTUALIZING 53

Common assets for providing context 55

Telling the story of UX 61

Getting good feedback 63

Summary 64

The "Presenting Without Contextualizing"
  anti-pattern 64

You know you're in it when... 64

How to break the anti-pattern 65

Patterns 65

  Prepare for presentation 65

  Be present to present 66

*Casting* feedback  66

Set scope expectations  67

Actively confirm understanding  67

The Half-Silvered Mirror  68

Tell them what you told them  68

If others inflict this anti-pattern on you  68

Terminology explained  70

Additional resources  72

References  72

Takeaways  73

5  BEING IN THE ROOM BUT NOT PRESENT  75

What is your job?  77

New software development processes,
    new collaboration models  78

Collaborating in iterative
    environments  82

Focus in an open-plan world  83

Summary  86

The "Being in the room but not present"
    anti-pattern  86

You'll know you're in it when ...  86

Patterns – how to be a better collaborator  87

Push for in-person access  87

The stenographers' pattern  87

The life in mono pattern  88

Carve out a space  88

The scary face pattern  89

Mind-body considerations  89

Sensible scheduling  90

Simplify your tools  90

Turn off the information firehose  90

The rear view mirror pattern  90

What to do when someone is locking you out of their silo  91

Terminology explained  95

References  95

Takeaways  96

6   NOT HAVING A CONSISTENT
    DESIGN LANGUAGE  99

Say what?  100

Buzzword Bingo  101

A consistent design language  104

If you liked it, you should have put a label on it  105

A note on labeling files  106

What do you do?  108

A step too far  108

Summary  109

The "Not Having A Consistent Design Language" anti-pattern  109

You know you're in it when...  110

Patterns  110

Be mindful of your language  110

Put a label on it  110

Present in context  110

Own the process  111

Label police 111

Buzzword bingo swear jar 111

Playback 111

Make a toolkit 111

If others subject you to this anti-pattern 112

Terminology explained 114

Reference 114

Takeaways 115

7 THROWING DELIVERABLES OVER THE FENCE 117

Tearing down the fence 118

Of fences and other obstacles 119

Code quality 122

Making the case 124

Find a shared rhythm 129

Collaborate across the project timeline 130

Deliver awesome products 131

Summary 131

The "Throwing Deliverables Over The Fence" anti-pattern 132

You know you're in it when... 132

Patterns 132

Take the battle to the planners 132

Make the value proposition obvious 133

Meet and greet 133

Breaking down the fence 133

Be the champion of design  134

Bring your defense  135

Sharing a rhythm  135

Track inefficiencies  135

What to do if others throw deliverables
over the fence to you  135

Terminology explained  136

References  136

Takeaways  137

# 8  LIVING IN THE DELIVERABLES  139

Best-in-show deliverables  140

Conversations, not lectures  142

The increasing difficulty of documenting
digital experiences  143

Beware the IKEA effect  143

Collaborate, collaborate, collaborate  145

Make space for collaboration  146

Leaner, meaner... UX  148

Prototyping  149

What if you work in an agency?  151

Collect user feedback  151

Summary  152

The "Living in the Deliverables"
anti-pattern  153

You know you're in it when...  153

Patterns  153

Dead Poet Society pattern  153

Embrace the creativity of everyone  154

Spring clean  156

Fast feedback  156

Toolbox bonanza  157

Push the changes upward  158

If others inflict this anti-pattern on you  158

Ask how it works  158

Suggest gathering some quick user
feedback  158

Sketch on the wall  158

If stakeholders demand pixel-perfect
mockups before they'll sign off  158

If the quality of the design is measured in
the deliverable, not the problem
solution  158

If procurement is buying documents, not
design solutions  159

Detailed discussions about the documents
procured, not the project outcomes  159

Terminology explained  161

Additional resources  161

References  162

Takeaways  163

9  ASSUMING OTHERS DON'T GET DESIGN  165

A note from the authors  166

Creating design and understanding
design  166

Pretentious little jerks  167

Pitchslapped  168

We live in a designed world  169

"Creative" isn't a noun  170

How can you make sharing easier?  170

    The not-invented-here bias  171

Feeding back  172

Well-intended suggestions  172

Get the HiPPO on board  173

Some people view creativity as risk  173

The "Assuming Others Don't Get Design"
  anti-pattern  174

You know you're in it when...  174

Patterns – making sharing easier  174

    Collaborative workshops  174

    Sketching  175

    Storyboarding  175

    Moodboards  175

    Paper mockups  175

    Word association  176

    Dot voting  176

    Design the box  176

    Role-playing  176

    I-invented-this pattern  177

    Kate Rutter's skills map  177

Patterns – principles to strive for  177

    Transparency  177

    Respect  177

    Use everyday language  177

    Frame of reference  178

    Facilitation magic  178

Pairing for design and development 178

Empower the nondesigners 178

If others inflict this anti-pattern on you 178

Terminology explained 179

Additional resources 182

References 182

Takeaways 183

## 10 INSISTING ON PERFECTION 185

Delivering on your vision 186

Defining objectivity 186

Setting expectations 187

Introducing a functional grammar 188

Trade-offs 191

Sustainable pace 192

UX debt 193

Knowing when you're done 193

Take inspiration from start-up entrepreneurs 194

Launch your idea in 3 hours, 24 hours, a weekend 194

Summary 195

The "Living in the Deliverables" anti-pattern 195

You know you're in this anti-pattern when... 195

Patterns 195

Checking in with yourself 195

Design/UX debt 196

Divide form and function 197

Sketch + code  197

Pairing with developers  197

90% rule  197

If others inflict this anti-pattern on
you  198

Terminology explained  198

References  200

Takeaways  201

## 11  RESPONDING TO TONE, NOT CONTENT  203

Nonverbal, not unimportant  205

Tone varies with culture  206

Caveat  206

Gaps in understanding  206

Who you are and who you're perceived to
be  208

The IKEA effect strikes again  210

Respondent fatigue  210

Summary  210

The "Responding to Tone, Not Content"
anti-pattern  211

The patterns  211

Set expectations  211

Paraphrased playback pattern  211

Yes, and... pattern  212

The power of silence  212

Mind-body considerations  213

Break it up  213

Mirror, mirror pattern  214

The meeting before the meeting and the meeting after the meeting 215

Encourage feedback at natural breaks 215

Subvert the script 216

You'll know when you have encountered this anti-pattern, because ... 216

What to do when someone is being confrontational or misunderstanding your tone 216

Tips 217

Terminology explained 218

References 218

Takeaways 219

**12 DEFENDING TOO HARD 221**

Spotting this type of client 223

The hidden cost 225

Business theater 225

Summary 227

The "Defending Too Hard" anti-pattern 227

You'll know you're in it when ... 227

The patterns 228

Choosing your battles: Don't get attached 228

Choosing your battles: Let the silence speak 228

Choosing your battles: Concede gracefully 229

Choosing your battles: Tactical retreat 229

Positive disagreement: Get to
the why 229

Positive disagreement: Embrace
and extend 230

Positive disagreement: Get them
to expand 230

What to do when someone keeps
repeating the same objection 230

Tips 231

Terminology explained 232

References 235

Takeaways 236

# 13

## NOT DEFENDING HARD ENOUGH 239

Everyone's a critic 240

What is the right decision? 243

Using the Five Whys to understand
business value 245

Framing the Five Whys 245

Asking the Five Whys persuasively 246

Closing the Five Whys 247

UX Value vs Business Value 248

Shortcut: Always defend user
research 249

Summary 251

The "Not Defending Hard Enough"
anti-pattern 251

You know you're in it when ... 251

The patterns 251

    Arrive via MoSCoW 251

    Beginning, middle, and end 252

    Snap the elastic user 252

    Letting the client/stakeholder fail 253

How to remedy a wrongly given-up
  point 253

Tips 253

Terminology explained 254

References 257

Takeaways 258

## 14 IDENTIFYING AND FIXING YOUR OWN ANTI-PATTERNS 261

The tip-off 262

The cool-down 264

Get an outside perspective 264

Find the common factor 265

Forgive yourself 265

Identify some patterns 265

Make it a habit 266

Keep going 266

Reference 266

## 15 RELAXATION TECHNIQUES AT WORK 269

In the moment 271

Breathe 271

Stay present 273

Fake it until you become it  274

Lifestyle  276

Eat for well-being  276

Meditation  278

Yoga  279

About the author  282

Additional resources  282

Reference  282

## 16 GROUP DESIGN TECHNIQUES 285

How many people to invite?  286

How much time to budget?  287

How to facilitate a group  288

In the room  288

Try out new formats  289

Elevator pitch  289

Business model canvas  291

Design the Box  293

Role-playing a service  294

Map the experience  296

Storyboard scenarios  298

Design studio  299

Moodboarding for personas  302

Hypotheses testing  303

Retrospectives  305

How to prioritize  307

Dot voting  308

Prioritization matrix  309

Additional resource 309

References 309

Conclusion 310

Glossary 313

Index 321

# FOREWORD

At the end of the movie "Soylent Green," Charlton Heston famously cries out, "It's people!" when he discovers the primary ingredient in the food system. Every time someone sends a goodbye note on their final day at a job, they always say, "I'll miss the people the most."

At the center of a great user experience design effort is – you guessed it – people. In the case of the UX project, the people are our customers and we function as their main advocate in our agencies, companies, and teams. We study them. We observe them. We learn their motivations and their needs. We figure out how to help them and ensure that our solutions meet their needs. We know how to speak to them. More often than not, we also know how to speak to each other. Why then do we struggle as a profession to make compelling conversation happen with our colleagues in other disciplines, our leaders and executives, and our clients?

Technology shifts in the last decade have made conversation with our customers increasingly easier, faster, and richer with insight. Capturing this insight and translating it to our colleagues and clients is core to our goal of creating delightful and usable products. It's also core to building successful collaborative teams. It is these highly engaged, cross-functional teams (made up of UX designers, visual designers, content strategists, software engineers, product managers, QA engineers, marketers, and others) that can properly respond, in a timely fashion, to this vast trove of insight now available to us. The more effective these teams are, the more responsive the organization can be to changing customer needs.

UXers are uniquely positioned to take advantage of this new reality to bridge the gap between individuals and interactions while shedding the constraints of processes and tools.

This new opportunity is often seen through the lens of facilitation. UXers are the most qualified individuals on a team to take the lead in facilitating productive, meaningful team discussions. We know how to take input from various sources, synthesize it into something meaningful, and present it back to our customers for feedback. Yet we struggle to do this with our own teams and stakeholders.

It is the tactics covered in this book that will help you make, and continue to make, a bigger impact on your organizations. They will teach you to translate your work into language your audience cares about. You will learn how to take data and metrics, and use them to not only inform your design process, but to make a compelling case for the decisions you've made.

Martina and James have put together a treasure trove of tactics and insights to ensure that UX is at the center of these Agile, collaborative teams. And it is with this know-how that we, together with our colleagues in other disciplines, can continue to build amazing products moving forward.

—Jeff Gothelf, author, *Lean UX*,
August 2014, New York, NY

# ACKNOWLEDGMENTS

Many thanks to our great editing team at Elsevier, especially Meg Dunkerley and Lindsay Lawrence, for making this book happen.

A special thank you to all our contributors who shared their stories with us: Aline Baeck, Chris Downs, Chris Nodder, Eli Toftøy-Andersen, Evgenia Grinblo, Jonathan Berger, Sarah B. Nelson, Richard Wand, Sophie Freiermuth, and Jeff Gothelf.

Many thanks for the feedback and patience of our technical reviewers: Darci Dutcher, FJ van Wingerde, Linda Newman Lior, Richard Wand, and Spencer Turner.

Chris Rain contributed the design of our playable card game, for which you can find downloading instructions in Conclusion. We're so grateful that he shared his graphic design skills with us to create such a beautiful card deck.

Thanks also to all of our friends and colleagues who agreed to take and pose for photographs. And to Pivotal, Method, Immediate Media, and Proximity London: thank you for your understanding of our time and space needs while we worked on this book.

Martina wants to thank Ed, her parents, and her friends for the inspiration, love, and support to make this project a reality.

James wants to thank Melissa, his parents, and the UXers of London for the support, solace, and sanity-checking. He also wishes to apologize to the many, many people on whom he has researched his own anti-patterns over the years.

NO
UNDER-
STANDING
ANY
TIME

richard tipping

# INTRODUCTION

As creative actors in the world of digital product development, UXers and designers are expected to combine our training and experience in the pursuit of great outcomes. But all too often, the focus of that training and experience is on the technical aspects of creating design, leading us to fall short when it comes to the other important aspect of our roles: *explaining* our work to the people who are developing and paying for it.

When the technical side of the role takes all the focus, good design can end up being rejected because it's not sold-in well enough for the buyers to see its value. In more extreme cases, the relationship between the business and the designer can be seriously harmed. The worst case of this the authors have experienced was in 2001, when James was a web designer working for a startup that had hired an external design agency for branding and graphic design. The relationship was turbulent, with the design agency struggling to adapt from their comfort zone of print design to a transactional website. Usability tests demonstrated that many of the designers' favorite ideas needed to be toned down or rethought for the ultimate product to be clearly related, but not identical, to their comps.

At the go-live, the startup invited the agency to review the implementation. The designer they sent was annoyed by what he saw as the startup's lack of adherence to his design vision and refused to listen to the reasoning behind the changes. Finally, as James tried to explain why it was important to let the user scroll, the designer held up his hand to stop him and said, "If you were a designer, I'd listen to you."

The agency was fired the next day.

Since those early days of the web, we have built many digital products for many different organizations. While it's rare to encounter such an extreme outburst these days, we still regularly encounter the attitude that design is us-and-them, with "our skill" battling "nondesigners' ignorance." This attitude can come from third parties, clients, and, yes, even ourselves. Many UXers and designers seem to believe that people who don't have the word "creative" in their job titles aren't capable of judging creative work (and, by reflection, that they themselves are incapable of turning in anything but perfect work). Even we are sometimes guilty of falling into that trap. You can believe it when we say that many of the lessons we've put into this book have been learned through firsthand experience.

But these supposedly "noncreative" people are still *creating* digital products. They're specifying, building, and – most importantly – *funding* our design work. Building a fence around "creativity" cuts these people out of a process they have every right to be involved in. It leads to a toxic environment, and not just for that project. People who have had a poor experience with designers will take that experience, and the after-work horror stories it gave rise to, to their next project. And the project after that. They'll work with unfortunate designers who, regardless of the quality of their work, always have to begin by justifying their involvement. That's a situation that leads to shackled creativity and further poor experiences on both sides.

It is possible to work in a different way – one that helps business-focused minds see the real value of design, that gives us better outcomes for loosening our iron grip, and that builds a foundation for ongoing collaboration. But to get to this way of working, we need to address the negative patterns of behavior that we learn – or at least, never unlearn – over the course of our careers.

None of us are formally taught how to communicate. We learn how to speak through a sort of osmosis in our early lives. Then, at school, we're taught how to read and write, but meanwhile there's a whole social thing going on that you have to muddle through on your own. This organic way of learning how to address others and participate in a culture forms a set of communication patterns that we rely on in our day-to-day interactions. Like many other aspects of our brains, these patterns let the brain filter and process the vast amount of information it constantly encounters by making assumptions about what's important and what's not. For the most part, our trial-and-error process of anchoring these patterns allows us to make friends, function in daily life, and avoid major conflicts. But when, as makers, we come into the workplace, we're suddenly doing something that we haven't done in a serious capacity before: building together.

The same patterns that might work for us in social or learning contexts, around like-minded people, aren't always suitable for communicating with parties who don't share our outlook, don't have the same context as us, or have unknown factors skewing their own attitudes. When patterns fail to work as expected, our social monkey brains get stressed, and this can lead to conflict. Being challenged in a core belief is an example of a pattern challenge that leads to defensiveness, argumentation, and conflict. At this point, we usually rely on more negative patterns to deal with the situation. However, patterns are so ingrained into our psyches that we either experience cognitive dissonance when this happens – "Bob couldn't understand my perfectly rational argument, so Bob is stupid/evil/hates creativity" – or, even if we do recognize the cause, we can't simply reprogram our brains to accept it.

In this book, we've taken the thirteen most common negative patterns that we see affecting projects every day and put names to them to help you identify them. For each of these anti-patterns, we've also provided a selection of positive patterns that you can use to displace the negative pattern, and lots of other helpful guidance. We want this book to be a practical guide to creating positive working relationships, with the understanding that the "work self" we create is built upon the learned behaviors from our younger lives.

We don't want you to think that the advice we give you in this book means you need to make your personality disappear under a veneer of "business-ness." As a designer, your entire professional life is about communicating: communicating the product proposition to the customer, communicating the interface needs to the user, and communicating your decisions to the people who will decide whether and how they'll be implemented.

Our advice seeks to make sure that every time you're communicating in that last context, you're doing it in a way that effectively relays the value of what you're doing, without being obscured by misplaced social gaffes. Equally, our advice will help you identify when you're suffering from other peoples' anti-patterns and turn those interactions around. Ultimately, we want to give you the tools to create a working relationship based on mutual respect and trust between you and your colleagues, one that really allows your design work to be valued and to shine in execution.

If you can get to that place, then you don't need the MBA, sharp suit, and smooth line in doublespeak. Colleagues who have learned to see the value of great design will also know how to recognize a great designer.

## About the authors

**Martina Hodges-Schell** is a London-based digital product and service designer who specializes in user-centered design, experience strategy, and qualitative design research. She has been creating interactive experiences for web, desktop, TV, and mobile devices since the mid-1990s. In her practice, she focuses on bringing a balanced team together with a shared empathy for users, business, technology, and design.

Deeply fascinated by how people work together, Martina has conducted research into methods for multidisciplinary collaboration and adoption of user-centered thinking to support creativity and innovation for her MA in Applied Imagination from Central Saint Martins School of Art and Design in London.

Martina mentors entrepreneurs at Seedcamp and Lean Startup Machine, and teaches user-centered design at Birkbeck, University of London. She helps companies large and small establish more user-centered, Lean, and Agile design skills and facilitates the cultural and organizational change required to collaborate and take risks more effectively. She has helped Fortune 100 and startup companies across a wide range of sectors develop new products and services, or measurably improve existing ones.

Her clients include Amazon, eBay, Microsoft, Yahoo! Mobile, O2, Vodafone, Expedia, Barclays, Lloyds, Not on the Highstreet, EDF Energy, and a growing number of startups, among many others. She has worked for boutique UX consultancy, creative agency, world-leading dot-com, and startup environments including Flow Interactive, Method, and Pivotal Labs, and has experienced a wide range of team and stakeholder constellations.

She shares her enthusiasm for UX as a member of the UK UXPA Committee, and regularly organizes and speaks at events, such as IA Summit, Interactions, UXPA, Agile, and Balanced Team events.

**James O'Brien** has spent the last twenty years designing and building digital products in roles that always seemed to spill over the edges of the job title. Known at various times as a webmaster, web designer, web developer, front-end developer, and UXer, he has always been dedicated to getting the best possible experience into the users' hands.

He graduated with a BSc in Media Technology and Production from the University of Bradford in 1999 and worked with several fledgling startups during the first web boom, usually in very broad roles that involved design, development, product strategy, and "tame geek" responsibilities for explaining the tech to management.

From 2002 to 2014, James freelanced with agencies, consultancies, and businesses in and around London, working with clients that included Disney, Channel 4, Aardman Animations, ThoughtWorks, Auto Trader, Royal Mail, and too many more to mention. He is currently the lead UX architect for Immediate Media, one of the UK's largest magazine publishers.

He is a builder and maker, and is most fascinated with finding new ways to make large teams both efficient and fun to work in. He keeps a foot in both tech and design camps to ensure he can always speak to the whole delivery team in the most appropriate dialect.

James was introduced to Agile in 2006 and immediately understood the benefits of the approach, then spent several years learning about the complexity of applying it to real-life projects. He's known for revealing the "big lies" about Agile, including identifying the cracks in the "no big design upfront" philosophy that provide space for UX and design to get a running start before the software begins to get built.

James speaks publicly at events in London and further afield on topics such as UX, Agile, and interpersonal communication. He's spoken at UXPA events, UX Camp London, IA Summit, UX People, UCD London, and Agile London, and loves to mentor new speakers.

## Why we wrote this book

The authors began collaborating on the topic of interpersonal anti-patterns in 2011 during a session of sharing our career woes. Martina was working at an agency that was finding its feet in terms of how it differentiated UX from design, and James was working in-house at a place that was just beginning to embrace Agile, and he was struggling to demonstrate UX value in the fast-moving but unstructured process. As we shared our latest horror stories, we realized that the same types of problem were cropping up over and over again. As we got more mature in our careers, we were finding new ways to solve them – and new traps to fall into.

We lamented that these traps are so endemic to the space where design and business people collide, so much good design *and* business value must be lost every day.

Both of us had been studying design patterns and software patterns in the course of our careers and, in a Eureka moment, we realized that behaviors have patterns, too – and we could immediately see how the common problems we'd encountered were examples of the corresponding anti-patterns.

We are both passionate about seeing great design embodied in great products. Loss of design and value upsets us on a philosophical level. We decided to put a talk together to pitch to conferences that would help designers and UXers identify and solve the most common and damaging anti-patterns that we'd seen in ourselves and others. We've made this presentation at several major conferences to great audience engagement and feedback, but we could only fit a small amount of advice into the format of a talk. We knew that there was plenty more experience that we could draw on and lots more patterns we could popularize if we put the work into a longer form.

Our hope is that, if we can help UXers and designers communicate their contributions better, then not only can we make their work more efficient and effective, but we can help them demonstrate the real value that design and UX bring to businesses and get more creative voices heard at the right level. If we succeed, more great products will make it to production. We can't wait to see what you create.

## How to use this book

This book can be read from beginning to end; many of the themes and patterns build on each other and you'll have a greater understanding of the whole landscape that way. But this book is also designed so you can dip in and out when you come across an interpersonal situation that stumps you, or you need to offer specific advice to a colleague or friend. Each chapter is self-contained, focusing on a single anti-pattern, exploring it, and offering corresponding positive patterns to help you get back on track.

In many anti-pattern chapters, we've included case studies from collaborators whom we admire. These will help you see how the anti-pattern (and often its solution) can play out in a real-life scenario. They'll also show that none of us are perfect communicators and that, no matter how senior we get, we all still fall into the same traps.

We've also included some broader guides toward the end of the book that will help you set up working practices and spaces within your organization to foster creativity and share understanding and empathy among your colleagues. These will help you put many of the patterns into practice, and ideally also make your job more fun and productive.

Most importantly, if you find yourself still expressing an anti-pattern after you've read about it in this book, don't be too hard on yourself. Patterns and anti-patterns are all habits, and it takes time to unlearn bad habits and learn good ones. Don't expect to transform yourself overnight. Treat the patterns as exercises to be strengthened whenever you have a meeting or presentation. Celebrate the successful outcomes and learn from the unsuccessful ones. Before you know it, you'll be a seasoned, successful communicator of design.

## A word about job titles

As a young discipline, UX has lots of different job titles that describe parts or all of the space we work in. At the broadest, you might find *experience directors, UX architects,* or *UX consultants.* Narrow the focus a little and you'll discover *information architects, UI designers, UX researchers, ethnographers,* and many more. Examine the Venn diagram closely and you find *graphic designers, digital designers, business analysts,* and *product managers* overlapping into the space UX occupies. So many job titles!

All of these roles come under the umbrella of *user experience,* and there are benefits that each of them could take from this book. To be as inclusive as possible, we've used the term *UXer* to refer to anyone who works in the sphere of UX, regardless of job title. Where we use the term *design,* we use it in a broad sense that encompasses all the creativity that it takes to get from project inception to product delivery, rather than just the creation of wireframes or mockups.

## Why anti-patterns?

If you spend a lot of time around software developers, you may notice that they often talk about *patterns.* The concept of patterns arises from the field of architecture, where they are used to provide proven solutions to common problems. For example, think about a theater. At the end of a performance, lots of people will want to leave at the same time, so it's a common pattern to have multiple staircases that lead to exits spread around the outside of the building – everyone leaves by their nearest staircase and ends up in a smaller crowd overall than if there were a single exit, and it all happens without a slow-moving and potentially dangerous crowd forming. Whenever an architect begins to design a new theater, they can take this pattern on board and use it to guide other design decisions they will make.

In design and software, patterns have exactly the same role. Some places where you would see patterns being used in software products might be the structure of a database designed to deal with user data; login/logout forms and processes; a shopping cart and checkout process; a credit card processing back end. All of these are actually difficult problems when approached from scratch, but the existence of patterns allows us to leverage the accumulated experience of all the people who have built these types of product before us.

The wonderful thing about patterns is that they are *implementation-agnostic*. Once I've identified the right pattern for my login form, it doesn't matter whether I'm building it in Ruby, PHP, or Java: the same principles apply and I can use my own tools to implement them.

So what is an *anti-pattern*? An anti-pattern is an obvious way of solving a problem that crops up again and again, but unfortunately, it is a poor or even destructive solution. For example, a common security anti-pattern relates to "forgotten password" functionality. It seems obvious that, if I have forgotten my password, the simplest thing to do is just send me an e-mail with my password in it. Because this answer is obvious, it frequently makes it into product discussions (and occasionally into production). However, this means my password has to be stored in a recoverable form on the server, and is therefore vulnerable if the server is ever hacked.

The frequency with which this idea appears, combined with the damage it can do when it does, it what makes it an anti-pattern. The corresponding pattern, which we're sure you're familiar with, is to send the user a link to enter a *new* password, which is then irreversibly hashed on the server. This (or a close variation) is the way almost every website handles forgotten passwords – a great demonstration of how a well-designed pattern can *push out* an anti-pattern.

How, then, do patterns and anti-patterns relate to interpersonal communication? Well, a communication pattern is something we adopt for a certain type of interaction. For example, when you're telling a joke, you fall into a certain mode of speaking

– your words have rhythm and timing; your voice takes on an edge that communicates you're not being entirely serious; you make eye contact and smile. You don't consciously think of performing these actions: you're just telling a joke. Giving a presentation is another example – while you may still be talking to the same friends or colleagues, you're in a very different mode of interaction from a simple conversation. Joking around and presenter mode are usually quite positive patterns, but where there are patterns, there is the potential for anti-patterns.

A communication anti-pattern arises when we fall into a type of communication that is our usual way of dealing with a situation, thinking it will result in the outcome we want. However, what makes it an anti-pattern is that we neglect its effect on the other party, and may not realize that the interaction is being harmed by its use. For instance, think of a design disagreement where the designer tries to assert his domain experience by saying, "I've been designing for ten years and this is how it's done..." To the nondesigners in the meeting, this can come across as dismissive and condescending, and they may fight *harder* to see their own solutions adopted instead. Worse, anti-patterns like this can cause the discussion to spin off-track, killing any potential for productivity that the meeting originally had.

We think targeting your anti-patterns is a great way to improve your interpersonal communication style. In the same way that software patterns are implementation-agnostic, communication anti-patterns are *expression-agnostic* – that is to say, the same anti-pattern can be exhibited in many different ways. By zooming out to the level of the anti-pattern, we can help you identify and resolve a much wider range of damaging behaviors.

Equally, anti-patterns remove blame from the equation. Anti-patterns arise naturally from good intentions and personal perspective: it's nobody's fault if someone suffers from them (and believe us, we've yet to encounter anyone who doesn't). Anti-patterns will help you look at your own behavior objectively and then find a range of positive patterns to help you overcome any negative aspects.

Anti-patterns also help you target your behavioral changes very carefully. This isn't one of those business manuals that seeks to rewrite your personality into a cookie-cutter corporate billable resource. Your personality is an integral part of your creativity and you absolutely must retain it! Instead, what we hope is that by making you more successful and confident in your interpersonal interactions, we can help you actually bring more of your real personality and thinking to the table, and showcase the importance of creative thinking to your organization more effectively.

Finally, how do you work out whether you're under the spell of a particular anti-pattern? Each chapter has a section called "You'll know you're in it when…" that lays out some common outcomes for that particular anti-pattern. If any of them sound familiar, then have a closer read of the chapter to see whether the high-level themes could be enabling any familiar behaviors. Later in the book, we'll show you how to figure out any other anti-patterns that might be in your repertoire that we haven't covered.

## How to use the patterns

For each anti-pattern, we offer a range of patterns that should help you replace the negative aspects of the anti-pattern with something that will give you a positive outcome. Ideally, you should be able to spot the moments when you're about to fall into an anti-pattern, or just have. While there's still time, you can switch to a pattern you've already chosen for that scenario, or choose one there and then.

This, of course, is easier said than done, but it boils down to two key aspects: recognizing when you're in the anti-pattern, and "calling up" the corresponding pattern at the right time. The "You'll know you're in it when…" section of each chapter should help you with recognition. To help with calling up, each pattern has a specific and memorable name. You can use this like a mantra to remind you of the behavior you want to express, use it as an memory aide when you need to reverse out of a situation and choose a pattern quickly, or even write it out when you're planning a strategy for those difficult sessions.

The patterns work best with practice, and the more practice you give them, the more they will become second nature. Try them out even in moments when you're not at risk of falling prey to an anti-pattern. Think of it as training for the big game.

For more tips on applying the patterns, see Chapter 14.

## On the importance of understanding your own style

In the same way that our use of anti-patterns allows for a generalized approach to identifying interpersonal conflicts, so too are the patterns that we offer to overcome them relatively general. It's important to understand your own communication style so you can best apply the patterns and ensure that other people don't feel you're following a script you're not comfortable with.

"Having a style" really just means being confident enough in yourself to be comfortable in your natural mode of speaking and acting, and being able to cast effective communication into that mode. The more natural you seem in your interactions, the more people will trust what you're saying – a lifetime of exposure to advertisements has taught us all to associate a natural style of delivery with authenticity and wisdom.

Politicians spend large portions of their working lives understanding their style. Think about the difference between how Barack Obama sounds in public from Mitt Romney. Regardless of what they're saying, the words they're using, or their own cadences, what they both have in common is that they believe what they're saying and they project their passion through their speaking. These techniques or attributes are also the ideal building blocks of a business interaction style.

To take the authors as an example, James and Martina are different personality types, but they can each use the same patterns in their own way. James is brash and jokey, so he uses the patterns like a showman or ringmaster – to play with the concept and build support. Martina is methodical and warm, and she uses the patterns in a very welcoming way – to draw people into discussions and build understanding. These are, of course, broad strokes and, when the situation calls for it, either of them can tweak their style into what's most appropriate for the moment. The important thing is that they can each take the general aim and content of the pattern and present it in a way that's natural.

Understanding your style means, to a large degree, understanding how it presents you to other people. What do they like about how you communicate, and what do they dislike? Being confident in your style means being sure that you're hitting the positive notes and the people around you are enjoying the interaction (or not caring if they don't; but this book wouldn't be very helpful if we took that stance). You can understand your style with experience and soul-gazing, but it's quicker to do it with the help of external observers. Ask your friends and colleagues what works and what doesn't – or, if you're already doing 360 reviews, really take on board the observations and recommendations. This can be challenging, but it is an important aspect of personal growth, and one that it's far better to be in control of than to be controlled by.

## Pattern zero

Before we get into the nitty-gritty of actual anti-patterns, there's one pattern that we'd like you to bear in mind that *always* applies.

### Address the person first and the requirement second

While we'd all like to believe that business is about rational people weighing up pros and cons and coming to reasoned, evidence-based decisions, we UXers in particular should know that's not true. People (including us) are subject to all manner of social effects, cognitive biases, and hidden motivations. In particular, people carry their social expectations into business interactions.

If you forget that you're talking to a person, you can set yourself up for all sorts of trouble. Always remember that whoever you're arguing, collaborating, or negotiating with is a person, and treat them the way you'd like them to treat you. Whether you're happy or unhappy about the conversation you're having, give the other party the respect of making eye contact, actively listening and letting them finish, and framing your responses politely. It's far easier to sway the opinion of someone who feels respected and, in turn, they will feel respectful toward you.

Conversely, make sure the *content* of your argument focuses on the requirements of the task under discussion. Referring back to old battles, perceived slights, or "unfairness" doesn't engage the other party's empathy or reasoning; without either of those, you face a greater challenge to get the content of your argument across. Better still, map the requirement to outcomes to help the other party understand the whole context of your position.

## Edge cases

The advice we give in this book generally assumes that you and your colleagues are pulling in the same direction. However, there are edge cases where that may not be the situation. There may be politics at play that you're not aware of, and you are being deliberately stalled or misled. You may have colleagues who, for whatever reason, have judged you and decided not to give you an easy time (if they do this as a form of discrimination, we urge you to seek help from your manager and HR). There may be people whose view of their role in the company is extremely self-focused – they see any form of communication as taking time away from them "actually" doing their job.

If the patterns we show you don't reach these people, it's not a failure of your implementation. Some parties can't or won't be reached. Work as much as you can with the people around these edge cases to keep the process flowing, use the structures within the business to ensure you are not bullied, and keep trying. Whatever happens next, the right people will remember the contribution your communication skills made.

## The anti-patterns

In writing this book, we've chosen the thirteen anti-patterns that we most commonly encounter in our practice. Some of these deal directly with conversations – presenting and interacting one-on-one or with a group. Others identify a seemingly desirable *lack* of interaction and the unintended fallout that can result.

### Speaking different languages

Domain-specific language has great value within a team, but it can cause friction when used across departments. The same word may have two different meanings to two different people, leading to speaking at cross-purposes or setting unexpected expectations. Alternatively, an important term in one department may mean nothing to someone from another, leading to serious considerations being missed.

Misunderstood requests and requirements can send UX and design off on the wrong path at considerable cost. Jargon-heavy design explanations can lead the business to draw incorrect conclusions or misinterpret the value of design.

### Having different KPIs

This anti-pattern is often imposed upon us externally. Businesses set each division a target in its specialized area, to measure and motivate them. But when divisions form a cross-functional team to create a product, this can lead to specialists being unwilling to consider the holistic view, seeing it as an impediment to their simple success metric. Everyone also has their own intrinsic motivation that drives their outlook on the project, and these can conflict in fundamental ways between colleagues.

For us to successfully design a complete product, we must recognize that it is our job to understand and resolve these various Key Performance Indicators (KPIs). Failure to do so can lead to political issues and disempowerment of the UX and design department.

## Not embracing everyone's goals

Recognizing the various motivations and targets of other parts of the business is only the first part of the puzzle. If we don't learn to wholeheartedly embrace them – and, more importantly, demonstrate that we are wholeheartedly embracing them – then our design solution will be viewed with suspicion and every choice we make will be questioned at a fundamental level. Hard design decisions about priorities and compromises will be subject to imposition by committee, restricting us in the area that should be our core competence.

## Presenting without contextualizing

We all complain about the lack of consistency in feedback – every week, stakeholders contradict their own previous comments – but stakeholders don't have the same level of contact that we do with the work being presented. It's hardly surprising that they don't have perfect recall from one week to the next. If we want better feedback, it's up to us to provide an environment that encourages it.

If we don't tell the story behind our outcomes, then all our audience can react to are the superficialities of appearance, resulting in feedback that doesn't resolve underlying issues and leaves us at risk of major rework when they eventually arise.

## Being in the room, but not present

We all need to focus sometimes, but putting on our headphones and disappearing into the tools all day, every day, creates a division between us and our teams. If we seem unapproachable or snap when someone pulls us out of the zone, the team will, with the best of intentions, start to make decisions without involving us. Focusing entirely on the work in front of us can lead us to forget that much of our work lies outside the deliverable – in gathering context and explaining the vision.

Virtually separating ourselves from the team in this way also makes it harder to build cohesion. If the rest of the team doesn't build trust in us, it becomes harder to communicate the value of UX and design, and the less-obvious aspects of our work – voice and tone, delighters, and so on – will be lost in the volume of competing requirements.

## Not having a consistent design language

As you begin to create a product, you need to identify features and interactions in explanations and reviews. If we allow the names to form organically in discussion, people will choose their own names for a feature, leading to a Chinese-whisper effect where everyone in the business has a different name for a thing. This makes feedback confusing and can potentially lead to misunderstood requirements, such as a different feature being amended while the original problem goes unaddressed.

## Throwing deliverables over the fence

The pace of modern software delivery is often under such time pressure that it's tempting to finish up a deliverable and ship it out so we can focus on the next thing. However, no deliverable can ever properly encapsulate our thinking, and the longer and more detailed we make our specifications, the more we risk the recipient missing a detail in the sheer weight of information.

Developers who receive these weighty documents also come to see design as rigid and dictatorial, and can get frustrated when assumptions we've made in our work can't be brought to fruition or require rework. If no conversational relationship exists between the developers and us, they have to either fix the assumption themselves and then justify their choice, or halt work while they wait for a change request to pass through the system. Ultimately, developers who are repeatedly frustrated in this way will lobby for a new process to be put in place that can result in the design process becoming subordinate to development.

## Living in the deliverables

A naïve view of design (especially UX design) is that it just involves creating the deliverables, so we're only being productive when we're creating the final document. Oddly though, this view can be held by designers as well as nondesigners. We don't feel productive unless we're creating wireframes or comps, polishing our work until it shines. However, scope change is inevitable in any project of reasonable size and investing time into the deliverables early on leads to a risk when change is required. Because the cost of change seems high, we see it as being more responsible to defend the sunk cost and argue against the change, rather than embracing it and moving our designs forward.

If we don't ensure that our deliverables are well-organized and able to respond to change, we risk letting the cost of change dictate every design decision. This is no more creative than having a team of accountants dictate all our decisions, but cognitive biases make it seem as if we're defending the design instead of harming it.

## Assuming others don't get design

We invest huge amounts of time and energy into learning the craft of design, but if we're not careful, this can lead us to develop a dismissive attitude that casts nondesigners as ignorant. This inward-turned view can cause us to create designs that only other designers can appreciate – a recipe for great art but poor consumer products.

When we forget that design has to work for everyone, we build a wall around our domain that excludes stakeholders and customers, and casts us as defenders of perfection rather than solvers of real problems. We grant ourselves the right to dismiss feedback at a trivial level, rather than truly respond to it. However, the rest of the organization will begin to see design as a subjective discipline, and won't see its connection to real value.

## Insisting on perfection

We want to see our designs built, but it's easy to forget that when we hand over to the developers our work is full of assumptions. We make guesses about what is technically possible, what can be made performant, and what can be fitted into tight development timeframes. Forgetting that these are only assumptions can lead us to tremendous disappointment when they are tested.

If we're not open to the possibility that perfection can't be achieved, then our work won't have the ability to flex when compromise is required. Design will find itself slipping down the priority list in favor of more achievable goals, and we will become disillusioned as our hard work fails to make it into the product.

## Responding to tone, not content

In the heightened environment of business, it's easy to misinterpret a colleague's tone as harsh or sarcastic. Responding in kind escalates the emotion, leading to a negative feedback effect. Agreement becomes impossible as both parties, seeing it now as a matter of pride, dig in. The environment becomes toxic when both sides see every design review as a skirmish in a war of attrition. Politics enters the equation as stakeholders seek ways around what they see as an obstructive process.

We can't keep emotion out of our interactions, and we shouldn't allow ourselves to be bullied, but we can maintain cool heads and learn to be wary of our initial interpretations.

## Defending too hard

Like the client who demands every piece of text be made bold "so it all stands out," arguing about every design decision makes it impossible for stakeholders to know when we have a serious concern versus when we're insisting on a less-vital aspect of our design vision. With no mechanism to gauge severity, they fall back on the axiom, "When everything is high priority, everything is low priority" and play it safe by disregarding our concerns.

Further, the time spent on defending decisions makes the design process inefficient and time-consuming, and leads stakeholders to avoid feedback sessions because there is such an interaction cost. When something really isn't working, they resort to imposing a decision by fiat, or making an end run around the designer. In extreme cases, designers can find themselves redeployed for the sake of productivity.

## Not defending hard enough

If we don't know when to defend, and how to do it effectively, then we risk letting our work become meaningless by allowing an incomplete understanding of the user to dictate interaction decisions.

Choosing our battles doesn't mean giving way every time a suggestion is made. By understanding where our domain knowledge and experience have the most value, we can choose the moments where a well-stated defense can improve stakeholders' understanding of the link between design and business value.

**desideratum** aim, aspiration, dream, ─────, goal, heart's desire, hope, ideal, lack, ────, objective, *sine qua non*, want, wish

**design** *verb* 1. delineate, describe, draft, draw, outline, plan, sketch, trace ~*noun* 2. blueprint, delineation, draft, drawing, model, outline, plan, scheme, sketch ~*verb* 3. conceive, create, fabricate, fashion, invent, originate, think up ~*noun* 4. arrangement, configuration, construction, figure, form, motif, organization, pattern, shape, style ~*verb* 5. aim, contrive, destine, devise, intend, make, mean, plan, project, propose, purpose, scheme, tailor ~*noun* 6. enterprise, plan, project, scheme, undertaking 7. aim, end, goal, intent, intention, meaning, object, objective, point, purport, purpose, target, view 8. *often plural* conspiracy, evil intentions, intrigue, machination, plot, scheme

**designate** 1. call, christen, dub, entitle, label, name, nominate, style, term 2. allot, appoint, assign, choose, delegate, depute, nominate, select 3. characterize, define, denote, describe, earmark, indicate, pinpoint, show, specify, stipulate

**designation** 1. denomination, description, ────, label, mark, name, title 2. appoint──

# CHAPTER 1

## Speaking different languages

"Working with other people is simple: figure out what they want, and make sure they understand what you want. The rest is a rounding error."
—Mike Monteiro, founder of Mule Design and author of *Design is a Job*

Imagine this: You are at an impasse in a design review meeting. You've explained your point numerous times. The other party, similarly exasperated, is staring you down as if you have clearly lost your mind. The time of friendly team play has long passed. You sigh and find yet another way of rewording your concerns – and all of a sudden, the other party is delighted that you've *finally* cottoned on to their view. "Wait," you say, "we've both arguing the same point this whole time?"

This is a painfully common scenario. In the course of the authors' careers, we have seen it derail progress far too often. We hasten to add that it's not always designers who are misunderstood. This can just as easily arise between any two participants. If you could add up the cost of all that time spent accidentally disagreeing over a common position, you'd be horrified at what it adds to a project's bottom line.

One of the most common reasons for this is that each discipline that contributes to product development has its own *business dialect*. This is a vocabulary and way of speaking that, while based in the group's native language, subtly changes the meaning of words and terms to be specific to the aims of a single discipline. This gives them efficiency in communicating their goals within the group, and a common language for working with in-sector groups outside the organization. To an observer from outside the group, a business dialect can sound like a collection of jargon, buzzwords, and nonsensical use of normal words (think of how marketers use the term "reach" to talk about the number of people who view a campaign). This can lead to a gap in understanding when two groups with different dialects discuss their goals.

Sysadmins regularly talk about *fingering*, *unzipping*, *stripping*, and *mounting*. To the rest of us, this may sound like sophomoric humor, but to an HR rep, they sound like the kind of coded language that leads to disciplinary action. This is a somewhat extreme example of how differing dialects can cause offense (although see later in this chapter for a real-life example of how it can happen), but most often, the result of clashing dialects is that parties end up with differing expectations of what's going to happen next. At least one of those parties is being set up for disappointment.

The first and most basic of our anti-patterns is to carry on a discussion based on what other parties are saying, without understanding what they *mean*.

## Crossing wires

Even when we do the same jobs, we can often have different vocabularies from our colleagues in other types of business. Think of a UX strategist in a consultancy-type organization building a customer-facing portal, and someone in the equivalent role at a marketing agency building a campaign for a large brand. The former will talk about the value of a feature by addressing its *business value* – whether it is worth the cost of implementation for the return it will bring. However, the latter might refer to what *return on investment (ROI)* it will bring – having paid for this feature, will the business see any benefit from it? Close investigation will show that these are the same metric from different viewpoints.

Dialects also change depending on the development stage of a project. At the implementation stage, a UX designer who is reserving space in a wireframe needs to know whether a piece of advertising is a banner, skyscraper, takeover, or MPU. However, early on, when a UX strategist was calling the shots, these all came under the generic heading of "display advertising."

More insidious is when the same, or similar, terms, mean different things to different groups. The classic example is the stakeholder to whom "user experience" means "user interface design" or even just "usability," with its correspondingly limited scope of influence. Or take the word "engagement," which implies a certain depth of relationship to UXers, while a marketing person may just take it as meaning a user has engaged with an ad and followed its call to action.

Think back over your latest project and see if there are moments of disagreement or circular conversations that could be explained by this mismatch of semantics. Were there moments where you dismissed or failed to understand a concern because it was in a different dialect?

You need to be aware of this anti-pattern before it becomes a visible problem, because errors in translation often go undetected at first, but have a nasty habit of combining, multiplying, and blowing up in a bigger way at a later date. Failing to understand the nuance of a first round of feedback is troublesome, because the misunderstanding will invalidate much of the work that is done for the second round, leading to added time and cost. If the misunderstanding slips through the second round and makes it to the third, you'll have eroded the trust and confidence of that stakeholder in a serious way, in addition to escalation in the time and cost to fix the issue itself – and, when deadlines are tight, there simply may not be enough time to fix it at all.

Without a shared vocabulary, you won't have the right terminology to reassure your stakeholders, raising the risk of your explanation making the matter worse. The more basic you have to make your explanation, the more it risks coming across as patronizing – "users know how to scroll" answers questions about the fold, but doesn't address the information architecture challenges the stakeholder is really clashing with. Multiply these difficulties across the many stakeholders a typical project involves, and you're in a lot of trouble.

## Bitter experience

James: How damaging can this anti-pattern be? Let me share with you a story I once witnessed. I was on a team building a new public-facing product, and we were in a sprint demo. The team had just demonstrated a new feature to support an upcoming marketing promotion.

"We'll need tracking tags added to the pages," said the marketing representative in the room.

The front-end developer, looking down at his notes as he captured the requirement, said, "Uh-huh. That's trivial."

To a developer, the word *trivial* is positive. It identifies the kind of feature request that's so simple it doesn't need a card on the wall, the type of request where you leave the meeting and the confirmation e-mail that it's in production is in your inbox before you're back at the desk.

But to a marketer, hearing their request called *trivial* can be an insult. It implies that it's unimportant and won't be made a priority. Worse, the developer delivered his response without making eye contact, and with an ambiguous term of agreement: "Uh-huh." This could mean "Yes, I will do that" or "I acknowledge that you've made that request." He made the classic mistake of addressing the request, not the person.

Piqued, the marketer shot back, "It might be trivial to you, but it's important to me!"

Now the tone had been raised and the developer was aware the marketer had been somehow offended, so he tried to explain: "I can check that in today, and it will go in the next drop." In developerese, this is a strong commitment to delivering the feature: "I'll make this my priority and it will be done today."

But the marketer didn't know the term *check in*, meaning to commit code to the version control system for inclusion in the release, and she didn't understand the term "drop" as meaning the release. She understood this as meaning that he would "drop it in" when he had time.

Neither was willing to push the matter further, so it was left there, but a lingering trust issue had arisen. The marketer henceforth saw the developer as naïve and unhelpful, and the developer saw the marketer as volatile and demanding.

Both parties here were suffering from the anti-pattern. The developer used domain-specific language that the nontechnical marketer misunderstood to have negative connotations: he addressed the request, not the person. But equally, the marketer didn't test her understanding of the terms she heard, even when she heard several terms that she had no reference for. Both sides of this fence are easy for UXers to get caught on.

Business dialects are troublesome, but they're a blessing as well as a curse. As professionals, we often deliberately push our vocabulary into more technical terms that grant legitimacy to our ideas. For example, it can be easier to get a stakeholder to buy into the idea of "cognitive fatigue" than "A messy layout makes the user tune out." We call this gain in credibility from using technical language the "$5 word" effect. But these specialized dialects also exist because disciplines form around core sets of new ideas, and those ideas need a way to be communicated for the core concepts they are.

To take a simple example, imagine the word "wireframe" had never been coined; would you really want to talk about a "low-fidelity schematic of the user interface" a hundred times a day? Now imagine that same scenario replicated across every piece of UX jargon that we use among ourselves. Jargon serves to simplify intrateam communications, so the resulting linguistic efficiency repeats itself within every department of an organization. Further, once everyone in a team or discipline is speaking the same jargon, it has a powerful bonding effect, defining that group as a tribe and promoting intrateam support.

For all their positive effects, there are further downsides to business dialects beyond just the cost of argument. When a team becomes too comfortable with its own jargon, it can lose the ability to communicate core concepts to the outside world. When they come to embody it in a user interface, the jargon has a tendency to seep through into labels and category names, resulting in wayfinding and calls to action that confuse users who have never come across those terms before. And, as jargon generally supports a team's culture, jargon in the interface is also a sign that the underlying navigational model and information architecture of the site is based on the organization's needs, not the user's.

Of course, UX and design have their own dialects – dialects that, if anything, are more complex and cliquey than most. Design is a well-established discipline and UX is an ambitious young one, which gives us an odd situation where we often have several terms for the same thing. For instance, where exactly is the line drawn between a *sketch*, a *scamp*, a *comp*, a *wireframe*, a *mock-up*, and a "*static*"? The distinction may be clear to you, but imagine being a stakeholder encountering UX for the first time; without context, it would seem like a whirlwind of very similar terms being thrown around, but each must have a different and important function, because each has a different name.

This anti-pattern has an insidious trap for us, because we learn in our careers that speaking with authority is the way to make others trust our designs. And the $5 word effect often does work, except that, when it doesn't, suddenly it causes people to disengage, to see design as exclusive and difficult to understand, and to question how it ties back to their "bread-and-butter" business needs.

When this happens, we usually pull back and try to restate our point in simpler terms, but simplify too much or choose the wrong metaphor and your audience can just get more confused. If, instead, we know their dialects and can translate our point directly, we'll gain trust and help the audience understand that our terminology and design concepts are well-grounded.

There's good news here, though: Design is language in visual form. That means that, as designers, we have the perfect toolkit to collect the dialects of our organization, translate them into a simple visual form everyone can understand, and capture them in a common vocabulary for the life of the project. For example, user journeys, iconographic maps, and personas are all methods of taking a complex verbal concept and recasting it into a form that is easier to understand and prevents elastic interpretation. Ultimately, when we do our job well, the outcome of our influence is to ensure that the common vocabulary the team adopts is the language the user speaks.

If we just extend this role as a translator into our business relationships, we can combat this anti-pattern and, as a bonus, earn the trust of our colleagues and even become the go-to people for facilitating decisions within the project scope.

## Summary

Departments within an organization develop their own internal dialect for the purpose of efficient communication and team bonding. However, each department's dialect will be slightly different and sometimes words overlap but meanings don't. If we don't truly understand what our colleagues are *really* saying, we can't understand their motives or the questions they ask of our designs. We'll answer the question we hear, not the question that's asked. Or we'll answer incompletely or with the wrong focus, leaving the questioner's concerns unanswered and eroding their trust in us.

## The "Speaking Different Languages" anti-pattern

Everyone in a cross-functional team brings not just different abilities and experience, but also a different dialect formed around their specialist area. Two different dialects may use the same word with different meanings, call the same thing by a different name, or one may not include the specialized use of a common word from the other. These can lead to mis-set expectations, confusion, and disappointment that, if left unchecked, can derail the development process. Unless you check for understanding

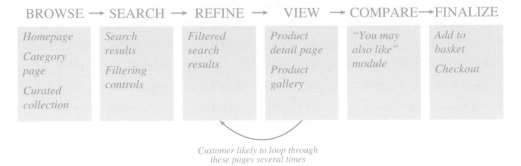

**Typical Purchase Journey**
*(Simplified, focusing on page nomenclature)*

BROWSE → SEARCH → REFINE → VIEW → COMPARE → FINALIZE

| | | | | | |
|---|---|---|---|---|---|
| *Homepage* *Category page* *Curated collection* | *Search results* *Filtering controls* | *Filtered search results* | *Product detail page* *Product gallery* | *"You may also like" module* | *Add to basket* *Checkout* |

*Customer likely to loop through these pages several times*

*Figure 1.1: Journey Map: Putting the journey into a visual form ties down the language used. (Photo credit: James O'Brien.)*

and ensure that everyone has understood not just what's been *said*, but what was *meant* by it, this anti-pattern can come back to bite the whole team later down the road.

## You know you're in it when...

- You find yourself suddenly resolving design issues by realizing that you've been arguing on the same side as the other party.

- Your answers to a question are met by *"yes, but..."* and a reframed version of the same question.

- Stakeholders start asking design questions of the project manager instead of you.

- You struggle to frame your answer in new ways when it's clear the other party hasn't understood.

- You *know* you've answered the other party's question correctly, but they haven't grasped your terminology.

## Patterns

We can be proactive about this anti-pattern, ensuring that we're exposed to as much of the business as possible and being omnivorous about what each department needs and why. Understanding of the need, and the language to describe it, should grow in tandem. Be interested in everything your company does – it will teach you the languages and ensure that your design responds more holistically to the company's needs.

## Stakeholder safari

Usually when we become involved in a project, it happens in the form of a kick-off meeting for all the involved parties. These are great for getting requirements on the table, but they're often the first time everyone meets. As a result, they don't do much to facilitate learning the dialects of other departments or promote a team bond. Some stakeholders can seem as remote and unapproachable as lions on the Serengeti, so, wherever possible, it's important to find a way to interact with them in their natural habitats. You can do this after the kick-off, but it often helps to go out on a safari beforehand if you know who will be involved. If you're in the same building, head up to their desk to have a chat about their needs and their expectations from the project. If not, try and get some time on the phone or video chat. The important thing is to seek them out proactively.

*Figure 1.2: Stakeholder Safari: Seek out your stakeholders to better understand their language and needs. (Photo credit: Katy Dickens.)*

This interaction is designed to work two ways. You're learning about their language and key needs. They're gaining trust in your ability to understand them and, in many cases, they'll also be learning about what UX is, and what it can do for them. It's not uncommon, especially in siloed organizations, for other departments to be unclear about the role and capabilities of UX. This technique really helps them understand it, because you can use your newfound fluency in their dialect to explain it in terms that resonate with them.

The difficulty with running unstructured sessions like this is that, in some organizations, they can be seen as unproductive and frivolous. It can be hard to convince a project manager of the need to make time in the schedule for them, or the stakeholders themselves may not make time to be available. In the first case, recast the safari as "requirements validation and refinement" sessions; this more formal description still describes what they do, but can be easier to see as a risk-reduction strategy. In the latter, it's important to be persistent. Doorstep the stakeholder if necessary: arrange a lunch or find (or create) a social opportunity. Remember that it's hard to turn down someone who comes bearing a gift, so if you can find out what kind of coffee or tea they like and bring them a cup to open the conversation, you have a better chance of making your advance stick.

The initial round of stakeholder safaris is important in opening the dialogue and setting expectations. But don't let them slip away once the requirements are set and understood. Regular facetime with your stakeholders is vital to not be blindsided by changes. Watercooler conversations are another of those communication aspects that seem trivial, but can actually give you advance warning of situations that can affect the project, like budget cuts, staff changes, or things happening in the wider business landscape. It's far better to know and prepare for these things as early possibilities than to have them delivered as *faits accomplis* by someone who hasn't been made sympathetic by shared chats.

The next few chapters contain lots of useful goals and techniques to pursue during your stakeholder safaris.

## The meeting before the meeting and the meeting after the meeting

Meetings are a special beast in the world of business. They have their own rhythm and etiquette and, as the place where business dialects crash into each other, they also have their own special dialect. When you're in a meeting, you tend to slip into a different communication pattern, with or without noticing. This makes meetings very powerful, but also extremely susceptible to this anti-pattern. But there are two other special aspects to a meeting where the possibility exists to interact in an unstructured way and break out of this pattern: the on-topic but casual time while everyone is gathering, and the time when the meeting is over and people disperse.

### Proceed with caution

As we mentioned in the introduction, the authors generally work in quite flat organizations in the US and Europe. This anti-pattern works well for us in these environments, but in more hierarchically led organizations or cultures, this pattern may be seen as an insulting end run around the proper structures. Observe your organization's culture carefully before deciding how to apply this pattern.

At the meetings before and after the meeting, the normal etiquette isn't in play, but any agreements that are made will usually feel to the bargaining parties like part of the meeting itself in retrospect. This means that these moments are a great time to set up your argument for the meeting with stakeholders who might be sympathetic with the right priming, or to crystallize actions based on a decision that's been made.

## The meeting before the meeting

It's important to enter a meeting knowing the outcome you expect. Before the meeting, you can engage in conversation with the other attendees present to give them a positive sense of your ideas. If you've done a stakeholder safari, it should be easy to understand how to cast the conversation in ways that will resonate with each stakeholder. You can also affect the shape of the meeting by priming them for certain topics: "I hope we'll get a chance to discuss the navigation today; we really need to get moving on that." Agreement (and especially discussion) to a statement like this in the meeting before the meeting means that you'll be likely to get support when you raise it in the meeting itself, and you'll know from which direction, too.

## The meeting after the meeting

In the dispersal after the meeting, you'll have a chance to choose which stakeholders to re-engage with. Usually a meeting will decide *what* will happen, and the meeting after the meeting will decide *how*. Those moments in flagship political dramas, where people follow each other down corridors trying to sway their decisions, are examples of how important the meeting after the meeting is.

Again, it's important to understand what outcome you need. Which stakeholder could support the right process, and might be open to a conversational nudge? That's the person whose ear you want to catch as you leave the room. Engage them positively and explain that you have a few ideas about how you can achieve the agreed-upon outcome that you'd like to briefly bounce off them. Treat it as striking while the iron's hot and the discussion is fresh in everyone's mind, and the stakeholder should see the sense of discussing it at that time.

The meetings before and after the meeting have lots of extra uses, too. They're great for smoothing over any frictions that have occurred, restating your dedication to the project and a stakeholder's needs, or just opening up the opportunity to carve out a time for safari visits. Once you recognize the existence of these moments, you'll begin to see plenty of opportunities in them for yourself. Next time you're in a meeting, observe the room before, during, and after it happens. What are the topics and who are the actors at each stage? Who's grabbing whose ear as you leave?

Using these conversational spaces this way may seem a little manipulative. But it's important to understand that most stakeholders of any seniority will understand this aspect of meetings and use them for their own ends. This pattern just brings you up to parity with them, and we trust you to have the best intentions.

## Lowering the wall

By the time we reach the workplace, we UXers have generally been in creative spaces for at least a few years, as part of a design degree or involvement in other creative aspects of business such as coding and business analysis. Experience of that creative environment is vital, but it can lead us to forget that not every department of every organization works in the same way we do. The confidence that we gain through presenting our ideas can be intimidating to people who don't see their roles as creative. The implication of readiness for critiquing that goes along with presenting our work can be missed. And terms that we use for efficiency or to cast our ideas with authority can feel like a wall being built between us and the other party.

However, when we speak with too much authority, it can feel like we are presenting ourselves as the masters not only of experience, but of the entire business. This can lead other parties to think we implicitly understand all their terms and the background of their requirements, or to feel that we cannot be challenged on those occasions when our knowledge is incomplete or wrong. It is necessary to find a way to expose the gaps in your knowledge in a way that encourages others to contribute positively.

It is, of course, vital from a credibility point of view to present with confidence and to be conversant with the business dialect of design. How do we ensure that this doesn't tip over into alienating stakeholders or coworkers? The more informal communication opportunities you take outside these times, the more options you have. When you're very comfortable with the other parties, you can step in and out of formality during a meeting, keeping the wall low and allowing the other parties to understand that they can step in any time to ask questions without losing face. If that level of informality hasn't been reached, then you can keep the wall low by checking for buy-in on concepts – "Am I making sense when I say 'affinity mapping'?" – and by actively inviting critique.

In the introduction to this book, we introduced the importance of knowing your style. This pattern is one of the places where your style is vital to how you use it. For example, James grew up in England and is comfortable using self-deprecating humor as a way to lower the barrier (in early drafts, he wanted to call this pattern "Call me stupid..."). Martina finds that her sense of humor doesn't translate from German in this context, so she uses a warm, inclusive tone to encourage other parties to engage. It's important that you choose a way of doing this that feels comfortable to you. If you're not, stakeholders will be able to sense your discomfort and you risk raising the wall instead of lowering it.

It may seem counterintuitive to suggest that showing "weakness" in a business context can be a positive and productive way to work. However, remember that creativity has its own needs, which many businesses are now finding themselves rushing to embrace. In businesses that develop products, the maxim "fail early, fail often" is used as a way of admitting the boundaries of our experience as we push into unknown territory, and minimizing the risk of failure. As designers, we can expose the boundaries of our experience to give the business permission to focus on being good at what it does, and demonstrate that design will not impose undue risk by investing too heavily in incorrect assumptions.

## Step back

Many anti-patterns arise from rushing in to answer questions or challenges rather than taking a moment to look at the problem from a different perspective and empathize with the other party. The pattern that underpins everything else we talk about in this book is to hold back on your initial response and take a second to evaluate what you've heard before responding.

In the case of this anti-pattern, Step Back is important in giving you the time to translate the dialect of the challenge into terms that are natural to you. Never try to answer a question or challenge without doing this first, because you will almost certainly answer a question that wasn't being directly asked. Or worse, you may end up defending a point that wasn't actually being challenged.

Taking a step back also gives you the opportunity to remember that the deliverable you brought to this meeting is not intended to be the perfect answer, but rather an embodiment of your current understanding to facilitate conversation. Once you have this view, it's a little easier to be empathetic to other parties who challenge it. It opens up the possibility that, rather than your work being *bad*, it just reflects contemporary assumptions within the business that are now being tested. Whether that's true or not, it offers a better headspace for you to collaborate in.

## Play it back

Check the quality of your translation by playing back what you heard. This gives the other party a chance to confirm or correct your interpretation, and helps them get a hold on what you mean when you use particular terms. We'll expand more on this in Chapter 12.

## If others inflict this anti-pattern on you

UX would be an impossible discipline if we didn't have a dialect of our own, but this does mean that the same problem we have with other departments can affect their understanding of us. Your stakeholder safari and lowering the wall will help share understanding with other groups, but there will always be times when, despite our best intentions, we can't find the right terms to explain our thinking.

If this happens, it's tempting to explain using a metaphor, but although a well-chosen metaphor can illuminate the point like a bolt of lightning, we recommend you tread very carefully on this path. Metaphors about UX goals have a habit of taking over the argument, giving the stakeholder the opportunity to disprove the metaphor rather than engage with the underlying point – for example, "We need the site to feel solid and dependable, like the way a Volvo's door goes *thunk* when you close it" can easily turn into an argument about how the stakeholder's aunt once owned a Volvo and the door fell off it. They also risk sounding patronizing if too simplistic, or making the misunderstanding worse if too complex.

Start by playing your understanding back in as much of their dialect as you can, and test understanding of any UX terms you can't translate. Don't try to simplify common UX terms too much – for example, if you try to simplify the term "persona" by calling it an "example user," a stakeholder could miss the link to research and understand this as a single person rather than a composite. Instead, get to a common base of understanding and then lead in with a needs-based explanation of the gaps. For example, "To understand why Ravi isn't converting, we need to know what's going on inside his head. To help us empathize with what he's seeing, thinking, hearing, and doing, we use a tool called an empathy map."

Conversations are a high-bandwidth method of communication, but they get an extra boost when sketching is also involved. Consider your sketching practice not just as design exploration for yourself, but also communicating ideas simply to nondesigners – the first step in creating the visual language we described earlier. Getting your explanation out as a sketch, and inviting the other party to sketch their side, is the best way to build common understanding, bar none.

If you're still struggling, remember the meetings before and after the meeting. Use these to humanize the other party's view of you and find ways to align your approaches.

## Terminology explained

$5 word effect

Accidental disagreement

Business dialects

Cost of argument

Playback

The meeting before the meeting

The meeting after the meeting

# CASE STUDY

Speaking different languages in software development

*Figure 1.3: Eli Toftøy-Andersen. (Photo credit: Eli Toftøy-Andersen.)*

I think understanding the words we use to describe the work we do and the complex domains we deal with is key to success in cross-functional teams. If the word "design" is already in use by five different experts, clarification is necessary. It's part of my job as a consultant and as a designer to make sure we all understand each other. In workshops with designers, clients and end user representatives, I always encourage "stupid questions" regarding the domain and the words that we use on all sides of the table.

### How to learn the client and project domain

As an interaction designer, I know that the words that you use in an application are important. In 2010, I worked at Norway's largest Agile project, the PUMA project at the State Pension Fund. Both working within the domain of pensions and the idea of Agile were new to me. In my first day at the project, I was walking around and stopped, looking at the different whiteboards.

Suddenly somebody told me that I was "standing in the middle of their standup." I had no idea what that meant at the time, but figured I had to move out of their way. Over the next few days, I was bombarded with new words. I had to design user interaction with values I knew nothing about. When I asked what "erhvervskoffisient" meant, I was told that it was a value between 1 and 10; usually between 1 and 2.

For an application for a hospital, I had to learn words like "diurese" and "cardio" and understand the responsibilities of the different departments. For an application for the Norwegian Department of Defense, I had to learn the difference between "ETA" and "ATA" and the rules for foreign ships that cross into Norwegian waters. Designing such applications would not be possible without knowing the words.

I've learnt the words by observation, talking to the people who work there, reading books, the intranet, brochures, and just spending time learning the client's business.

### Multilingual projects

In multilingual projects, the risk of misunderstandings is even greater, not just because of the different words that we use, but also because of the cultural differences. The need for clarification and explanation of the way we work, what we mean by design and what we deliver will always be there.

The differences in the words also come into the applications and websites that we design. When working with the multilingual learning environment Fronter, I learned the hard way that words in different languages "build" differently. For instance, a typical sentence takes up more space in Norwegian or German than in English. When it comes to languages like Finnish, the order of the words might be so different that just replacing strings in broken-up sentences will not work at all. And where do you place the lefthand menu when the reading order goes from right to the left?

### Conclusion

I find that studying languages and being interested in languages is a big plus for interaction designers.

As a UX person in a company with lots of engineers, you need to be prepared to keep explaining what you do and what the words that you use mean. To clarify the words and ensure you speak the same language as your audience – making sure that new team members and the stakeholders know what you are talking about – is part of your role. You have to do your part to help with getting to the common understanding that is necessary to work together in a good and efficient way.

**Eli Toftøy-Andersen, team manager, User Experience, Steria Norway**

*Over the last seven years, I've been working as an interaction designer and team manager at one of Norway's largest IT consultancies. Even the word "design" is a source of misunderstanding at such companies. Architects are designing, infrastructure consultants are designing, and I've met project managers and sales people who think it is perfectly OK to ask an interaction designer to "make it look pretty."*

# TAKEAWAYS

1. Different departments speak different dialects for good reasons. To engage fully with them, it's up to us to learn how to speak their language.

2. Engaging with colleagues outside traditional business contexts gives us the ability to humanize ourselves and lower the wall between "creative" and "serious" parts of the business.

3. Meetings are a special space with their own dialect that must also be learned.

4. Around the edges of meetings, there are lots of opportunities to bend the social rules to gain or seed understanding of terminology between groups.

5. Never answer the question you *think* you heard. Take a second to process it before answering. If necessary, play it back to the other party to test your understanding.

6. Remember, you were aware of the imperfections and assumptions in your work when you were designing it. Don't get flustered when they are tested in presentation.

# CHAPTER 2

## Having different KPIs

Why do the kinds of specialized business dialects that we discussed in Chapter 1 exist in the first place, if they plague the development process with such inefficiencies? One of the reasons this specialization occurs is because not only does each department have a different area to focus on and innovate within, but they also have different ways of measuring success – embodied by their Key Performance Indicators (KPIs).

## How organizations measure success

Where do KPIs come from? It's hard for the people at the top of the organization chart to take a holistic measure of an entire organization, so they break the process of measuring the whole into easily digestible chunks. Typically, each department that contributes to a product is given its own individual criteria for success – chosen from the areas they can influence. Then, for ease of analysis, a subset of these measures is chosen for performance monitoring – the measures that are most emblematic of that department's influence scope. Thus, each department ends up with a simple set of KPIs, which, in the organization's eyes, determine whether its contribution has been successful.

For example, the sales team probably gets a bonus for picking up new business, marketing might be measured based on a traffic uplift, developers on the number of new features delivered per release. Very rarely is the entire blended product team measured on the same set of criteria, and even more rarely do these criteria have much to do with an overall view of the product. Once a team's KPIs have been established, their dialect will naturally begin to shape itself around them. This is where business dialects arise: they are all about communicating the most important concepts quickly and concisely to one's coworkers, and KPIs are, by definition, the most important concepts. Because KPIs differ between teams, their dialects soon begin to drift apart.

Viewed from 1,000 feet up, this strategy looks efficient: every team is working its hardest to meet a set of KPIs that is tightly tailored to each particular sphere of experience. But it leads to a great deal of friction when, for whatever reason, those KPIs clash between different teams. To get its traffic uplift, marketing *could* insist on an irritating advertising campaign that brings more visitors to the site just to see what it's about, but has them arriving in such a negative state of mind that it's impossible to design an experience that converts them into customers. As a measurable outcome, conversion rate is one of the most common KPIs to be targeted in UX work. In this case, marketing could meet its own KPI, but damage the UX KPI at the same time. However, the department may not even be aware that the conversion rate KPI exists.

While the more benign instances of this anti-pattern can lead to time-consuming negotiations and damage to team cohesion, in more serious cases, it can put departments at war with each other. When marketing knows that the *only* way to get traffic uplift is with irritating banners, and considers any suggestion to try something else as a rejection of their strategy, they are being positively motivated to damage the product (and the KPIs of the rest of the product team).

And, of course, for "marketing" in the previous paragraph, you can just as easily substitute "UX." We're not immune to this effect, either. But we can be the ones to identify and solve the problem.

## Intrinsic motivation

In our experience, it's rare for UX designers to be directly motivated in the way that, for instance, a sales team is (this may have something to do with the fact that it's simpler to count successful sales than to measure the softer aspects of a successful experience). However, it's not unusual for us to self-motivate through a natural desire to deliver exceptional experiences. When this desire butts up against career or financial incentives working in the opposite direction, it creates a damaging clash of ideologies where we see the opposing argument as being motivated by financial gain, and the other party sees us as commercially naïve. Whoever wins this argument, it's not good for the end product.

We *need* sales, marketing, development, and all the other people who are involved in turning an idea into a product. The idea doesn't become a product unless it can be sold to a buyer. It doesn't become a product if no one ever finds out it exists. And it doesn't become a product if no one understands how to build it. And if it doesn't become a product, then how exactly are our wages going to get paid?

We aren't suggesting that every team other than UX is callous, self-interested, and motivated only by money. Without doubt, the piecemeal provision of incentives we describe here is a broken system from a product point of view, but even in a fully integrated company, there can be friction between KPIs just because every player wants to do the best job possible.

## When KPIs clash

Of course, we can't do the impossible when a KPI conflict deadlocks us between two mutually exclusive goals. In these instances, you may need to appeal to a higher power for a realignment of the project goals. This can happen in concert with someone who has responsibility for delivery, such as a product owner. Even better, you can work with the stakeholder whose KPIs you're in conflict with to come up with a plan that you can both present.

### Defining success

Most of us are familiar with asking the question "What does success look like?" It's one of the best ways of running a backtrace from a solution to a business need, setting expectations, or establishing the immediate direction of a project.

However, always remember that, when you ask the question, the answer you get will be shaped by the role of the person you're asking. A project manager may have a very different answer from a product owner – and, of course, a UXer would have yet another.

Sometimes this is down to the specific lens through which a role encourages people to view a project, and sometimes it's because they just don't have any vision of success metrics beyond their own area of expertise.

Success metrics also come in two flavors: externally imposed metrics such as "*Conversion uplift of 30%*," which is what we traditionally mean by KPIs; and self-imposed success metrics, such as "*I want to build the best experience possible.*" It's always worth doubling up the question of what success looks like by asking, "On a personal level, what do you really want this project to achieve?" Not only does this give you greater insight, it demonstrates to stakeholders that you really are committed to their needs.

Just as you should be omnivorous about learning other team's dialects, you should always be trying to understand what they need to get from a project. The sooner you understand that need, the sooner you can start demonstrating your understanding and bringing skeptical stakeholders on board with your solutions. Gaining trust early is hugely valuable when you may later have to negotiate different solutions to meet that stakeholder's targets.

Always remember that being *seen* to understand everyone's KPIs is just as valuable as actually understanding them. This is where widespread buy-in comes from, and it gains you valuable goodwill from the team.

## Bikeshedding

One of the most difficult aspects of understanding other parties' KPIs is that people naturally tend toward a behavior known as bikeshedding.

Bikeshedding comes from C. Northcote Parkinson's Parkinson's Law[1], a well-known essay on management. Parkinson observed that project groups tend to over-discuss trivialities and minor risks while waving through the largest and most potentially risky aspects almost unquestioned.

Parkinson explained this using the example of a nuclear power station. Very few people understand the intricacies of nuclear reactor design, so, on a cross-discipline committee, most members will simply agree with the experts when the subject comes up. However, when the subject comes around to the employees' bike storage shed, that's easy for everyone to picture in their heads. Because everyone can understand it, everyone suddenly has an opinion to present. And because everyone wants to do a good job and add value, they all want to pitch in and argue for what they see as the best possible solution.

This tendency to offer the greatest volume of opinion on incidental matters can make it very difficult to expose another party's KPIs. They'll reveal (explicitly or implicitly) their opinions about matters that everyone understands, but keep quiet on more specialist areas. This means that we can believe their focus lies on trivial matters, yet ultimately we can end up treading into those specialist areas in our work without being aware of the expectations attached to doing so.

Regrettably, bikeshedding seems to be one of those things that dispropor-tionately affects design, because everyone feels qualified to have an opinion on the visible face of a product. However, this doesn't mean that every piece of design feedback is bikeshedding. Falling back to that assumption every time is another version of what we discuss in Chapter 9, "Assuming Others Don't Get Design."

Learning to spot and defuse bikeshedding is difficult, but if you can master it, you'll find meetings become more productive and stakeholder motivations become much more visible. In Chapters 12 and 13, we'll in-troduce some techniques that are helpful for diagnosing bikeshedding and defusing it.

## Summary

We count success or failure of a product according to processes that usually happen in software design and development, but for any sufficiently large product, many departments are working outside that process. We need to learn and embrace the ways they measure success, because the product can't be successful unless all of these goals are met. Stakeholders who truly believe we're working with their interests at heart will be engaged, helpful, and willing to negotiate. Those who feel we're ignorant of their interests or opposed to those interests will be the most difficult to persuade.

## The "Having Different KPIs" anti-pattern

A valuable part of our self-image is that we are the users' champion. However, we can easily forget that our job is to marry the actions of the user with the needs of the busi-ness. We fail if we don't serve the user, but we also fail if we don't serve the business. In fact, if we fail to serve the user, we may get a chance to re-engage them on a later occasion, while failing the business could mean an early end for the project. Failing the business could be worse than failing the user.

We can't satisfy the needs of the business without understanding *all* of its drivers, not just the ones proximate to delivering user journeys. The drivers that aren't proximate will still shape the company's goals and responses, will still bring users to the product, and will still make sure the company can keep the lights on. When we treat drivers that fall out of our realm as irrelevant, we're being as derelict in our duties as if we had ignored a chunk of the userbase when doing research.

What's more, the stakeholders whose performance is measured by those other drivers will still be involved in discovery, feedback, and delivery. If they see our designs failing to embrace their goals, they'll raise the issue to the people above our heads. And because the squeaky wheel gets the grease, what we might have considered minor issues will blow up into major ones.

## You know you're in it when ...

- Stakeholders outright state that their needs aren't being met.
- Stakeholders you've never met before appear during or after your review sessions.
- Departments begin to send extra stakeholders to review sessions for moral support.
- Feedback e-mails after reviews talk about concerns you weren't aware of.
- Stakeholders push back repeatedly on something you consider trivial.
- Someone takes what appears to be a disproportionate amount of interest in what should be an incidental detail (but watch out for bikeshedding).

## Patterns
### Diligent discovery

While you're learning the dialect used by other teams in the business, sound out those teams on what they need to get from the project as well. Remember to examine not only their stated KPIs, but also their self-imposed goals.

Test your understanding by playing back what you've understood from the conversation. If you can immediately see conflicts, don't raise them there and then, but do explore the general area to deepen your knowledge and confirm that there's a risk of conflict.

Don't allow the other party to say "I'll know it when I see it." Push back politely by pointing out that that's too broad a response and that you need some direction from an expert to get started. Don't insist on hearing an answer right away, but do be prepared to chase after it. If, after a couple of rounds of chasing, they still can't give you direction, escalate the problem.

Pull quiet stakeholders out of their shells and ask what you can do to meet their aims, even if (today) they think they're orthogonal to design – some day soon, you might expand into an area that does touch them, and then they'll have something to say!

Leave on a high note by confirming your understanding and assuring the other party that you'll consider their needs as you develop the solution.

## Tu casa es mi casa

Demonstrate your adoption of other parties' KPIs by referring specifically back to how they are served by specific aspects of your work. We've often found that it helps to caption the presentation in a way that separates user benefit from business value, explaining the link between the two.

When stakeholders feed back on something that doesn't seem to be in their area of responsibility, check it against their KPIs as a way of understanding what they're really asking. There may even be something you weren't previously aware of that now affects the work.

## Don't butt heads

If you need to challenge someone else's KPIs, remember that you can't just expect them to drop their objectives. Be prepared to work with them to find a way of satisfying the needs of both parties. If changing KPIs means going to a higher authority, you have a much better chance of succeeding if you go together, with a plan for success, rather than appearing separately simply to demand change.

Remember that everyone's KPIs are set for reasons that make sense to their spheres of influence, even if it's opaque to you. That can make it hard to understand the underlying business value that another party's KPI serves. The only way to undercover this value is to work with the party to understand it. Treat the conversation in the same way as you'd tease out a research subject's motivation: openly, not leading, with no foregone conclusion in mind.

In the same way, the value behind your KPIs can be opaque to other parties. When you identify a conflict, make the other party aware using nonjudgmental language and tone, and without an expectation of outcome. "There's a conflict here that makes it difficult for me to deliver my part. Can we work on a solution together?" is much better than "You have to change this because it's hard for me." Be prepared to explain how your KPI relates to business or UX value and, if it's a pure UX value issue, be ready to justify why this is so important. Go in prepared: have an elevator pitch ready that explains the route from visible KPI back to obscured value.

## If others inflict this anti-pattern on you

The motivations of design disciplines like UX can be extremely hard for other areas of business to understand. We tend to be self-motivating, quality-driven, and subject to a whole external set of measures, born of experience in the craft, that sometimes make it hard even for the people setting our goals to understand where we're coming from. For example, our responsibility to bring the user's perspective into the mix can make us seem to be completely at odds with traditional business goals.

That makes it easy for this anti-pattern to play out against us. Our KPIs are so hidden relative to our outputs that it can be extraordinarily difficult for other parties to tie them back to what they understand as business value. If we don't explain this gap well, it leads to a perception that the work we do *can't* be tied back to business value. Stakeholders who believe this see design as unquantifiable and subjective, and designers as perfectionist and naïve about business.

In business, things that are unquantifiable constitute risk; a typical delivery process has an overall aim of minimizing risk and several roles explicitly dedicated to removing it. If design effort becomes equated with risk, this is a toxic situation to be in. No design decision under those circumstances can be allowed to stand on its own feet. Ultimately, an organization needs to *trust* design because it understands the inherent value of design.

### Don't try to handle organizational change singlehanded

Getting a whole organization to understand the value of design is not something that happens overnight. Experience of the process has taught us that it takes around eighteen painful months of organizational change before large companies can fully accept methodologies such as Design Thinking into their cultures. Cultural change on this level is also not something that can be driven from the bottom up. In the long term, this kind of organizational change is a valuable goal to sell in; wherever possible, through pilot projects and lobbying the higher-ups. However, without short-term tactical solutions to break this anti-pattern, you won't have the proof to demonstrate that the change can be successful.

*Figure 2.1: Driving organizational change can feel endless when done singlehanded. (Photo by: Davide Ragusa.)*

In Chapter 11, we'll explain the importance of presenting with context to demonstrate the solid rationale behind your decisions, and we'll introduce frameworks for understanding when and how to defend your decisions. These are powerful tactics for breaking out of this anti-pattern.

When someone challenges one of your KPIs, you should be able to do more than just explain it – you should be able to *sell the value of it*. Remember the power of the elevator pitch. An elevator pitch is not just explaining something in 30 seconds; it's a story that you tell in 30 seconds to make someone believe.

### Constructing an elevator pitch

Elevator pitches originated in Hollywood, where aspiring screenwriters need to be on the lookout for opportunities to get their ideas into the hands of high-up executives. Such a pitch is designed not only to say *what* a script is in the 30-second span of an elevator ride, but also *why* it's destined to be a huge hit. In a UX context, the elevator pitch is a useful technique for times outside of structured discussion, like those magical moments before and after the meeting that we discussed in the previous chapter.

Start with a goal: *What* do you want the stakeholder to buy into? Remember that this is not the design element itself – it's the *rationale behind* the design element. Once the stakeholder buys the rationale, the element becomes the solution to the need. For example, maybe you're selling in a gradual engagement strategy. What you're defending with this elevator pitch is *not* the lightweight initial registration form, directly. You're selling the need to demonstrate value to the user before asking for a commitment. "*So here I am, at the point where I can create my first note with the system, and I have this encouraging prompt to get me to start.*"

Add a challenge in the form of a question. Our brains always try to answer any question that gets asked, so this is a powerful way to get the other party to put themselves in our shoes, or the user's shoes. For example, you might ask, "*As Sue the hard-pressed mother, why would I take the time to register right now?*" Using a well-understood persona here makes it easier for the stakeholder to empathize with the customer need we're serving.

Finally, wrap up the goal and challenge by tying them together with reference to business value. "'*Well, actually, I wouldn't, because I don't feel like I know whether this product does enough for me yet. But if I get further and put a little bit of my own energy into the product, suddenly I feel a bit of ownership and yes, now I want to protect that ownership, so I'll register.' And that's how we achieve our conversion uplift target by using gradual engagement.*"

Crafting elevator pitches is a creative skill like any other, and the more you practice them, the more persuasive they'll get. So don't wait for a challenge; start practicing as early as possible. To get you started, think about how you answer when someone asks you what you do for a living. That is an ideal opportunity to test an elevator pitch for UX itself.

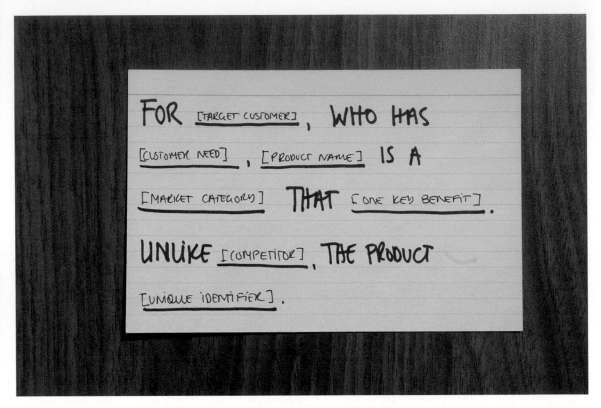

*Figure 2.2: How to Construct an Elevator Pitch. (Photo provided by Martina Hodges-Schell.)*

## CASE STUDY

*Figure 2.3: Aline Baeck.*

Closing the KPI gap

Designers often use customer-based KPIs such as Net Promoter Score (NPS), task completion, and error rate and satisfaction. Engineering organizations, meanwhile, are often judged by their on-time delivery and bug counts. A KPI gap, which occurs when different measures of success create tension and conflict in product teams, can feel like an insurmountable chasm.

How can this gap be reconciled?

The best closure I've seen of a KPI gap happened on a team I led a few years ago. We'd been asked to reduce customer attrition, and were expected to define a solution to implement in the next release.

Our research showed that an uncomfortably large number of customers bought our product but stopped using it within two months. An initial analysis of data, combined with ethnographic research, revealed a complicated set of interconnected causes with our new customer process, ranging from misleading marketing messages to overly complicated terminology in our setup wizard. We mapped these issues on an end-to-end customer journey and felt despair. As a design leader, my main goal was to increase our user's satisfaction, thereby reducing attrition. But the need to significantly reduce that attrition in our next release meant pressure from engineering to define incremental changes that could meet the predetermined release schedule. The KPIs were at odds because design and engineering did not measure success in the same way, and the resulting conflict on the team was almost paralyzing.

To resolve this conflict, we stepped back as a team to reexamine what we were trying to accomplish. Ultimately, we needed to reduce attrition in our customer base, and our design-based KPIs and engineering KPIs were our own perspectives on how to reach that business goal. By focusing back on the business goal we shared, we were able to radically rethink our approach and reach a solution.

We recognized that the complicated landscape of product issues could not be solved in the timeframe defined for the project, so, instead of solving the underlying problems, we asked ourselves, "What if we provided a service-based support system for users that effectively smoothed out the speed bumps and reduced attrition of users from the product"? This could provide a short-term solution to meet the overall business goal and give us more time to solve the deeper issues.

We quickly defined a service that we were able to test with minimal engineering investment. Since it showed potential, we then gave this service a limited trial run, iterated, and launched in the timeframe originally defined for the project. The result was a service that significantly reduced attrition, as well as increased the long-term value of those users to the company.

The turning point was the team's recognition that our KPI gap was limiting our thinking. By refocusing on the ultimate business goal, we were able to see a solution that had been hidden by the function-specific KPIs. Most importantly, the business goal gave us a single, shared KPI that enabled us to create a much better experience for our customers.

*Aline Baeck has applied her passion for design to big data, small business, national defense, medical devices, telecommunications, and consumer applications. Originally from Silicon Valley in California, she is currently living in London and working at eBay.*

## Terminology explained

Bikeshedding

Elevator pitch

KPI

### REFERENCE

1. Northcote Parkinson C. Parkinson's Law: The Pursuit of Progress. London: John Murray; 1958. ISBN: 1906821348.

# TAKEAWAYS

1. One of the biggest problems when working across different teams is that each team has its own distinct incentives. The incentives of other groups can't be ignored or negated; they must be addressed.

2. People are explicitly motivated by KPIs, and implicitly motivated by the personal desire to do a good job. Both sets of motivations must be understood and addressed.

3. A product that only meets some of the business' KPIs cannot be a successful product, no matter how great its design.

4. When a KPI conflict arises, it must be resolved. This is easier to achieve if you can work collaboratively with the other party to identify a solution.

5. Our motivations can appear unbusinesslike from the outside, and we must work to make the value that underpins them visible so the business can begin to trust design.

# CHAPTER 3

## Not embracing everyone's goals

## Onto the right path

Once you learn to recognize and understand the different motivations that exist within your organization, you're on the road to successfully designing a product – but, for the organization to begin to completely integrate design thinking into its processes, there is a further step that has to be taken: you need to build trust. It's possible to recognize and respond to other parties' motivations without fully embracing them, or treating them as integral to the design solution, but not integrating everyone's goals into your design goals leaves stakeholders wondering if you can be trusted to lead the product development and have their best interest at heart.

If you're like the authors, you've definitely been in the situation where nondesigners treat UX and design as a veneer that can be applied late in the day after the "important" parts have been put to rest. We've also been guilty of treating marketing, technical, and business needs the same way in our design solutions. Jamming a required feature wherever it fits into the information architecture, grudgingly leaving space for standard banners, or treating content and social marketing as necessary evils – these are all ways of responding to a KPI without really embracing it.

In many ways, these kinds of response are the worst of both worlds: we feel that we're compromising our design, while our stakeholders feel that our commitment to their needs doesn't go beyond shallow lip service. We may be getting sign-off, but we're not building the deeper level of trust that is the hallmark of a design-centric organization.

## Trust is magic

One of the themes that we find ourselves coming back to time and time again as we write this book is the sense that, to those outside traditional design roles, design and designers can appear intimidating, unquantifiable, and having a different set of rules. Trust is the magic that bridges the gap between "their world" and "our world."

If the other parts of the organization don't have trust in us and our work, we end up simply seeking acceptance. Acceptance is valuable: it means we get sign-off to build our design. But it should only be a portion of the relationship we establish with stakeholders – and a minor portion at that.

Design means change. Change means risk. And risk makes people worry about their paychecks. Under these circumstances, it's natural for stakeholders to proceed cautiously in embracing our ideas, but this often means pulling back on key aspects of design work and watering down the impact. When the experience is eventually delivered, there can be a sense of "so what?" because the compromises have stripped away so many of our capabilities. Merely accepting design's contribution to creating a product creates a situation where only the parts that design can justify are seen to have value.

On the other hand, when we build trust in an organization, stakeholders begin to understand that adding to UX and design doesn't mean taking away from other areas; indeed, it means adding to those as well. User-centric thinking comes to be seen as a merit in its own right, because of the resulting benefits to the whole organization.

Looping "nondesigner" stakeholders into the creative process is one of the most powerful ways to build this trust. In the beginning, it demystifies our process and exposes our commitment to business value. As time goes on, including stakeholders in the creative process becomes a virtuous cycle: they see the value, they contribute to the value, they see the value flowing back to their own areas of influence, and that drives further trust in our creative process.

It's no coincidence that many of the patterns we cover in this book involve co-creation and involving stakeholders in creation. We believe that successful design stems from an organization-wide culture of understanding and trusting design practices. Lack of trust is the ultimate anti-pattern, but by involving stakeholders and demystifying our processes, it is possible to fix this.

Trust runs both ways, of course. Why should an organization full of stakeholders trust design if they feel as if the designer doesn't trust them? How can we hope to embrace the needs of other business areas if, on some level, we believe they don't have the best outcome at heart? How can we be fully integrated into a structure if we build barriers around us?

It's not enough just to understand and respond to KPIs from other areas of the business. We need to commit to them and ensure that our solutions embody them with the same level of integration as our own goals. In addition, we need to be *seen* to be doing this by the owners of those KPIs, because there is an odd effect at play when we do this.

## The sore thumb paradox

When we sloppily integrate a stakeholder's needs into our solution, it can often stick out like a sore thumb. Some stakeholders will observe this, recognize the design compromise, and request that the need be better integrated. Others will be delighted that their need has been recognized with such prominence and visibility. The important thing is that both camps have *seen that their need has been recognized.* Ironically, a properly integrated response, without this in-your-face lack of subtlety, can often be misinterpreted by the responsible stakeholder as the designer de-prioritizing their KPI, or even failing to realize that the response has been made at all. The Sore Thumb Paradox is that bad design gets noticed.

When we respond properly to a stakeholder's requirements, it's important that we do as much as possible to demonstrate how our solution meets the needs of both parties. This is one of those key moments where being able to speak to a stakeholder in their own dialect is vital in demonstrating understanding and building trust. It's also important to introduce your solution in the context of the stakeholder requirement and with the story of why this solution serves everybody's best interest. We'll fully unpack the importance of presenting in context, and introduce some useful patterns for doing so, in the next chapter.

## Summary

It's not enough just to understand and respond to stakeholder needs. We must give them the same level of consideration as our own. However, this can lead to a Sore Thumb Paradox situation where a better-integrated answer is not as visible to stakeholders as a quickly added afterthought. Instead, the jarring bolt-on seems to be a more prominent response to their request. Therefore, it is vital to also communicate how the solution embraces the stakeholder need and balances with the many competing demands within a product. Succeeding in this approach leads from a situation where your UX work is aiming for acceptance to one where UX has the trust of the organization and more resources can be dedicated to exploring better experiences.

## The "Not Embracing Everyone's Goals" anti-pattern

If we don't work as hard to integrate the needs of other stakeholders into our solution as we do with our own, then at best we gain acceptance, rather than building trust across the team. In the long term, this lack of trust results in products built with a conservative attitude to UX. It can result in a situation where every UX input into product development has to be justified in quantifiable terms (e.g., Return on Investment [ROI]) rather than being understood to create qualitative value across disciplines.

However, the better we integrate these needs, the more we need to highlight and explain how our solution serves them, or the stakeholders who own them can feel that their needs have not been addressed.

## You know you're in it when...

- It can be hard to identify this anti-pattern because you can successfully gain acceptance for individual solutions even while you're suffering from it.

- In general, stakeholders don't seem to trust UX; they seem to insist on seeing the benefit of every feature you add.

- You're just doing the things that you know will get an easy sign-off.

- You're not truly embracing the feedback you're getting in design reviews and as new requirements emerge; you're dismissing them as not that important.

- Stakeholders who are not particularly sold on the benefits of UX will agree in terms that make UX seem like a market requirement or a fad: "I suppose if everyone else is doing this, we need to as well," or "If you need to add your trendy bits, then go ahead." These are signs that you need to build trust and demonstrate integration with the wider business aims.

## Patterns

### Be the canonical source of why

If your project is of sufficient complexity that it has many external stakeholders, then it's almost certain that nobody outside the delivery team has a complete understanding of what it is that you're delivering. There's a great opportunity here for someone who can speak the language of different departments and has a fully formed understanding of the many different needs that are being embodied in the product. You can become the trusted source of explanation for *why* anything on the project is happening. Being able to explain choices in terms that make sense to the person asking results in them trusting you; trust that will be reflected back to your UX work.

Of course, it's not always convenient to explain everything face-to-face, and your project might be so complex that you need a reference to remember everything. In these cases, it's helpful to have your work on the wall both as an aide-memoire and reference, and for others to see and internalize as they pass through your space.

### Active agreement

Treating your stakeholder and their opinions with the appropriate level of attention from the start of the process is a vital method of building trust at the source. It's far easier to maintain trust when it's been established early than to try and build it out later in the process.

When you're seeking out stakeholders' needs (see "Diligent discovery" in the previous chapter), make sure that they understand your commitment to them.

NOT EMBRACING EVERYONE'S GOALS   **CHAPTER 3**

- Take notes – even if you have a photographic memory, note-taking indicates to the other party that you're taking what they say seriously.

- Make eye contact and use positive gestures such as nodding.

- Probe their requirements and methods until you're sure you have a full picture.

- If you have external insight that you can use to play back your understanding, be sure to mention it.

- Suggest techniques that you can apply to their requirements, but don't try to solve everything there and then – present options rather than leaping directly to an answer.

Make a verbal commitment to your stakeholder's requirements. Saying something out loud not only offers confirmation to the person being spoken to, but also primes you to form a stronger memory of the event – and the self-herding tendency, as described by Dan Ariely,[1] means we make decisions based on our memories of how we acted before.

## Consciously internalize

Remember that trust flows both ways. It will be easier for the business to trust you if it feels like you trust them. However, sometimes people within the business will get their approach wrong, come to unsuitable conclusions or appear to trample on our decisions. The first part of building trust within ourselves is to give people who do this the benefit of the doubt. You can make a conscious effort to do this by having a mantra to remind you. We like to use a variant of Norm Kerth's[2] Retrospective Prime Directive, which reads:

> "Regardless of what we discover, we understand and truly believe that everyone did the best job they could, given what they knew at the time, their skills and abilities, the resources available, and the situation at hand."

For our purposes, this would be something more like:

> "Regardless of this situation, I understand and truly believe that everyone is working to make the best possible product, given what they know now, their skills and abilities, the resources available, and the environment we are working in."

Just like the previous pattern, repeating this out loud and not just in your head creates a powerful priming effect that puts you in the right frame of mind to treat an awkward stakeholder without blame or frustration. Repeat it to yourself before difficult meetings and design reviews, and see what a difference it makes to your approach.

## Stakeholders are people, too

It's easy to mistrust a role, but harder to mistrust a human being, so it's important to try to understand the person behind any decisions on a human level. Team lunches, after-work activities, and other social bonding rituals are important to building trust within a team and an organization. If they aren't happening where you are, make sure you work to get them going – or start them up yourself.

It's also valuable to let a little bit of your own personality show, so the people you deal with understand that UXers are normal people, too. We don't insist you should go as far as James and the reversible disco-ball jacket he is famous for, but letting your passion for the craft of UX shine through is a great way to show your personal side. Organizational and cultural context permitting, being able to reveal some unlikely fact about yourself in an unguarded moment is also a great way to open up conversations beyond your role on the project.

An extension of this idea is to have a "game face," which is to say an outward expression of committed concentration for serious business moments. Donning your game face in important meetings and one-to-ones demonstrates your commitment to the issue at hand, but allows you to discard it and be a little more yourself during less-critical times. Just make sure your game-face expression comes across as natural.

## Present in context

Structure your design presentations so attendees are led through the process, rather than just presented with the outcomes. For more details, see Chapter 4.

## Co-design

Allowing "nondesigners" into your process by inviting them to co-design workshops on their requirements is a great way of demonstrating the process by which you turn their needs into features within the greater experience framework. This builds trust

*Figure 3.1: James in his awesome jacket. (Photo credit: Melissa Fehr.)*

and confidence that you're not just designing for design's sake. We've included a guide to running co-design sessions later in this book.

## If others inflict this anti-pattern on you

In the general case, this anti-pattern takes the form of other stakeholders not understanding the goals of UX and design, which are themes that we deal with in several other chapters of this book, in particular, chapters 12 and 13. However, this is an anti-pattern that can affect UX and design even when they're only caught in the crossfire between two or more stakeholders inflicting this anti-pattern on each other.

Some of the biggest challenges can arise when two or more stakeholders have conflicting requirements and, as the designer, it falls to you to reconcile them. This can manifest simply, as conflicting sets of requirements in the product backlog, or in a more complex political form, where stakeholders try to cajole you into supporting their view, monopolize your time so you can't work on the opposing option, or seek the assistance of higher powers when they perceive that you're favoring the other side of the argument.

The first line of defense against this situation is to meet with the stakeholders concerned, either individually or together. Explain, without blame or recrimination, that there's clearly a mismatch in requirements that is making it tricky to deliver on your part of the job. Offer to broker a solution by understanding both sets of requirements and agreeing on a way to make the best compromise. Use the patterns we've shown in this chapter to build trust on both sides as the requirements are explained, but also to keep control over the meeting – don't let stakeholders challenge each other's requirements during the explanation.

Once the requirements are understood, discuss where the conflicts exist. You may be lucky at this point and find that, with everything laid out on the table, the conflict disappears. Otherwise, move to start figuring out a solution, engaging both stakeholders and visualising possible solutions through sketching wherever possible. Gain positive agreement on the way forward from both parties as a way of finishing the meeting. Remember to document the agreement and e-mail it to both parties so everyone has the same baseline for future engagements.

If you're not able to resolve the situation like this, you will need to escalate. Having two key stakeholders with conflicting sets of requirements is essentially the same as having an incoherent product vision. Fortunately, there will be someone in your organization whose job is to ensure the delivery of the project against its vision – if the vision is not resolvable, it's their job to fix it. This may be your project manager, the product owner, one of their sponsors, or perhaps a member of senior management. Regardless of who it is, routes upward through the governance of the project should allow you to raise the problem to the level where someone has the authority to drive consensus.

## Terminology explained

Sore Thumb Paradox

Retrospective Prime Directive

Self-herding

Canonical source of why

Game face

### REFERENCES

1. Ariely D. The Upside of Irrationality: The Unexpected Benefits of Defying Logic at Work and at Home. New York: HarperCollins Publishers; 2010.
2. Kerth NL. Project Retrospectives: A Handbook for Team Reviews. New York: Dorset House; 2011.

# TAKEAWAYS

1. It's possible to get a good design into production by only shooting for acceptance from stakeholders, but you can get a great design into production, with less struggle, if you can build trust instead.

2. It's much easier to build trust at the start of an engagement, by demonstrating commitment to stakeholder needs, than to try to regain it if they feel neglected or misunderstood.

3. Involving "nondesign" stakeholders in the creative process is one of the most powerful ways of building understanding and trust (More in Chapters 9 and 16).

4. Try to build empathy for the person behind the role, and let them see a little bit of your own personality, to help trust grow.

5. Use a mantra to consciously internalize the sense that all parties involved have the best intentions of the product at heart. Repeat the mantra before difficult interactions.

6. If you get trapped between two fighting stakeholders, you can use a co-design session to attempt to resolve the conflict, or escalate the issue through your project governance framework.

# CHAPTER 4

## Presenting without contextualizing

"Out of mind as soon as out of sight."
—Fulke Greville[1], Lord Brooke

Talk to anyone whose job is to produce creative solutions and you'll hear the same story: stakeholders give feedback in one direction at the first session, and then directly contradict it in the next session. One week, they're musing about how there's not enough blue, the next week, there's blue everywhere and it looks terrible – take some of the blue out!

Why are clients and stakeholders so mercurial? There is certainly a subset who micromanage design through the feedback meetings, trying out whims and exploring at the wrong level of fidelity. However, we'd like to believe that these are in the minority and the vast majority of people you'll present to in your career have the best interests of the product in mind. The problem is really an imbalance of contact time with the design.

Wherever possible, we like to give our clients and stakeholders as much involvement in the design game as possible. That can mean pairing, active exploration of design during requirements sessions, and getting the work up on the wall for maximum visibility. But it's not always possible – for example, if you work in an agency environment, it's unlikely that the client will be constantly present and you may have to fall back on periodic review sessions. Similarly, if you have a large and/or busy group of stakeholders involved in the product, you may only be able to bring some of them into the process and will still have to present to the others.

Put yourself in the shoes of these attendees. They may not have seen the work for a week or two. In the meantime, their focus has been on other aspects of their jobs. You'll talk them through the current state of the work and ask for feedback, with only a minimum of contact time. No wonder the resulting feedback is often superficial and doesn't take into account the full context in which the design solution was prepared. Equally, having given off-the-cuff feedback, it should be no surprise that the feedback doesn't stick in their minds for the next session or that, if it does, it doesn't match the exact form of the solution they originally proposed.

This contact gap can be very dangerous to your design aims. It can rob your work of depth by focusing only on the immediate impressions. The more complex the product you're building, the more risk shallow feedback poses. The missing ingredient in providing that depth is *design context* – the set of user insight, feedback, reasoning, and assumptions that led to the solution being presented.

Resolving this *context imbalance* means more than just walking through your solution. It means explicitly telling the story of the background insight that led to the solution, and making the evolution and original feedback response clear. It means telling the *what* and *why* of the paths that weren't taken – because these will inevitably come up as suggestions if you don't. To do this effectively, you must prepare more than just the design collateral for feedback sessions: you need to work out the story you're telling, and also prepare the assets that allow you to tell that story visually.

## Common assets for providing context

We produce a lot of artifacts during the UX discovery and design process, but often these fall into disuse once created. Remember that stakeholders have fallible human memories and may forget the detail of assets that have been signed off or are not being used. Keep these up on the wall and visible, to act as a reminder and reference.

*Personas* are probably the device used most often to provide design context in UX. They're an encapsulation of the research, a reminder of contradictions within various aspects of the audience, and a reminder of the service boundaries the product will live within. We attach all of these purposes to a realistic-seeming face and name – the persona – so they stick in the memory of everyone working on the project. This helps us keep stakeholders focused on the needs and abilities of the end user when prioritizing features.

*Maps* of various kinds are vitally important in providing the underlying requirements for our design solutions.

**Process maps** explain why there may be more or fewer steps to a given journey, highlight external dependencies that force design solutions, and demonstrate how confusing situations have been avoided.

*Figure 4.1: Persona Example. (Photo by: Martina Hodges-Schell.)*

**Experience maps** help lay out stages in a user's engagement with a product and the user's needs and goals at each stage. They also show how each service touchpoint is integrated into the customer experience. On a larger scale, these evolve into **Service maps**, giving context of bigger systems.

**Empathy maps** capture snapshots of a persona's experience and help teams better understand their context and identify goals of their users. This insight is used to design products and workflows that help users achieve their goals more effectively.

**Story maps** act as an interim step in developing an information architecture. A story map is an affinity-grouped set of user actions (for example, one affinity group would be the actions around registering, logging in, logging out, and managing a profile). These are a fantastic way to show the range of abilities a user will have on a site without committing to a fixed structure or initial scope. Story mapping is also a great way to help development teams break down work into bite-size chunks. When the information architecture is formalized, the story map evolves into a **Site map**.

## Core User Journey
Batch Jobs

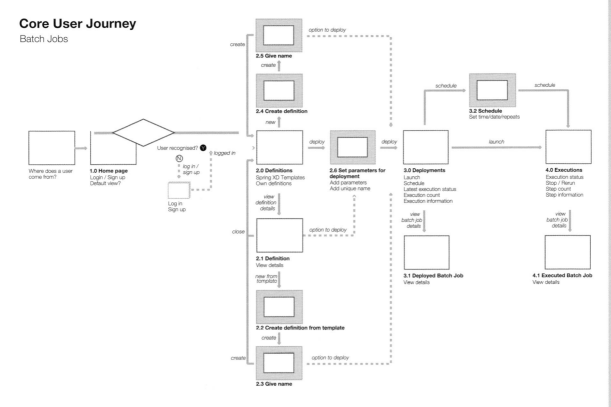

Figure 4.2: Process Map. (Photo by: Martina Hodges-Schell.)

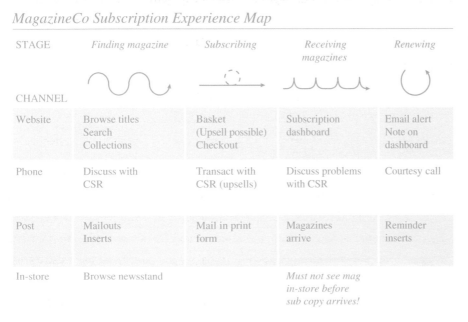

*MagazineCo Subscription Experience Map*

| STAGE | *Finding magazine* | *Subscribing* | *Receiving magazines* | *Renewing* |
|---|---|---|---|---|
| CHANNEL | | | | |
| Website | Browse titles Search Collections | Basket (Upsell possible) Checkout | Subscription dashboard | Email alert Note on dashboard |
| Phone | Discuss with CSR | Transact with CSR (upsells) | Discuss problems with CSR | Courtesy call |
| Post | Mailouts Inserts | Mail in print form | Magazines arrive | Reminder inserts |
| In-store | Browse newsstand | | *Must not see mag in-store before sub copy arrives!* | |

Figure 4.3: Experience Map. (Photo by: James O'Brien.)

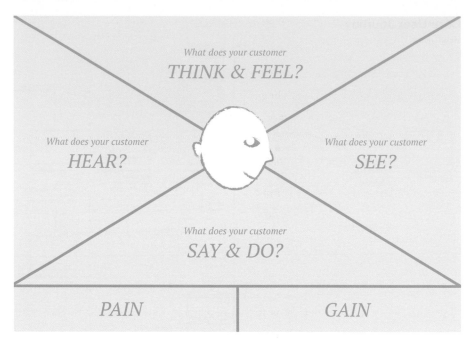

Figure 4.4: Empathy Map. (Photo by: Martina Hodges-Schell.)

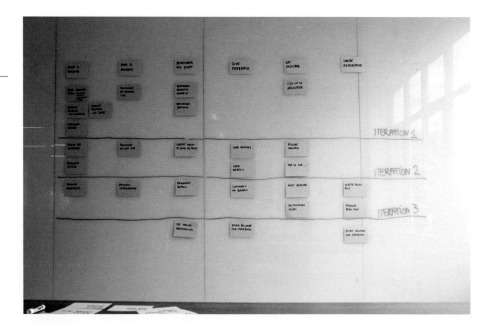

Figure 4.5: Story Map. (Photo by: Martina Hodges-Schell.)

Along with these maps, here are some other useful artifacts that help expose the insights driving our decisions.

The **Customer Life cycle** maps the entire journey that a user goes on over the course of engagement with the product. Beginning with initial awareness of the service, the life cycle follows through discovery and understanding, to repeat use, habituation, and advocacy. For a service that has a defined end-of-engagement, the life cycle also defines how a customer will disengage in a positive way.

**Experience principles** act in a complementary fashion to personas: they assert the personality of the product being developed. By acting as an agreed-upon frame of reference to guide design decisions, they give us permission to pursue quality and a benchmark for UX success.

Once design reviews have begun, the **sign-off from the previous review** provides a vital line in the sand for decisions that have already been made and therefore are likely to incur a higher cost to change. It also shows the framework within which the current round of work needs to operate, and helps direct feedback expressed in the form of solutions to be coherent with the existing work.

*Figure 4.6: Customer Experience Life Cycle. (Photo by: James O'Brien.)*

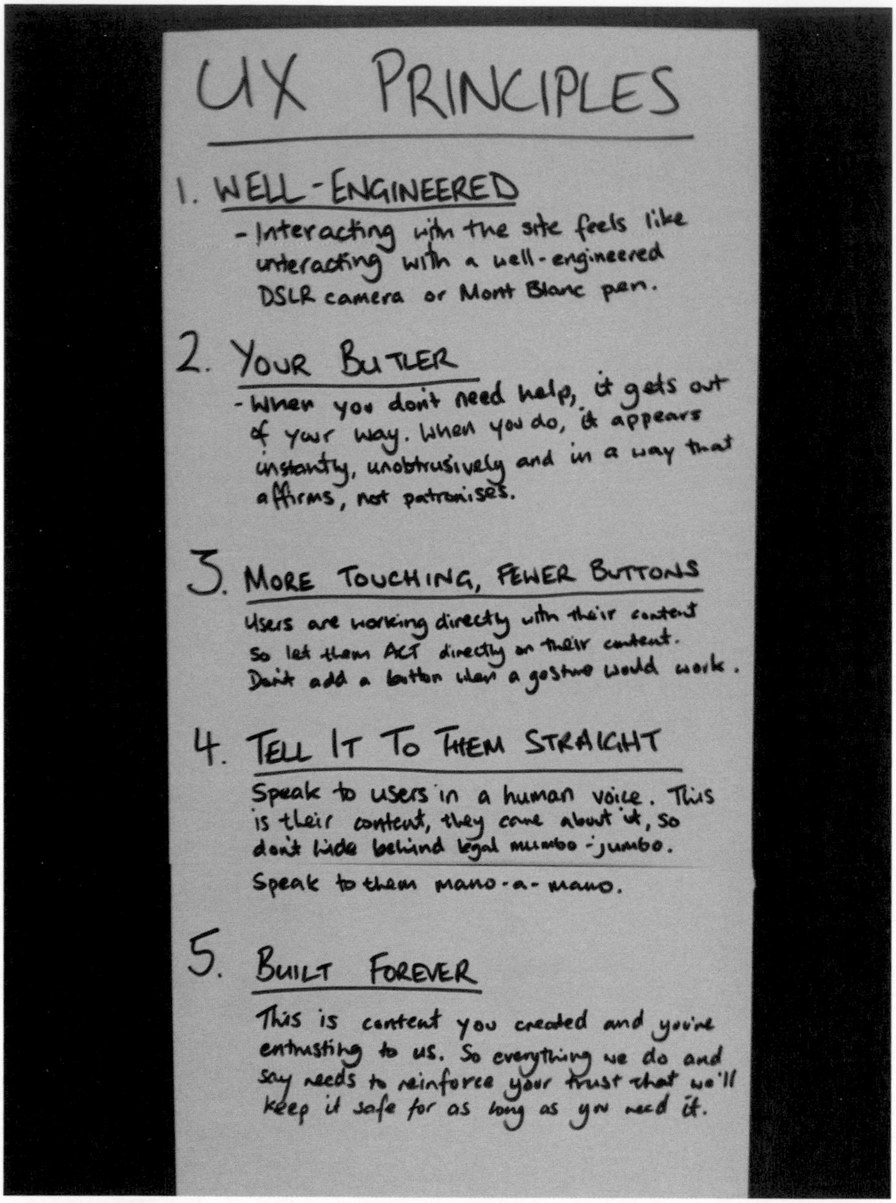

# UX PRINCIPLES

## 1. WELL-ENGINEERED
- Interacting with the site feels like interacting with a well-engineered DSLR camera or Mont Blanc pen.

## 2. YOUR BUTLER
- When you don't need help, it gets out of your way. When you do, it appears instantly, unobtrusively and in a way that affirms, not patronises.

## 3. MORE TOUCHING, FEWER BUTTONS
Users are working directly with their content so let them ACT directly on their content. Don't add a button when a gesture would work.

## 4. TELL IT TO THEM STRAIGHT
Speak to users in a human voice. This is their content, they care about it, so don't hide behind legal mumbo-jumbo.

Speak to them mano-a-mano.

## 5. BUILT FOREVER
This is content you created and you're entrusting to us. So everything we do and say needs to reinforce your trust that we'll keep it safe for as long as you need it.

*Figure 4.7: Experience Principles. (Photo by: James O'Brien.)*

## Telling the story of UX

In the authors' careers, we've sometimes found ourselves starting in new workplaces and being treated like celebrities whose mere presence will solve a host of entrenched problems. However, this "rockstar," "ninja," or "wizard" status often goes hand-in-hand with a lack of understanding about how UX has to integrate with product development and company culture. It places us in an outsider role, where our deliverables are seen as having a magical ability to make people understand experience design, without needing to see, understand, or adopt any of our process.

There's nothing magical about what we do – we use research, heuristics, and exposed assumptions to make decisions and document them. This can only feel like magic if the research insight and heuristic basis are hidden and the assumptions aren't exposed. An organization like this is not a bad place to be, but you need to make it your mission that the people you'll be working with begin to understand your processes in the context of more than just the end result.

The most powerful rule of thumb we have discovered in our UX careers is "when in doubt, tell a story." As social animals with powerful memories, humans are innately primed to respond to the structure of a story. Indeed, in *The Science of Discworld II: The Globe*, Terry Pratchett, Ian Stewart, and Jack Cohen make the argument that, far from being *Homo sapiens,* the wise man, our social structures and biology make us more suited to be *Pan narrans,* the storytelling chimp.[2] Further, they argue that we were *only* able as a species to build civilization because of our ability to share a vision by creating and telling stories. If stories can manage that, they can definitely get you through the next review.

A narrative must have several features to become a story. First, every good story has a **beginning, a middle,** and **an end**. To apply this to an experience, think about the story that a signup form, or a progress indicator tells: here's where you started; here's where you are; here's where you should be going next.

Stories need a **focus** – a character or event that everything else flows from. We often speak about making a piece of content "the hero" of a layout, or a key feature that defines the whole product.

Finally, stories need to live in a **setting** that makes them feel real. Think of the personal details we add to personas to make them seem more plausible, in exactly the way that a novelist or screenwriter will bleed backstory into a character.

From these parallels, it emerges that, consciously or unconsciously, we tell stories all the time in our work. However, all too often, we expect stakeholders to jump into the middle of the narrative – *here's where you are* – when it's been awhile since they read the previous chapter, and they're a bit fuzzy on what the ending is supposed to be.

It's also vital to do the hard work of *editing* your story – showing only the aspects of the work that move the narrative forward. Low-fidelity wireframes are a great example of this editing; by not including visual design, they prevent stakeholders from feeding back on an aspect that is not intended to be included in the discussion. Use editing to *guide* your stakeholders to give the right level of feedback at the right time. Match the fidelity of your review deliverables to the level and subjects of feedback you expect to receive. For example, when you're looking for feedback on a user flow, show a zoomed-out view of the flow, not fully designed concepts of each individual page. Be careful not to show solutions when you're still defining which problem you're solving.

Don't allow stakeholders to break out of context, either. Eager (or combative) stakeholders will often jump ahead on the boards or in the handout to ask questions about something that hasn't been presented yet, or ask flow-breaking questions that require unpacking before your narrative can continue. Structure your presentation so those present can only see the currently contextual deliverable, and respond to questions that jump the gun with "I'd like to do a complete run-through to tell the whole story first. Make a note of any questions or suggestions you think of, and we'll do a second pass, step-by-step, to address them in depth." It's even better to establish this at the start of the session (or with an agenda in the invitation) so the expectation is set within the group, and anyone breaking it is crossing a social boundary. Ensure that each deliverable has a recognizable title or reference that stakeholders can make notes against.

Another powerful method for focusing feedback is to ask stakeholders to capture their thoughts in writing during the first pass. Run the pass so they have enough context to follow the flow, but do not explain every aspect of the design. Go relatively slowly so they have a chance to view the design and capture any thoughts. These can then be used as a springboard for subjects that need further expansion on the second pass. Capturing feedback in this way not only focuses the topics and volume of feedback, but also avoids groupthink by preventing all the stakeholders present from jumping onto the back of the first spoken comment.

## Getting good feedback

Good feedback is vital to developing successful products. We as UX designers rely on the experience of specialists in the business area of the product, just as those specialists rely on us to provide the UX domain experience they lack. But poor or nonactionable feedback is triply damaging. First, it crowds out useful, actionable feedback that we could use to angle our work closer to the goal. Second, it erodes the trust relationship between us and our stakeholders. Third, when it's not actionable, it leaves us staring at a round of work with no direction to follow. Feedback is so vital to the process, failing to provide the environment in which everyone's feedback can be of optimum quality is a dereliction of our duty as UX designers.

The "work" aspect of UX often feels like the production of deliverables, with presenting them being no more than an interim or endcap activity, or possibly even a chore or distraction. An extra hour spent on the production of deliverables, rather than the preparation of how they'll be presented, feels more like legitimate work. But this is a close-horizon view of the process. At its best, feedback should improve the quality of the experience for the user, but if you present your work poorly, you invite feedback on the quality of your explanation instead. Responding to feedback of this type means compromising the experience in favor of making it more obvious to the stakeholder, not necessarily better for the user.

The user is better served by getting quality feedback on concepts that are well-understood by those reviewing them; quality feedback is something that does not arise of its own accord. Switching that hour to preparation instead of production may not produce a tangible document, but it may result in a better experience in production. And that, however it is achieved, is our *real* job.

## Summary

While the product needs to speak for itself in front of end users, the interim assets we create can't be expected to do so in front of stakeholders with different concerns and targets. The solution itself needs to be the central character in a story that explains the wider context of its history, the evolution of the solution, and the end goal. Without this, stakeholders will respond to superficial aspects of the design, with little investment leading them to remember their motivations at the next round of reviews.

## The "Presenting Without Contextualizing" anti-pattern

Our work competes for attention and priority in our stakeholders' minds. We can't expect them to have perfect recall to retain all the detail from review to review. A context imbalance arises when we spend a lot of time with the work, but only show it to stakeholders periodically at design reviews. If we present carefully reasoned detail without refreshing our stakeholders' view of that context, we invite feedback that serves stakeholders' need for better explanations, rather than the users' best interests.

## You know you're in it when...

- Stakeholders give contradicting feedback in successive rounds of review.
- Stakeholders give feedback only on a superficial reading of the deliverables.
- Much of your work seems to be tweaking or fiddling on a minor level, but there are unresolved major issues.
- You follow feedback suggestions to the letter, but the stakeholders making those suggestions aren't happy with the results.
- You spend more time in review sessions correcting misconceptions about the design intent than presenting the work.
- Stakeholders take the work and present it themselves, leading to nonactionable feedback from the people to whom it was presented.

## How to break the anti-pattern

The realization that you're in this anti-pattern tends to come right in the middle of a design review. However, this can also be the most dangerous point to try and fix it. The realization usually comes as part of an emotionally draining process and, while it can be tempting to identify the context imbalance to the group, that can all too easily come across as belittling their present concerns.

If you do choose to deal with this head-on in the review itself, several patterns in Chapter 11 can help you choose the right wording and tone.

If it's early enough in the review, you can take a step back and use some of the patterns below to *recontextualize* the attendees – for example, **Setting the topic** and **The half-silvered mirror** can be used in-flight to bring stakeholders up to speed, especially if they're introduced with "OK, let's take another run at this..."

However, the best way to break out of this anti-pattern is to be in control of the review from the start. Get to the end of the present review, and use the full arsenal of these patterns to start out right the next time around.

## Patterns
### Prepare for presentation

*Tell them what you're going to tell them; tell it to them; tell them what you told them.*

Go into every presentation knowing what story you'll tell, and with your deliverables in the right order and with the right support – annotations, alternate views, Post-it notes – to follow the narrative. Ensure that the story is told end-to-end before collecting feedback; explain upfront that the session will be structured as a noninteractive run-through, followed by a step-through for in-depth assessment. Don't structure your presentation in such a way that stakeholders can jump ahead of you. Have on hand (or preferably on the walls) the artifacts that give context to your decisions – personas, maps, principles, and so on. Have a capsule explanation of the story to date for any new arrivals who haven't been involved in the process yet. When preparing your presentation, always remember the context imbalance and err on the side of letting the stakeholders dismiss excessive context.

## Be present to present

Some organizations have the explicit habit of sending the presentation deck to all stakeholders before the meeting so they can look through the content at their leisure. This can be useful if the audience is of subject-matter experts who know how to read the content. However, design reviews with out-of-domain stakeholders, especially the challenging ones, have to be handled differently. We must be able to set the context, tell the story, and guide the team through the feedback process to shape the product successfully. We recommend circulating an agenda with what you are going to cover, but no artifacts that could pre-empt a contextualized review of your work.

This happens after the presentation, too – often stakeholders or clients will request the design artifacts so they can present them onward or circulate them to their teams. This is a tricky request; ideally, we'd prefer not to have the work presented with such a risk of context imbalance. However, an agency (for example) can hardly tell the client that they can't take away the work they've paid for! In cases like this, try to offer an annotated deck, offer to be available for explanations or to resolve misunderstandings, accompany the deck with the already-captured feedback so duplicates are avoided, and request that the product owner pre-rationalize any feedback that results so the aims remain consistent.

## *Casting* feedback

Remember that context imbalance means stakeholders give feedback that isn't deeply considered or clearly held. Unpack the underlying concerns that the feedback embodies – for example, if their feedback is that the logo needs to be bigger, unpack their concerns with them to discover that, perhaps, they're concerned about brand visibility. Then capture *this* feedback (with their agreement), rather than the original feedback that has been resolved. In this case, rather than "make the logo bigger," you'd capture "we're worried that the brand needs more visibility," which gives you more scope to explore solutions that suit both the brand and the user better.

Importantly, once you capture feedback in this form, you must *stop* discussing it. The root cause has been identified and anything else becomes unhelpful attempts at solving the problem that will not only color your approach to the solution, but also set expectations among the stakeholders for how it will be fixed, limiting your ability to design freely. State the feedback, say that you'll look at it for the next review, and encourage the group to discuss the next item on the agenda. If a stakeholder tries to return to that individual piece of feedback, reassure them that the action is on your slate and the group is using its limited time to focus on the next item.

When you play back the results at the next review, *always* show feedback in the context of the previous stage. "Here's what we showed last time. The feedback *we took from this was that the brand needed more visibility*; here's" – and only *now* do you show the new version – "how we addressed that." Casting or positioning feedback like this has several major benefits: it ensures that the historical context of your new decision is correctly communicated; it prevents flip-flop feedback because the nonworking solution is clearly presented and discarded; and it makes stakeholders feel smarter for raising it that way.

## Set scope expectations

Know before starting which aspects of the work are ready for feedback and which aren't. Where possible, edit out the ones that aren't ready. Begin your presentation by introducing the areas that are up for discussion this time around: "Our focus this week has been on the sign-in and registration form, so that's what we're seeking feedback on today. You'll also see some changes to the navigation and the footer, but we're still tweaking those, so please consider them as not part of the feedback target today." If someone tries to lead feedback into an irrelevant area, then suggest that, "as it's not quite ready and we only have limited time in this session, we should probably park it until the next round."

## Actively confirm understanding

When presenting particularly complex solutions, or when understanding relies upon a particular set of knowledge that you assume everyone present has, it's OK to ask whether you've been clear on everything you presented. "Have I filled in all the gaps here?" "Is everyone comfortable that we've captured that process properly?" "Would anyone like me to unpack that a bit more?" It's important to phrase this in such a way that stakeholders can admit to needing more explanation without it seeming like a failing on their part. Many stakeholders feel that they need to maintain face, and will feign understanding rather than admit to ignorance.

### The Half-Silvered Mirror

Remember that our deliverables generally only show the user's side of interactions, so it's often important to remind stakeholders that what appears to be one thing to a user can have a very different meaning and motivation for the business. For example, surprise-and-delight elements can be seen purely from the point of view of the user as "a nice touch that makes me smile." Stakeholders who only have the user view of a delighter can easily write it off as an unwarranted cost, unless they understand the business view that this acts as the key to positive emotion, generating increased user engagement and making the user more likely to share the experience of the product with friends. Doing this preemptively the first time you introduce a particular element serves to remind stakeholders that you have business goals in mind.

### Tell them what you told them

Finish each review with a capsule of what you showed and what you learned in terms of feedback, so that everyone leaves with the same understanding of the actions to be taken. You can also send an e-mail message that sums up the review, along with your cast feedback, along with any other action items and their owners, which then forms the skeleton of the agenda for the next meeting.

## If others inflict this anti-pattern on you

Always be aware of potential context imbalances when reviewing the work of others, and be prepared to chase down understanding before submitting your own feedback. Always test to see if *you* can tell the story of what's been told to you – if you can't, you're missing something vital to your ability to respond.

One way this anti-pattern tends to play out is when stakeholders themselves are subject to shifting contexts. This often means the project is subject to incomplete requirements or is being governed by a divided set of owners who are changing direction with the wind. Resolving this is more normally the job of a project manager or product owner, but you can raise it to them if they're not aware of its effect on you.

Always be sure that you're being provided with the background you need to be able to do your job well, whether this is research, insight, business knowledge, or product vision. You can't communicate context if you don't know it yourself.

## *An example agenda*

### Goals for this session

What we're reviewing today, and the subjects we're looking for feedback on. What we're excluding, and why.

### Structure of this session

We're going to start with a noninteractive run-through of the whole journey. I'd like you to put your initial feedback on paper; I'll give you plenty of time. We'll have a second run-through where we examine each step in detail, and we'll review the feedback you provided during this phase.

### Feature-by-feature feedback

I'll explain this feature in terms of the design and business goals. Here's how it looked last week; this is the feedback we took from that session. We've responded to that feedback by taking the following actions, and here's how that plays out in the design. Here are the ways in which the user-facing aspects map to business goals. Let me start by asking the owner(s) of that feedback if we've addressed their concerns?

### Strategy check

With the individual components reviewed, let's step back and ensure that, as a whole, this design still meets the overall goals of the project. We'll refer to the business requirements, product vision, experience principles, and personas to ensure we're moving in the right direction.

### Wrap

I'll recap what we've shown here today. We explored these particular areas and we showed these particular steps. We took these key feedback findings from the group, and we'll be working on them before the next review, which is on _____. We'll send these round by e-mail shortly. Thanks for attending, and we'll see you next time!

## Terminology explained

Context imbalance

Design context

Casting feedback

Active confirmation

*Pan narrans*

Empathy map

Experience map

Feature map

Service map

Personas

## CASE STUDY

Chris Downs, founder of Live|Work Studio

*Figure 4.8: Chris Downs. (Photo by: Chris Downs.)*

At Live|Work, the service design agency I founded in 2001, it occurred to us that, when pitching new service concepts to clients, no matter how strong or compelling the idea was, clients would often respond by finding reasons not to take it on. We would often be briefed to deliver a disruptive service innovation, however, and we began to see a pattern. The more disruptive an idea, the more reasons a client would find *not* to invest in it.

We had a client that was in the widgets business. It was a truly global, family-owned business that had been established for well over 100 years. Over that time, it had amassed a huge product library of widgets designed to suit every known instance in every market. Their brief was typical for us. They needed radical, disruptive innovation because their business had become commoditized and they could no longer compete with their traditional widget sales business model.

Our team of design researchers spent a considerable amount of time on observing their customers and end users in markets around the world. What we came back with was remarkable. The vast product catalog that our client was so proud of was largely unnecessary. What customers wanted was less choice and much faster delivery. This, we thought, would be great news for our client. We could save them millions through rationalizing their products, which would also simplify their stock and supply chain management, which would enable them to deliver the widgets to their customers much more quickly. Fantastic.

The idea was simple and very compelling, but we were concerned. We were at their global board meeting and we were about to tell them to slash line after line of products their customers didn't really want or need. We knew that the executives would resist. We were preparing ourselves to hear of all the reasons why each and every product was necessary, how each market's needs had to be met, and how having a dramatically smaller product catalog would hand the advantage to their competitors, so we decided not to pitch this idea to them.

Instead, we "faked" the idea. We quickly "forged" artifacts that made it look as though the idea already existed. And what's more, we made it seem to be an idea owned by a competitor. We borrowed the design language of Easyjet and mocked up an extremely convincing website that we called EasyWidget. The EasyWidget website had just three widgets on it (dramatically fewer than the many hundreds in their existing line-up) and promised next-day delivery. That was it. For extra dramatic effect, we fabricated Google pages and sequenced them, so that, in the presentation, we could pretend to search for this "competitor" and then happen across their website. This was all very carefully stage managed.

When the time came to present our findings and our ideas, we told our client of the problem we encountered. We made up a story about some of their customers telling us about a new competitor. We opened up a browser for them to see and typed our search Easy Widgets into our fake Google page. When the EasyWidget page that we had faked appeared to load, the whole of our client's global executive team stood in stunned silence, mouths wide open. The chief executive simply said, "That's it. We're finished. We can't compete with these guys. They are going to wipe us out."

We, of course, were thrilled. This was the response we wanted. He had validated the strength of the idea for us. However, as we were about to reveal the fact that it was all fabricated and that the idea, in fact, belonged to them, the marketing director stood up. Pointing to the EasyWidget website we had forged, he said, "I know these guys. There's really nothing to worry about. I met them at a trade show, and they're no real threat. They're all show and no substance." We were stunned. He obviously didn't know them and had never met them, since we had faked the whole thing. In his effort to protect his professional pride, he couldn't let his superiors believe that this was happening without his knowledge, so he lied.

We managed to recover gracefully, but we learned a valuable lesson about being in control of a meeting like this. You can shape the course of the meeting – but you can never truly control it.

## Additional resources

1. Berkun S. #23 – How to run a design critique 2009. <http://scottberkun.com/essays/23-how-to-run-a-design-critique/> [accessed 17.12.14].
2. Knapp J. Nine rules for running productive design critiques 2013. <http://www.gv.com/lib/9-rules-for-running-productive-design-critiques> [accessed 17.12.14].

## REFERENCES

1. Greville F. Selected Poems of Fulke Greville. Chicago: University of Chicago Press; 2009. ISBN: 10 0226308464.
2. The Science of Discworld II: The Globe. Terry Pratchett, Ian Stewart, Jack Cohen. Ebury Press; 11 April 2013. ISBN: SBN 0-09-188805-0.

# TAKEAWAYS

1. Always be cautious of potential context imbalances.

2. Make sure stakeholders have the whole picture before they offer feedback.

3. People respond best to stories.

4. Always know what story you're telling before you present the work.

5. Keep the wider context in your "back pocket" in case you need to refer to it.

6. Be prepared to cast or present feedback in a form that is more actionable.

7. Make sure your deliverables are socialized so that everyone sees the context they embody.

# CHAPTER 5

## Being in the room but not present

In software development, we often talk about *silos*. Taking their name from agricultural silos (huge storage tanks each containing a single type of grain), these organizational silos each contain a single type of skillset – analysis, design, development, quality assurance (QA), and so on. Silos often arise in businesses that think departments are running most efficiently and with the highest quality when they're left alone to execute on their core function. However, many businesses find that, when new product development (NPD) enters the equation, these silos actually damage the process by impeding communication across functions.

In the ideal siloed model, each department is free to develop its aspect of the product to the best of its ability. Quality is maintained by passing detailed specifications across the silo boundaries. These detailed specifications can be understood by all parties and take into account all limitations and edge cases that any other silo may encounter. In the unlikely event that an unspecified limitation or edge case occurs, the specification can be amended quickly and simply by simply raising a change request and following the process back through the product development chain until it reaches the original source of the oversight.

This can be quite a disruptive process, especially in cases where the oversight happens to have domino-like effects on other large parts of the system. Therefore, this system works best when there is free and easy communication between silos about technical limitations, design assumptions, and the context of business decisions. Which, as it turns out, is one of the things this system expressly inhibits.

In the authors' experience, most businesses engaged in NPD now understand the need to break down silos and use the efficiencies of natural human communication and inter-team trust to build products. However, many of them are still learning *how* to break down the silos, in what can be a long and painful process of organizational change. In fact, there is such a strong relationship between NPD, user-centric design (UCD), and organizational change that the authors have a theory the three cannot be separated. Increasingly, UX is about organizing and facilitating teams so they can deliver on the user-centric goals we define.

As UXers, our position at the heart of the UCD process puts us in a unique place to enable and drive organizational change. But this necessary communication and change can't happen unless we fully engage with the team around us. We need to do more than just sit in the same room.

## What is your job?

As we will touch on in more depth in some of the later chapters, there are two opposing ways to define the role of UX design:

- UX design is the process of creating a set of deliverables that allow a business to create user-facing products.
- UX design is the process of doing whatever is necessary to put an experience in the user's hands.

The authors prefer the second definition. It gives us more freedom to adapt our process to the user, the product, and the team around us. It helps us find new efficiencies in the process and better ways to communicate the experience with our teams. Unfortunately, to many businesses and many UXers, the former definition is what actually counts as "work."

In this definition, we best serve the business and the user by creating as many deliverables of the best possible fidelity in the time available. To maximize productivity, we find ways of cutting out distractions and creating virtual private spaces – for example, shutting out the world behind a pair of headphones. But while this may increase our output rate for wireframes (see *About Flow* in Chapter 14), there is a whole set of conversations and decisions happening in the team around us every day. If we cut out this *buzz of the room*, we miss out on being a part of those decisions. By shutting out the team, we have placed ourselves in a silo of our own making.

Why do we make these silos? Because distraction, context switching, and human interaction all have *cognitive costs*. Over the course of a day, they can add up to a huge drain on your resources. However, intensive team interactions like co-creation and pairing can bring amazing results in buy-in, cross-team understanding, and product quality. In this chapter, we hope to help you spend your social energy in the most productive ways possible.

### Introverts vs. extroverts

You'll hear us talk about these two kinds of people a lot in this book, but what exactly do we mean by *introvert* and *extrovert*? Most people think they know the answer to this – extroverts are outgoing and energetic, while introverts are shy, withdrawn, and quiet – but the truth is a little more subtle. Introverts can be very outgoing and full of social energy, but they use up that energy in the course of social interactions. Extroverts, by comparison, gain social energy from interactions. Introverts, therefore, sometimes need a little time alone in their own heads to recharge before they can go back to being the life of the party. This is also not a black-and-white issue; there is a spectrum between the two extremes and everyone exists somewhere on the scale.

The best article the authors (who both strongly identify as introverts) have ever read about introversion is "Caring for your Introvert" by Jonathan Rauch in the March 2003 edition of the *Atlantic* magazine. Whether you're an introvert or an extrovert, it's full of great insight to help each end of the spectrum understand the other. Read it for yourself at http://www.theatlantic.com/magazine/archive/2003/03/caring-for-your-introvert/302696/

There is a cognitive cost to being pulled out of your private space for both introverts and extroverts, with varying levels of impact. The advice we offer in this chapter applies no matter where you are on the spectrum.

## New software development processes, new collaboration models

Everyone in the software industry has felt the change of pace in recent years. The Internet and various app stores have revolutionized delivery, increased the amount of competition, and continue to demand new ways of sating customer desire. As software products embrace these new opportunities, they ramp up the speed of new feature delivery accordingly, meaning that, across the market, we all need to run faster to keep up. The old models of software development can no longer compete, giving way to newer ways of creating software that embrace iteration, using it to respond quickly to customer desire.

In contrast to the established waterfall method, a linear process comprising spec–design–code–test–release (itself proposed as a development anti-pattern in the 1970s!), newer methodologies like Agile, and Lean Startup, create highly collaborative teams that are able to react to a rapidly developing marketplace and changing needs much faster and more fluidly.

## WATERFALL, AGILE, AND LEAN STARTUP

The waterfall model, where progress flows downward, arose in the 1970s as a way of translating existing physical product development methods to software. It consists of a series of sequential stages, beginning with conception, through to design, development, testing, release, and maintenance. There are usually sign-off "gates" between each stage so the business can be confident that its requirements have been met before proceeding to the next activity. Each stage outputs a specification that is taken up by the actors in the next stage for implementation.

While theoretically waterfall guarantees the software will be implemented "to spec," it offers no guarantee that the people writing the specification from one stage will understand the needs or realities of the other stages, nor does it allow implementers the scope to suggest better solutions for issues they encounter farther down the line. It also does not deal well with changes to business reality or product vision during the development phase.

Agile arose in the early 2000s as a formalization of many existing developer-led responses to these inefficiencies with waterfall. A very broad range of method-ologies sits under the "Agile" definition but, in general, what they share is a core of iterative processes, where software is "just-in-time" designed, developed, and released, by an integrated cross-discipline team that spans the whole business (including the client, if there is one) and is empowered to find its own ways to solve business needs. In Agile projects, there is supposed to be no defined end state – the job of the development team is to experiment and see what solutions provide the required market response. Rapid iteration means that the business can tweak the product as it goes, responding to changes in the business landscape far faster than waterfall. This model of iterative experimentation is known as "Build–Measure–Learn."

As Agile was originally developer-led, it can be hard to cater for a holistic design or UX vision within an iterative framework that expects to receive business needs and output code within the next cycle.

Lean Startup takes the iterative build–measure–learn process from the core of Agile software development and applies it to the entire business model, aggressively prioritizing product features until a Minimum Viable Product (MVP) emerges that can be developed quickly and put to market to test the core idea of the business at low cost, low risk and without wasting time. Market feedback from the MVP is used to redirect business priorities for further iterative product development. Designers working in Lean Startups often find that they encounter many of the same challenges that Agile presents, often made even more acute by the intense iterative nature of the entire business.

There are assumptions and processes that we have always taken for granted in digital design and development. Agile and Lean, with their acknowledgement that we can't predict the future, put an end to these. No longer can we specify the finished experience and expect development to proceed toward that goal after we hand off our deliverables. We can't hand over a finished document, move on to the next thing, and wonder what happened to our idea when we see the finished product after launch, sometimes barely recognizable from our intended blueprint.

As designers, we need to recognize that the same forces that encouraged developers to create Agile project management processes are the same forces that should encourage us to adopt them: Unless you can predict the future, a waterfall approach tends to make products and services that aren't as good as they could be.

Our mantra is that *our work is not an experience until users get to interact with it.* After the discovery phase is over, changes to the business landscape, tested assumptions, and reactions to development milestones will change the needs of the product in ways that your documentation can't possibly predict.

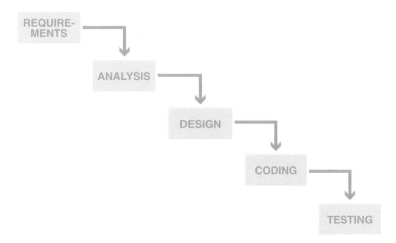

*Figure 5.1: The Linear Waterfall Process. (Image by: Martina Hodges-Schell.)*

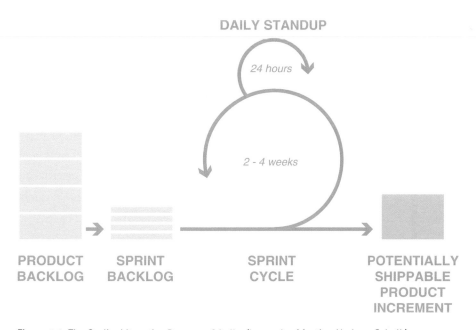

*Figure 5.2: The Cyclical Iterative Process of Agile. (Image by: Martina Hodges-Schell.)*

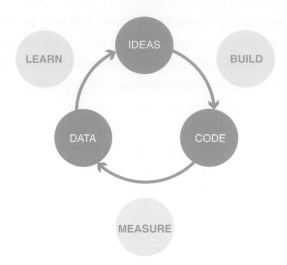

*Figure 5.3: The Iterative Build–Measure–Learn Loop of Lean Startup.*
*(Image by: Martina Hodges-Schell.)*

The only way to maintain user-centricity when this happens is for you, as a UXer, to stay in the process. If you leave the response to someone else, then what you have designed is not the experience; it is just your deliverables. When we divide responsibility for aspects of the product among parties who do not communicate, we create a silo – a place into which requirements flow and deliverables emerge, stripped of their surrounding context. The reasoning behind design decisions can disappear, giving those left to implement our work no reason to prefer it to their own solutions.

In different environments, we may be even further removed from the project flow and decision-making. The authors have observed and worked in design agencies, UX consultancies, and client-side (from dot.com behemoth to day one at start-ups). Often, designers have to collaborate with offshore teams, third parties, external client organizations, and a whole host of internal teams. It is no surprise that it can be difficult to move your ideas beyond your notebook.

## Collaborating in iterative environments

Once we recognize the importance of getting beyond the deliverables, the resulting need for collaboration demonstrates how damaging a personal silo can be. But others can perceive a silo around you, even when you don't intend there to be one.

Consider this example. Sometimes a developer will identify a place where the design does not comply with other pressures on the product. Ideally, the developer should approach you to discuss the problem, and that means you are going to be pulled out of whatever you were concentrating on. How you respond to this approach is critical. If you seem irritated, even only in your non-verbal signs, at having your concentration broken, that's a powerful signal to the other party, whether you mean it or not: *Don't do this again*. Do it a few times and you'll find the team starts to guess at solutions rather than collaborate with you. And this starts even before the developer taps you on the shoulder: if you have your headphones on and your head down, that is also a powerful signal: *Don't bother me*.

We use the example of a developer approaching a designer here as a sort of *mea culpa*, as both authors have experience with provoking development dilemmas with our design work. But the same is true for any relationship within a delivery team, whether it involves a project manager, a business analyst, a quality assurance tester, or any kind of project stakeholder. Just being in the same space does not make a group of people a team. You have to be in the same *headspace*. That means you need to know the direction you are all moving in and the importance of everyone's role in getting you there. Once you can agree that everyone's role is important, you can understand why it is so necessary to give every role the respect of your attention.

In the introduction to this chapter, we talked about the buzz of the room. If you are not tuned in to the discussions that are happening in the room, you are missing opportunities to engage in discussions that affect the experience. Your team may come up against problems that have simple user-experience solutions, but without the insight from a UX practitioner, they may not even realize that the possibility exists. This also works in reverse. If you want to inject your ideas into the design process, it is best to be present when your idea has the best possible opportunity to land: in the moment, when it solves a real problem for someone.

## Focus in an open-plan world

The flipside of the buzz of the room is the constant opportunity for distraction that exists in most modern office environments. We *need* our headphones. The authors are explicitly not recommending that you throw yours away. The challenge is balancing availability with deep concentration.

We're not the only ones who find this hard. Developers who have already paved the way with adopting Agile and Lean Startup ways of collaborating have a wealth of experience with the real-life challenges of putting this into practice. Many developers are used to the ability to shut out the world and concentrate on the code, and find continuous availability one of the most challenging aspects of Agile. This is great news. It means you have allies in setting up ways of dealing with all the related anti-patterns. You can suggest patterns in daily standups, and deal with a strategic solution in retrospectives and planning meetings. Being proactive in solving this problem is also a great way of demonstrating that your goals are aligned with those of your colleagues.

## Make collaboration sustainable

A few years ago, Martina volunteered to set up a fully collaborative project at a design agency with her client. She was used to working embedded in cross-functional start-up teams and looked forward to bringing her preferred working patterns to the agency-client relationship. Instead of seeing the client in weekly workshops or daily standups, she invited him to colocate with the team at the studio, sharing the same desk. She expected it would take the team some time to gel, as this was a new working pattern for all involved, but she wasn't prepared for how exhausted she was in comparison to other collaborative team setups she had managed before.

Acting like startup cofounders, she and her client had a quasi-equal relationship, with one key difference: she and her team were an expensive asset for the client, and being seen as less than 110% productive and engaged was not an option. This came into sharp contrast to the rest of the design studio's relaxed, yet hardworking, approach. So she got creative, experimenting with many different patterns to balance collaboration while respecting personal boundaries. There was no doubt that this approach delivered outstanding project outcomes and pointed to the future of how we would engage with our clients. It was a question of making it sustainable for the people involved.

We don't think Agile – as it is currently often practiced – is a perfect discipline, and we recognize that it brings significant challenges to the design process. But in our experience, the collaborative nature and the shared understanding of the business goals, user needs, and technical feasibility make those challenges much easier to address than the equally many unresolved challenges of the waterfall method.

But you are not always lucky enough to be working in that kind of environment, and sometimes silos will be forced on you, perhaps by the kind of business you work in (for example: a horizontally organized company structure) or by executive decisions about the shape of the project (for example: when the development has been outsourced).

How can you pass on context in situations like this? Robin Dunbar[1] of the Institute of Cognitive & Evolutionary Anthropology at Oxford University has compared various forms of communication to see what emotional responses arise from them.[1] He discovered that, when people communicate by voice, they smile and laugh more and come away feeling more positive than when they communicate by text-only means. But more importantly, when participants can see each other, they smile and laugh the most and come away feeling the most positive. Interestingly, the participants do not have to be in the same physical place – video chat is enough!

The implication here should be clear: push for access, even if that means only occasional Skype calls to the people to whom you hand on your work output. You can justify this ongoing involvement by pointing out the inevitability of change during the development program and promising a light-touch oversight of the response to change. As the UX guardian, you should be empowered to ensure the seamlessness of the experience as the product moves to release, so you should view a lack of ongoing access as a block to doing your job properly.

Continuous collaboration across teams and functions is key to happy people and a well-rounded product. You can harness this new emphasis on closer collaboration to make your voice heard, get your ideas across, and step into the process early to resolve design issues that would otherwise be able to make it into production against your better judgment.

## Summary

Although it may feel productive to shut out the world, it often results in the team building parts of the experience without our input. Without a free, open relationship with the rest of the team, where they feel not just free but actively welcomed to approach us, we risk allowing the final product to diverge from our intentions. It's essential to find ways to balance focus with availability, and clearly signal that balance to colleagues.

## The "Being in the room but not present" anti-pattern

Businesses continue to move to collaborative development models that demand more interpersonal interactions and leave us less time to focus. If we don't fully embrace contact with our colleagues, we won't be able to help them bring our visions to life and the end experience will suffer. If we don't help the business find effective ways to balance our availability and focus, those ways will be defined on our behalf by others, and we may not be able to work effectively with the result. And if we send signals to others that we're not to be bothered, they will work around us when there are important decisions to be made that we should participate in.

## You'll know you're in it when ...

- You notice decisions by the team get made without you, but you feel you should have had a voice.

- You are concerned about the direction of the project from one meeting to the next, but you have not involved yourself in the conversations beyond formal meetings that steer the direction.

- You spend the majority of your time tucked away in isolation to concentrate on your work:

  - headphones on, so you can't hear the buzz in the room

  - working from home regularly

  - finding a quiet corner in the office

  - in residency at the local coffee shop

- You can get quite exhausted with the extra demand of being continuously "plugged into the group" and/or you get irritable when team members interrupt you.

# Patterns – how to be a better collaborator
## Push for in-person access

Remember Robin Dunbar's rule and avoid trying to get agreement or consensus through e-mail or other text-based media. In such media, you risk your tone being misinterpreted or your reasoning being skimmed over. In-person communication makes your job easier by associating your arguments with positive emotions and expressions, and lets you guide and double-check the understanding of all parties. Even if you can't get in the same room, voice or video chat with the other party will help. Use e-mail afterward for documenting the things you agreed on; that is where it excels.

## The stenographers' pattern

This is one of our all-time favorite patterns because of how simple it is. Legal stenographers have the challenging task of transcription, which requires them to concentrate on two streams of information at once – what they hear and what they see. This leaves them no spare cognitive bandwidth during the task. Jumping around in their line of sight or waving to get their attention would certainly work, but it would pull them out of their focused state at the wrong time, interrupting sentences on the tape or making them losing their place in the document. These methods of attracting a stenographer's attention would be effective but disruptive.

Court workers know to simply place a hand on the stenographer's desk, in the corner of the field of view, and wait. As soon as he or she is are able, the stenographer will pause playback, remove the headphones, and turn to the interlocutor with a smile to show the interruption isn't resented.

This is an easy pattern to introduce to the team. In an early standup, you can simply say something like, "I'm going to have my head down in concentration today, but if you need me, please put your hand in the corner of my field of vision and I'll come up for air as soon as I can." You can also introduce it simply by using it on other members of the team when you need to approach them.

The benefits are so obvious that, in our experience, the whole team is quick to pick up and spread this pattern. If you are collaborating over online chat, a similar pattern is to establish a lightweight and noncommittal opening question. At Facebook, people use a simple "yt?" for "Are you there?" The implicit understanding is that people don't set their present/away status on as granular a level as their attention, so yt? can be answered at the recipient's leisure. The convention is that a person being pinged who isn't available to talk will answer with a number – 10, 15, 30, etc. – indicating being free to talk in that many minutes.

## The life in mono pattern

When you wear headphones, be aware of their effect and make sure they remain a tool of concentration, not a barrier to collaboration. Keep one ear free so you can still hear when the buzz of the room increases in reaction to a problem. Respond with a smile when someone breaks into your bubble. Better still, get the music out of your headphones and into the room itself. Most teams can be sold on the idea of gently adding some music to the ambience. A shared playlist will keep everyone happy and you might even discover some new music to love.

The authors have tried several approaches to the headphone problem. Open-backed headphones work well for letting external sounds through, but they tend to leak your music so others can hear a tinny version of it. Similarly, bone-conduction headphones give you excellent situational awareness but tend to buzz an audible bassline that others around you can hear (and your music won't sound as good to you). If your colleagues are OK with a little sound leakage, then these might be workable solutions, but we've had best results with well-sealed, closed-back headphones that allow for keeping the volume low, and one ear kept free.

## Carve out a space

The whole concept of patterns in software development arises from architectural patterns. Sadly, one of the things missed in translation was the idea of different spaces for different needs. A good architect will create a workspace with noisy collaborative areas and quiet contemplative areas. A good collaborative working setup should seek analogues. You can, of course, find another space – it's good for your body to change things around and curl up on a sofa in a breakout area to sketch, or stand at a whiteboard for a while. But sometimes you have to maintain focus in front of a screen or on a Wacom tablet.

You can also carve out time, either by working outside normal hours or by establishing blocks of time for focus. You can make this timeboxing more effective by granting yourself a reward when you're successful; a coffee or tea break if you manage to focus for 60 minutes. Some of the following patterns will help you find ways to carve out time on a regular or occasional basis.

## The scary face pattern

This is one of our favorite patterns of all time. James came across it at a design agency where everyone had photos taken and laminated of themselves making scary faces. When someone was busy and needed to focus, he or she put the photo where it was easily visible on the desk so colleagues knew to give them space. This is a pattern that is open to abuse – do not put the face up when you arrive first thing in the morning and leave it there until you leave at night! When applied with a bit of discipline, though, this lets your coworkers know that you are not being antisocial. This also applies to your messenger status (do not set it to "busy" by default and never change it, and don't go home with a *yt?* hanging).

This pattern works well in combination with the *Life in Mono* pattern – only have your headphones on both ears when your scary face is on display.

## Mind-body considerations

Sometimes the best thing you can do is not to prevent interruptions, but to maximize your concentration between the interruptions. Try exploring new ways of working to see whether you can influence your state of mind by changing your physical position. James uses a standing desk because he finds that standing to work puts his mind into a more alert and productive state than sitting down, which the body interprets as a resting position. It also removes the energetic barrier of standing up to leave the desk and talk to people. Martina finds that sitting by the open window/skylight improves her alertness, and she prefers to solve sticky problems while walking. Steve Jobs famously insisted on "walking meetings" much of the time because that was when his creative abilities were at their highest. Try some of these techniques for yourself and note the change in your output.

## Sensible scheduling

You can carve out time for focus by agreeing on a schedule with the rest of your team. One option is to block out a couple of hours at the beginning and end of each day where everyone agrees not to schedule formal meetings. You'll still need to manage incidental interruptions, but you will have some solid focused time available. You can even extend this to whole days that are meeting-free; this works particularly well in sprint-based development where known processes will be happening on set days.

## Simplify your tools

Make the most of your focused time by ensuring that you don't get distracted by the very tools you use. For example, you could open up a full-featured word processor and spend ages deciding which font and layout will be most effective for the document you're writing. Instead, open a simple text editor that forces you to focus on the content first. You can layer in presentation later. Find the part of your task that requires the most concentration and focus, and use the simplest tool you can to achieve it. When you move on to the other stages, you may find that distractions are less costly.

## Turn off the information firehose

Distractions don't just come from other people in the same space. The Internet is a highly refined distraction machine. Every e-mail notification, push notification, and half-glimpsed webpage in a background window is an opportunity to be pulled away from flow. Make the most of your focus time by quitting, or at least minimizing, the applications that distract you most often. If your phone has a do-not-disturb mode, think about toggling it on during your focused moments.

## The rear view mirror pattern

In hindsight, we're often smarter. We recommend that your in your post-project reviews include a detailed team discussion of what worked and what didn't work so well in terms of continuous availability. Lead the way in suggesting tweaks to your patterns or new ways to work together more. Repeat these intentions in any pre-project kickoff meetings to maximize the likelihood that they will be adopted by the team.

## What to do when someone is locking you out of their silo

Self-siloing is an extremely common anti-pattern, so you may be affected by it just as often as you affect others. If you're making the effort to be available and collaborative, but others are actively or passively shutting you out, here are some ways you can reach out.

- Explain that you value their input for the successful progress of your project. Highlight how other team members are making themselves available to work together more effortlessly.

- Make the collaboration process more engaging. As designers, our tasks lend themselves to co-creation work sessions. It helps to know what overall direction is important for the success of the project, but let team members (even the ones inexperienced in design) be part of that process. Use your expert knowledge to guide and prioritize this input. (See more tips on team workshops in *Chapter 15*.) Extend the input from formal sessions to day-to-day collaboration. For example, sketch out a solution to a question together on a whiteboard, instead of e-mailing back and forth.

- Create shared empathy for your *user needs* and *business goals* to facilitate more discussion as part of the decision-making.

- Encourage colocation if it is possible. Find a space where you can work and exchange ideas together. If possible, face each other. If you work in different locations, get creative with keeping a video chat open, so people can listen in and drop in without scheduling a meeting. If you work with external clients, invite them to your space as often as possible, not just for formal meetings.

# CASE STUDY

Sarah B. Nelson

*Chief Instigator and Igniter of Passions at Radically Human*

*Figure 5.4: Sarah Nelson*

Engaging employees in the design of a new HQ

When my client – a rapidly growing software company – came to me for design facilitation help, they were hip-deep in design for a new, state-of-the-art headquarters. As the team's plans developed, questions about the unique work habits of this company mounted. After months of work, design planning had come to a screeching halt. The executives refused to approve a furniture purchase until the facilities team could prove the chosen furniture system would support – not destroy – company culture.

The HQ team wanted my help to get through this hiccup. They had a strong concept for the new space, but had run into some sticky questions. In a classic design conundrum, they realized that they didn't know how their ideas would work when users – the employees – actually started working in the space. Short of a major design research initiative, they weren't sure how to answer the questions that had surfaced. The team decided to conduct a series of workshops with employees to answer the questions.

Moving to a new company headquarters is one of the most emotionally fraught events any organization faces. The physical environment in which people work affects more than just the work done – it can affect your livelihood. When companies start to re-design workspaces, employees get nervous. They start worrying.

After years of facilitating design projects, my experience tells me that, for multi-stakeholder design projects, the problem is really 30% about design and 70% about communication. Whenever a design project has a personal impact this deep, emotions run high. A corporate move has both many stakeholders – 1,600 in this case, to be exact – and a high emotional impact. A perfect storm.

Based on interactions with employees, the HQ team anticipated a potentially hostile workshop experience. The company prided itself on strong opinions and passionate people. At its best, meetings were vibrant and energized. At its worst, the loudest person in the room won. Consequently, the team was worried.

### Seek to understand rather than be understood

The first thing I did with the HQ team was to help them step into participants' shoes. I wanted them to recognize the emotional impact of a new HQ on employees. I also wanted them to imagine what participants might hope for when asked to participate in such a workshop. We brainstormed a list of potential expectations employees might have. Then we developed tactics to address those expectations.

### Before, during, and after

One of the mistakes I made early in my design facilitation practice was to focus all of my workshop design efforts on the workshops themselves. However, I've learned that what you do *before* the workshop and how you follow up *afterward* are as important as what happens *in* the workshop. While we spent time designing strong activities to help us understand employees' needs, I worked with the team to create clear messages about the workshop's focus (what was in, what was out of scope). Then we set a plan for post-workshop follow-up.

For instance, we set up post-workshop office hours with the HQ team to discuss discipline-specific work issues. We also planned executive meetings to walk the executives through the workshop results. We wrote e-mails introducing the workshop and reiterating key points, and set them up to go out before and after the workshop.

### Ingredients for engagement

With all workshop projects I do, I go through a mental checklist of elements that will promote maximum engagement. Engagement is not something you can force to happen – it's something you create space for so it can evolve.

First, participants need to understand why they are being asked to participate. With the HQ team, we got very clear on our goals. Then we made sure we communicated information about the workshop clearly several times before, during, and after.

Second, participants need to connect the workshop to a shared purpose. In this case, everyone cared passionately about the culture, so we placed culture at the center of the workshop. Anytime workshop participants got caught in circular arguments, we brought the discussion back to culture.

Third, participants need an accurate understanding of the impact of their input. Lip service is the kiss of death for engagement. Throughout the workshop, we were clear about what information we were going to use and how we were going to use it.

### The end result

At the end of the workshop series, we had three deeply engaged groups who knew exactly why they were asked to participate, were reassured that the core team was acting in their best interests and that their input mattered, and that they would continue to be a part of the design of the new headquarters. Because of this experience, these forty-five people and their teams are more likely to see themselves in the new headquarters – to see it as something they had a hand in designing. Finally, the core team, architects, and the executives had greater clarity on what was most important to the company and its employees and they felt confident that they could now tackle the design problem effectively.

*Sarah owns Radically Human. Radically Human believes that a product's user experience is a direct reflection of an organization's health. Through offsite facilitation, team building, and leadership training, Radically Human works with leaders to develop environments where creative teams can do their best work. www.radicallyhuman.com*

## Tips

Remember to pay attention to the link between body and mind. Hunger, dehydration, and caffeination can all affect your ability to focus and collaborate for better or worse. Find what works for you and structure your patterns around the times of day when these factors are optimal.

Explore alternate working methods to find ways that work for you. For example, some people find Pomodoro makes them more productive.[2] In this way of working, you set an alarm for a 25-minute "pomodoro," working intensively on a single problem until the alarm rings and then taking a mental break for 3–5 minutes. For every four pomodori, you take a longer break of 10–15 minutes. Proponents of Pomodoro find that the context switching helps unlock subconscious solutions. By combining this with the Scary Face pattern, you could even reserve one of every four pomodori as a time when you're completely unavailable to the team. Pomodoro doesn't work for everyone; some people find the context switching to be a constraint rather than an enabler of creativity. We include it here as an example of the many working structures that are worth exploring.

We recommend reading Lifehacker.com and 43folders.com to explore some of the other options and see what works for you. Pay attention to your own patterns and structure collaboration around that. Perhaps you need some time to get up to speed first thing in the morning, or have a slump in concentration early afternoon. Suggesting collaboration patterns to the group is a great way to organize work in a way that is sympathetic to your own peaks and troughs.

## Terminology explained

Lean Startup

Lean UX

Agile UX

Balanced team

Stenographer's pattern

The buzz of the room

Continuous availability

Architectural patterns

### REFERENCES

1. Vlahovic TA, Roberts S, Dunbar R. Effects of duration and laughter on subjective happiness within different modes of communication. J Computer-Mediated Commun 2012. Available from: http://onlinelibrary.wiley.com/doi/10.1111/j.1083-6101.2012.01584.x/full.
2. Cirillo F. The Pomodoro Technique 2006. Available from: http://www.pomodorotechnique.com/ [accessed 17.12.14].

# TAKEAWAYS

1. As our work processes focus on more and more continuous collaboration, we need to check in with our collaboration approaches and possibly fine-tune how we contribute to the team.

2. Seize the opportunity to communicate your design vision more and have more impact throughout the project process.

3. Make yourself available to all of the project team throughout the day-to-day interactions so your voice is heard when decisions are made as questions arise. Don't wait for formal meetings to catch up.

4. Check that you are not shutting yourself off from the team unintentionally when you seek some space to concentrate.

5. Reach out to individuals on the team who are creating silos. Unheard voices can create havoc further down the line.

# CHAPTER 6

## Not having a consistent design language

## Say what?

When Martina joined a new team, she was surprised about their interpretation and use of UX vocabulary, which was very different from the understanding she had established over the years as a user-centered designer and researcher. The UX team had never heard of something as fundamental to the job of experience design as a user journey! On further investigation, it transpired that they *did* make user journeys – but one person called them *user stories*, another *task flows*, another *experience journeys,* and so on. They each had a different name for the process of tying an experience together through a task flow and narrative.

Colleagues have spent an overwhelming amount of time on debating the finer details of what we call a user journey, user flow, task flow, work flow, experience flow, experience map, feature map, service blueprint, or simply boxes and arrows. How much more productive would we be if we had used that time instead to become more efficient with how we talk about our work?

Even as a UXer, it was confusing. Martina couldn't imagine how our clients felt; understanding what the emerging field of *user experience* is all about in the first place is hard enough without this added layer of complexity. If we, who are part of the discipline, can't express these concepts in a consistent way, how can we possibly hope to communicate understanding to those outside the craft?

There's enormous risk in not communicating clearly. Neither of us can remember the number of times we've confidently described a feature when a developer asks us, only to discover that, during implementation, the user story had a different term for something within the feature, resulting a technically "correct" implementation of the user story, but a broken experience.

Not using consistent language to describe our work leads to confused collaborators and poorer decision making because stakeholders don't have a clear idea what we are asking them to do.

## Buzzword Bingo

Buzzword Bingo is a fun game to play in meetings or conferences. Make a list of terms that are meaningless but fashionable in the domain under discussion, then make a bingo grid featuring those terms. Cross off each term as it's (unwittingly) mentioned by a participant, then shout "BINGO!" when your card is full.

When you explain or introduce a concept, imagine that everyone in your audience has buzzword bingo cards and will cross off a square every time they hear something that makes no sense to them – *even if it's perfectly meaningful to you.*

*Figure 6.1: UX has more than enough jargon and clichés to make its very own Buzzword Bingo card. (Photo credit: Martina Hodges-Schell.)*

## Buzzword Bingo

| ground-breaking | actionable | revolutionary | leverage | synergy |
|---|---|---|---|---|
| big data | unique | unicorn | robust | dynamic |
| offline | circle back | cutting edge | pivot | lean |
| agile | innovative | social | bring to life | gamify |
| cloud | app | framework | Maslow's hierarchy of needs | engagement |

Before using a technical UX term, be prepared to introduce it and look for understanding among the group. If you don't find that understanding, then drop into a plain English explanation of the term – both the *what* and the *why*. For example: "Have any of you encountered an empathy map before? OK, so an empathy map is a way of putting ourselves in the user's shoes and understanding what they see, hear, think, and feel at each stage of the journey. This helps us understand what kind of experience will resonate with them and make them feel supported." Alternatively, if people in the group have seen this technique before, you can check their understanding by inviting them to share in the introduction.

These comprehension checks are always valuable, even between UXers who use the same names for things. Often, we have come to UX through different routes where the same term might have been expressed slightly differently, and it helps to re-establish the baseline and create a shared vocabulary and common understanding.

*Figure 6.2: Comparing apples to apples is one thing, but we designers are great at taking it too far. (Photo credit: Martina Hodges-Schell.)*

## A consistent design language

We all understand the importance of a consistent and coherent visual language. We use patterns in our designs to help users understand clearly and easily how to use our product or service. And we often advise teams and clients to use simple and plain language to enhance the ease of use and user friendliness. Most of all, we insist on consistent labeling so as not to confuse.

But when it comes to labeling our work, and the words we choose to speak about it, we are often much less careful. We often neglect the task of translating our visual language into a consistent and coherent set of terminology. As our team builds a new product, we are calling into existence new features and ideas. If we don't give names to these, and make those names visible to everyone on the team, everyone will make up their own names – and no two people will settle on the same name for the same thing.

In Chapter 1, we talked about how hard it is to create a product when all the teams involved have their own particular language. Imagine how hard it is when that applies to every *person* involved.

The team and stakeholders will be looking to you to define the design terminology of the product and discipline you represent. If you fail to do that, confusion and disagreement will result, wasting time with unnecessary debate.

If two people have different names for a feature, a stakeholder has to learn four pieces of information: Alice's name for the feature, Bob's name for the feature; when Alice says X, it means Y to Bob, and when Bob says Y it means X to Alice.

If three people have different names for a feature, a stakeholder has to learn *nine* pieces of information: Alice's name for the feature, Bob's name for the feature, Charlie's name for the feature; when Alice says X, it means Y for Bob; when Alice says X, it means Z for Charlie, and so on... Interrelations grow as the square of the number of people in the group – and, in our experience, a product team generally includes more than three people.

Worse, if the team doesn't learn a common set of references from you, they'll take that looseness of language into their own discussions about a feature, further blurring the understanding when you're not there to guide the discussion back on track. Other business stakeholders will refer to these components without the visual reference in front of them and, without a name to anchor the object, its meaning will drift, be conflated with other things, or become elastic enough to include whatever the stakeholder thinks it should be. Eventually, this leads to differing definitions of what success means for a given chunk of functionality, grinding the project to a halt and requiring expensive rework when the mismatch is exposed later in the process.

We've witnessed many a project where the team failed to get to a consensus, or even a final sign-off, because of poor understanding and the resulting misalignment of expectations. This alone is damaging, but when you add in the loss of confidence that external stakeholders will take away from a team that is in linguistic disarray, it can have disastrous repercussions for the future.

## If you liked it, you should have put a label on it

Tie your language down as early as your initial sketches. Get a title on them – that will help you contextualize the sketches when you come back a week or a month later. Begin the naming process by referring to the identified requirements behind the sketch. A design kick-off session is a great way to set ground rules to ensure that everyone has the same name, role, and scope in their minds for every object you design and every process you employ.

This happens in a workshop for capturing the project needs and scope, and clarifying roles and responsibilities. If you are in an agency, this is a great opportunity to educate your clients on your process as well. Settling on names for the design objects and activities you discuss at this early stage will go a long way toward setting expectations and boundaries throughout the project. Make time to explain any terminology to your team and stakeholders, as some people will not reveal their unfamiliarity with some terms to save face. Present examples to illustrate what you mean. Budget enough time to go through these details, especially if this isn't already part of your agenda.

As the solution to the design requirement develops, you should be able to give it a simpler and more memorable name, and then ensure the adoption of this name across the project team. It will help this adoption and understanding if you continue to maintain the reference in the document to the underlying requirements, but always be sure to use the memorable name as a title and in conversations.

Give different design routes their own short, punchy names to make it easier to distinguish between them and decide between the routes more easily.

You're going to have to be diligent about this early on, but it really is vital to ensure the same thing has the same name across the entire landscape of the project.

That doesn't mean you can't change terminology on your project, but you need to do it by consensus. Once the team has adopted the names you created, those names are now owned by the team, not just by you.

Externalize your thinking. Put it on the wall. Give others the opportunity to see what you are talking about. Where possible, we build mobile project walls, using large pieces of foam board that can be easily brought to project meetings, to ensure that we are showing, rather than telling, the team about changes to the solution. Another trick we've used when onsite with clients is to have a project war room, preferably with glass walls. While sketches are being worked on, they face inward, toward the room. When they're ready to be socialized, we turn them around so they face the outside world. Sticky notes are available so passersby can leave feedback and suggestions. If you don't have a glass-walled room, set a routine where the outside world is invited into the room on a regular basis.

One of James's previous clients was a publishing organization where the print hierarchy was well established and the newly created digital team needed to bring hearts and minds on board. There was initial resistance from the die-hard print people to being involved with the digital process. Eventually, the team hit on the idea of turning the war room into a pub, complete with name boards and bar towels, every two weeks. Designers were on hand to pour drinks and talk visitors through the thinking behind the work on the walls. Print stakeholders may have walked through the door for no reason other than the free drinks, but they walked out engaged with the digital vision.

As a general rule, ensure that you always present your design elements with a solid name context and never refer to it by any other name. If someone refers to something by the wrong name, politely correct them without being rude or pedantic.

## A note on labeling files

This might seem obvious, but finding a meaningful and repeatable structure for naming all work is essential when working with a team and creating documents that will live through numerous revisions.

From experience, a lot of designers' folders look more higgledy-piggledy than their keen visual aesthetic would lead one to expect. Calling something "final" or "finalfinal," without including client names, dates, versions, or clues to the thing you are looking at are challenges to creating a common understanding of what you are looking at and talking about.

## FILENAME ELEMENTS WE NEVER WANT TO SEE AGAIN

- final
- latest
- new
- old
- USETHISONE
- DONTUSE
- readyfor[x]
- (designer's initials)
- and, especially, doubling up any of the above: e.g., "final-latest"

Companies that are ISO-9001–certified have very strict rules around filename structure, including internal and external version numbering. Expressing this link between quality and traceability can be a good way of getting the project team to want to adopt version numbering.

While not always technically ideal for the kind of non-text–based deliverable that we often create, version control solutions like GitHub can still be useful repositories that allow other team members to revert to earlier versions, branch for different purposes, and see the evolution and reasoning behind a deliverable's life cycle.

If you can't do any of that, then we recommend creating a common naming convention that lets you easily identify the purpose and completeness of every artifact, for example: 20141225-clientname-deliverabletype-version.

Set your folders up so there is a work-in-progress folder and a "good to go" folder. Documents in the good-to-go folder are ready to be used by others and should not be edited. Use the work-in-progress folder to update work, incrementing the version in the filename, and move it into the good-to-go folder for distribution.

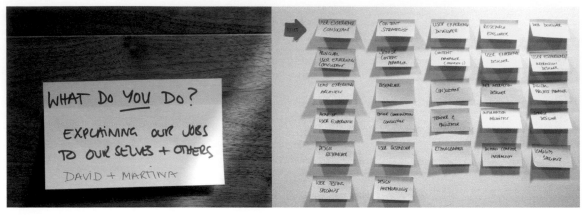

*Figure 6.3: UX encompasses a wide array of specialisms, each with their own technical names. (Photo credit: Martina Hodges-Schell.)*

## What do you do?

An important aspect of maintaining common terminology is to resist the urge to shift terms every time we see a more linguistically accurate description of something. This is an affliction that seems to be particularly pronounced among UXers. For a salient example, look no farther than the endlessly swirling discussion about job titles in our industry. Calling an apple an apple is one thing, but we usually go a step further. On the light-hearted side, it inspires jokes like the UX title generator (http://www.aaronwey-enberg.com/uxgenerator/) [accessed 28.12.14]. But in terms of communicating under-standing about our roles, responsibilities, and capabilities, it can be extremely damaging.

Martina was asked to host a session on "How do we explain what we do to ourselves and others" at UXcamp back in 2010. After years of perennially recurring debate on the topic, aren't we done yet? Shouldn't we know how to describe what we do and feel con-fident about it as a field? Critical engagement and continual improvement are vital to the growth of a new discipline like UX, but we must be careful not to allow our process of refining the vocabulary to look to outsiders like a conference of snake oil salesmen. It's taken a long time to build credibility for the craft of UX, and sometimes it's more important to maintain the trust than to be utterly accurate in the label we attach to it.

## A step too far

Martina remembers one project that encapsulates all that is wrong with designers not using consistent design language. None of these challenges happened because of client input, but because the internal team did not have a shared understanding of the terminol-ogy in use. This left us vulnerable to scope creep and setting the wrong client expectations.

1.  In the *statement of work,* a number of design terms got jumbled together, sounding as if we would deliver one piece of work. But careful dissection of the terms used made Martina realize that we would need to deliver three different pieces of work, at varying degrees of fidelity that couldn't be done in the given time.

2.  The practice lead introduced a new term for a deliverable without explaining what it was. He proceeded to angrily tell off a more junior project manager who asked for clarification. He alleged that the project manager was incompetent for not knowing what he was talking about. A quick straw poll in the office revealed that no one else had ever heard of this term, either.

3.  The team had agreed to supply a particular deliverable that has an established expectation for form and content. Martina was invited to support the team in getting the work done, but hadn't been involved in the setup. To her surprise, she was on a conference call, talking the client through a *service blueprint* that was mislabeled as a *user journey* in a document whose filename suggested it was an *experience landscape.* Confused much?

As much as we think we are clear and rigorous with our language and communication, things get out of control really easily. If it is confusing for us as practitioners, how do we even begin to help our clients and stakeholders with understanding what we do, and how best to input into this process?

## Summary

Be kind, share your vocabulary, put a label on everything you do, and keep using the same language consistently. Be the champion of common understanding within and outside your team. Resist the urge to shift terminology without a compelling reason – linguistic accuracy is not enough on its own!

## The "Not Having A Consistent Design Language" anti-pattern

We would never dream of subjecting the user to an inconsistent taxonomy, but when it comes to communicating with stakeholders, it's easy to do exactly that. When we don't keep consistent names for our processes, our deliverables, and the features we design, we set up confusion about what a thing is and where it has come from. Confusion adds lead time to everything we do, taking away valuable time that could be used to improve the product. In addition, every instance of confusion is a chance to trigger further misunderstandings and create friction in the team.

## You know you're in it when...

- People are referring to things by names you don't understand.
- The definition of success for a particular feature keeps moving.
- The team finds it hard to articulate which aspect of the product or process they're talking about.
- You have myriad labels for the same thing: in writing, on documents, and in conversation.
- You evolve your design language at too fast a pace, changing terminology without contextualizing the change and without evaluating whether it adds value to the overall quality of the communication.
- The names of established tools and deliverables get reinvented under the guise of "adding value" or "innovation."

## Patterns

### Be mindful of your language

Whenever you're speaking, be aware of your audience and the language you're using. What is the intention of the discussion: illumination, discovery, justification? Are you using industry-specific terms to hasten the discussion, or to assert authority? There are no right or wrong answers to these questions, just better and worse matches of language to purpose. Get used to holding these questions in the back of your mind as you converse with people and you'll find yourself better able to create an optimal fit.

### Put a label on it

Get into the habit of labeling your deliverables and being mindful of the words you use to describe your design tools and processes. You will set a solid communication foundation that will result in fewer surprises later on in the design process. Agree on a consistent language with all team members and stakeholders from the beginning of the project.

### Present in context

Remember the lessons of Chapter 4, and avoid context imbalance. Always explain what you are saying and showing in the context of previous conversation and action points. Build on the embedded understanding of your audience rather than assuming it's present by default.

## Own the process

Facilitate the conversation around nomenclature and own it. That means you are responsible for raising the topic and keeping the team aligned. Get the terms on the wall in a visible place and ensure they stay up to date. Invite the outside world to explore the state of the project and ensure that they also take away the right terms.

## Label police

Don't be coy about enforcing the naming you have agreed to as a team. It might feel awkward in the beginning, and your peers might find it a little pedantic at first, but this will help consistent language adoption.

## Buzzword bingo swear jar

Introduce a "swear jar" for the team to put money into when they use trendy jargon rather than plain language and the agreed-upon team terms.

## Playback

Don't fear sounding like a broken record. If someone uses a term that is not in your shared vocabulary, ask them to explain what they mean. You can then decide whether this is covered by a label you already use and share, and remind them of it. It also gives you the opportunity to adopt this new label to describe a distinct object or action.

## Make a toolkit

Method cards are a useful communication tool. They describe different tools and techniques from our design practice in a visual and playful way. There are a growing number of examples available, such as IDEO Method cards or Stephen Anderson's Mental Notes™ cards.

Make your own such tools for your company. The process of creating a shared definition of what you mean by a *prototype* or *user journey* and what it's useful for is a great internal exercise. You can clarify different artifacts, use cases, and create a common understanding of what they are and when they are best used.

## If others subject you to this anti-pattern

If people are changing labels out of ignorance or poor memory, be gentle in your corrections and add more memory aides to the deliverables next time around. However, you will sometimes get stakeholders who will rename objects to assume control or appear proactive. "I really like [new name]..." is generally a clue that these people are actively renaming things. It's difficult to push back on this in a meeting, so schedule a one-to-one with them to let them have input, adopt what's good, and use the cause of group understanding to push back on the rest.

## CASE STUDY

Evgenia Grinblo, user experience specialist at Future Workshops

*Figure 6.4: Evgenia Grinblo. (Photo credit: Evgenia Grinblo.)*

When I recall the biggest lessons of my first year in UX, a clear winner comes to mind: the time when I learned that clients couldn't read my mind.

It all started with great intentions. A new client approached our company for help with shaping their mobile strategy and was excited to base that strategy on user research. It was an exciting moment for us because other clients had been skeptical about user research. This time, we finally had a chance to plan a proper research effort for the project. We scheduled interviews with users and planned the method that Indi Young[1] describes in her book *Mental Models* to help summarize the data.

The Mental Model method was going to make a huge impact, we thought. It promised all the right benefits: a visual, concise overview of the data; the ability to align roadmap features with user insight; and a document that could be used for business insight as well as interface design. Plenty of late nights went into putting the Mental Model together. We carried out long interviews, drew some exciting conclusions, and were keen to share the insights with our client.

We soon learned that our hopes were premature. After sending the Mental Model over to our remote client (along with the summary of the project's discovery phase), we expected to hear a litany of questions. Instead, the research wasn't mentioned once. There were questions about the competitor research, the analytics conclusions, the user survey we had carried out. Nothing about the Mental Model. In those conversations, the Mental Model diagram was something between a ghost and an elephant in the room.

It wasn't our client's fault. They were missing context. To a UX practitioner, the diagram was a perfect tool. To our client, it was a sheet of paper with yellow columns and boxes, full of words that they hadn't expected to hear or see. We had chosen this method for a set of reasons, but had forgotten to explain the reasons to them, expecting the method to speak for itself.

This experience taught us a valuable lesson: we had to invite our clients into our thinking process of choosing methods. We learned to explain how each deliverable works (from layout to function), give examples of benefits, and explain what could be done with the document after that particular meeting.

When we created experience maps for the same client, we made two things clear: how the document informs product decisions today, and how it can aid the project tomorrow. We made sure to draw product insights from the data and leave room for a discussion of how they fit into the roadmap. We outlined the next steps to help clearly illustrate that the maps will be useful as the project progressed. We didn't wait for our client to guess that they can use our work beyond the current app iteration; we told them this ourselves.

The biggest lesson was to keep our UX hats on when dealing with clients. With users, we knew it was our job to make things simple and explicit. The surprise was that our clients were no different. Since then, we work hard to spell out even what we think is obvious: the context, the benefits, and the results of our work. Designers know so much more about the potential of the tools we choose because we study and use them everyday. Perhaps we even know too much, and assume others share our perspective.

Our UX process had users, too – our clients. When we presented without contextualizing, we asked them to fill gaps without the full extent of our knowledge about UX. The Mental Model incident was akin to a meta usability test that uncovered a limitation of our approach to UX: it's not enough to just do good UX work – we need our clients (and teams) to understand it.

## Terminology explained

Vocabulary

Nomenclature

Buzzword bingo

### REFERENCE

1. Young I. Mental Models: Aligning Design Strategy with Human Behavior. Brooklyn, NY: Rosenfeld Media; 2008.

# TAKEAWAYS

1. Use consistent language. As a profession, we are known for having a plethora of different terms to say the same thing, and even some practitioners are confused about UX and design terminology.

2. When introducing any UX terminology, explain what it means in plain language, with examples, and check that the audience understands what you are trying to communicate.

3. Label all your work as soon as possible and stick to that terminology.

4. If you need to change labels, consider the cost and value of this change, and socialize the change with the group.

5. Rigorous naming extends to filenaming as well. Set up a good practice to easily see what the latest file is, rather than adding a tail of suffixes like "final-final," "new," or "usethisone."

# CHAPTER 7

## Throwing deliverables over the fence

There are fences within and around every team. They mark out physical workspaces, they define spheres of responsibility, and they mark the boundary where "the team" meets "the world." This chapter doesn't attempt to argue the existence or value of these fences. We're more interested in what happens when you encounter one. Do you stare squarely at this impenetrable boundary of your world, or do you look beyond it so you can make the jump over it?

One of the tallest fences in the UX lifecycle is the one that lies between us and the next implementer – whether their role is in design, development, or some other aspect of the process. It's tempting to hand over a pack of deliverables to this soul, trusting that they will interpret it exactly according to our intentions.

If we want the end product or service to stand up to the love, sweat, and tears that we pour into it, we need to do more than simply pass the responsibility down the chain when the life cycle moves into the implementation phase. We need to shepherd the understanding along.

## Tearing down the fence

A few years ago, Martina started work with a new employer that had a very sturdy fence between the design and development teams – a half-height cubicle and a two-yard aisle in an open-plan office. Each team could see the other, but they simply didn't hear anything from each other. The design team was frustrated at how "poorly" the developers were implementing the design, and the developers were frustrated at how "ignorant" the designs were of the realities of implementation. Each side of the divide treated the other as *them*, at odds with *our* goals.

She got talking to Ed, one of the developers, in the break room – one of the few places where the two teams could mingle without an agenda. They quickly realized that their local frustrations were facets of the same larger problem: inefficiencies in the way the product delivery process was working. They made it their business to talk to each other about their goals for any brief and brainstormed ideas together. This approach quickly spread through their teams, giving the developers input and ownership of design ideas, and giving vital technical context to the designers' solutions. The outcome was better design solutions that were inspired by what tech can do, rather than just the limitations of what the tech team couldn't support. And they both rallied to get their teams working together at a larger scale.

Amazing things can happen when you tear down the fences. Ed and Martina got married during the writing of this book.

## Of fences and other obstacles

This anti-pattern is quite often a symptom of working in a waterfall-based delivery process or in an external consultancy where you don't get to collaborate with other teams. At a deeper level, projects planned in this way result from an intention gap between planners and doers.

**Planners** seek efficiency in the project *plan*, keeping everyone engaged at their core competency and optimum utilization. To a planner, on-schedule handoffs of deliverables are the key artifact of this efficiency: the discovery process, distilled down into a perfect description that the next person can pick up and immediately understand.

**Doers** seek efficiency in the project *implementation*. They know things on the ground are a little messier than the ideal, and that a handoff is only a starting point. Doers know that sometimes it's more efficient to have a quick chat, whip up a prototype, or sketch a theory in a workshop than to think, plan, and make a fully fledged deliverable.

Both planners and doers have important contributions to make to product development. But it's important not to let one or the other dominate. Planners can create a process that's entirely in service of the plan, and becomes so rigid that unexpected discoveries throw everything off course because there's no space in the plan for them (and, if the market landscape changes halfway through the plan, crisis ensues). Doers can be so free-form that the focus of the project is lost while they chase down

*Figure 7.1: It's time to break down the fences. There is no room for us-versus-them siloing in product development any more. (Photo credit: Martina Hodges-Schell.)*

the latest interesting train of thought – and there's no hope of getting a realistic estimate. Neither should hold the upper hand, but the existence of too many fences is usually a sign that planners have the balance of power.

Shifting to a balance of planning and doing means engaging in organizational change, which is scary to many organizations. But as designers with a strong interest in the outcome of production and a toolkit for involving people and explaining how and why to do things, we are in a strong position to help the organization evolve into a more creative endeavor. You can be the change agent that makes hurling deliverables over the fence a thing of the past. To do that, you need to be able to express the doers' hidden efficiencies to those with a planning-led mindset.

Why is this so important? When a UXer is given a brief with little to no explanation of how and why a given design task has come about, with someone else having already set the strategic direction, or even with explicit instructions on how to "solve" the problem, that UXer has been stripped of the ability to use their knowledge and experience to inject the user's voice into the discussion. UX is about marrying user needs with business goals. To deliver optimum value to the business, it has to be involved upstream of the point where the user interface needs to be designed.

As a community, we often ask how we can get a seat at the business table, so we can bring this user context into the strategic decision-making phase. But we can sometimes forget that the people who work on our projects after we hand off *also* have to make decisions on the user's behalf and need the context that we can give to them. For UX to deliver optimum value to the user, we need to make sure that context persists *downstream* from the point where the UI has been designed.

Be conscientious about what you produce, what decisions you make, who the recipient of these decisions is, and how the decisions get communicated. No one likes being landed with instructions on how to do their job, especially not badly communicated ones.

Make it your business to seek this change – to explore what's beyond the fence, even if that's not in your job description or it seems improbable. You'll be surprised at what you can achieve, and a little progress can open the doors for more.

> *"I don't care how smart you are. Every design solution you put out there is a hypothesis."*
> —*Jeff Gothelf*[1]

Software development always involves assumptions: the platform can support *this* method of accomplishing the task; the third-party service will be able to provide *that* level of performance. We have to design to these assumptions or we'd never make any progress. However, the time when these assumptions will be tested and proven right or wrong often arises during implementation. An early demo shows that the platform *doesn't* support that method, or that, in fact, the third-party service *can't* provide the real-time updates you hoped it would. When this happens, your deliverables won't be able to do the thinking for you. You need hands-on time with the problem.

Even if you're not *living in the deliverables* (see next chapter for more details on how to approach this challenge), it's easy to see your job as being "done" once they're handed over to the next link in the chain. Especially during busy periods, it's tempting to let them be someone else's problem while you move on to the next interesting or pressing piece of design work. But this can have a serious effect on the implementers: they may see you as being elitist and unobtainable, which dissuades them from approaching you to resolve questions.

It can have a detrimental effect on you, too. By disengaging once your deliverables are "done," you can come to see future reviews and signoffs as an unwanted distraction from whatever new thing you're working on. This can make your feedback overly pointed and brusque, or lead you to forget the original intent behind the design and miss important details that have been incorrectly interpreted.

Make it a priority to stay involved in the project outside your own box in the development plan. Just as much as we don't like being handed requirements by other teams without knowing the whys and the hows, we need to make sure we help the rest of the team understand our piece of the puzzle as well. Otherwise, this breakdown in communication can lead to products being built without proper understanding of your blueprint for it.

Throwing deliverables over the fence results in other people involved in the product development process not understanding your decisions or intent as embodied in the design. It also strips you of the opportunity to feed back in the build process. There are plenty more design challenges to be resolved in production. If you can, collaborate with the build team. Along the way, you're going to find some unexpected pressures on the user experience that you could never have foreseen without being embedded in the development process, and you're going to have to think on your feet to fix them.

## Code quality

It might seem to fall outside your comfort zone, but code quality is absolutely a UX concern. By that, we don't mean that you have to write production-ready code, but we want to encourage you to be involved in the quality assurance (QA) review of the code that gets built so you can have a say in whether an element is built to satisfaction. If you don't review how your design work is being translated into code, you don't have any say in how arising challenges get resolved or how your design intent was simply misinterpreted or had to be re- or de-scoped for time or cost reasons. As a result, you might see a product being launched that you barely recognize from the wireframes you handed off.

The challenge is that, if we don't have a relationship with everyone involved in delivering the product, they won't feel empowered to discuss our work. If they can't explore our design choices this way, they won't trust those choices. It reaches behind

## What does code quality have to do with UX?

Isn't it a little arrogant of us to claim domain over the developer's output as well as our own? Perhaps a little, but it's important to understand what we mean here. We're not proposing that UXers do code reviews! A team can *feel* when it's producing good quality code in ways that directly benefit the experience being delivered. Conversely, when code quality is poor, there are lots of ways it slows progress and affects the experience.

For example, keeping code quality high means:

- It's easy to change the product's behaviors without affecting a web of interlinked functionality (enabling responses to A/B testing and user feedback).

- Regressions are rare, with output focused on delivering new value-bearing experiences (meaning users encounter fewer frustrating bugs).

- Technical debt – a suboptimal solution that is "thrown in" to get a feature released, but requires fixing properly later on – is managed and not allowed to have an impact on the quality of the experience (you don't end up hearing "We can't follow the design because the library we 'temporarily' threw at the codebase six months ago clashes with it, and now it will take three months to unpick all the dependencies on the library" from the developers).

- Recent builds of the application are easy to deploy, so you can take them to testing.

- The product meets the right performance metrics but, if it ever doesn't, it can be optimized until it does (so it feels responsive and snappy to the user).

These are some of the outcomes of code quality that affect the experience and that it's important to challenge the team to deliver. In our experience, good developers want these same goals for their own benefit – and they want to deliver a great product experience. If code quality is taking a hit, work with developers to craft a case to take to management.

to stakeholders, and ahead to the development team. Since no deliverable is a perfect encapsulation of your design intent, there are always going to be questions. You may not be deliberately putting yourself in a silo with this anti-pattern, but the recipients of your deliverables may well see you as being shut off from them anyway.

## Making the case

You can be proactive about this anti-pattern by ensuring that you develop a trust bond with the entire team, handing over design with a proper implementation brief that ties it back to the business aims, and actively stressing that you're available for further conversations to clarify understanding or respond to arising challenges.

One way to improve communication is to understand how the development team will work with your design deliverables. What kind of deliverable do they need? Do they need a detailed spec? Words are rarely enough to describe interaction design, as we have already discussed. But without facetime, what formats do the team need? Most likely, a development team will work with user stories to manage their scope, estimates, and delivery. If so, you should be involved in writing the user stories to ensure that the interaction behaviors and business-design links are properly exposed. Get information from your development team on what they consider a well-written user story, and share it with the others involved in creating the stories. Don't assume that, because you understand what you write, it works well for development as well. One of the main complaints we hear from developers working with designers is that the quality of user stories creates a struggle in the implementation.

### How to write good user stories

User stories are a common (if not the most popular) tool to gather requirements in Agile methodology frameworks like Extreme Programming or Scrum. They document a user need and help the team scope and prioritize the software development effort to getting the product or service built.

This sounds pretty good from a UX viewpoint (user-centered requirements-gathering – yay!), but here are a few tips on how to write user stories so they are useful for developers working with them.

Use index cards and a Sharpie (or marker pen of your choice) to capture user stories. Similar to UX advice for writing on Sticky notes (one concise point per one note), write user stories on index cards to limit excessive rambling or multiple stories.

Capture user stories from the perspective of the most appropriate personas; for example, if the UX aim is to cut down on registration steps, then "Susan the time-pressed working mom" is a good choice for getting developers to sympathize. Anonymous "users" all too easily become elastic to the point where they think and act like the developer handling the story.

Using paper cards makes it easy to collaborate. The user stories should facilitate a conversation for the team. Face-to-face conversation trumps any documentation in Agile[2] and user stories are a great conversation facilitator.

### The core structure

Our preferred way to write stories is known as behavior-driven design (BDD), which has a *narrative* and *scenarios*. In the narrative, an actor (for example, a user, an admin, or the business) has a need, which, when served, will fill a business goal.

"As a (user role), I want (function) so that (benefit/reason/business value)."

> Example: **As** Jane, the personal assistant, **I want** to book flights on behalf of others **so that** I can manage my boss's travel tickets.

The second part of a BDD story is at least one scenario describing how the software meets the need that has been identified. This is written in the form given-when-then.

"Given (a prerequisite), when (an action is taken), then (the outcome)." Clauses within the scenario can stack using *and*.

> Example: "**Given** Jane has logged in **and** has credit in her account, **when** she books a flight, **then** her credit is debited by the cost of the booking **and** she is shown a confirmation message on screen **and** an e-mail is sent to her with the booking details."

The story card (or its virtual counterpart in the tracking system) can contain as many scenarios as necessary to deliver all the functionality.

On the back of each card, include acceptance criteria. The code has to function to support these goals.

> Example: Can include third-party name & e-mail address. Can pay with credit card not associated with traveler.

BDD is a way of taking a narrative description of a feature's behavior and breaking it into chunks that can be encapsulated in code and will give a yes/no result when tested. This makes it easier for developers to estimate and deliver the story, and gives QA a solid basis to pass or fail the resulting feature. It combines extremely well with wireframes and/or design mockups to describe both the visual and behavioral aspects of a feature.

Writing optimal user stories

- Story writing is team work. This is your opportunity to involve the business and build teams to capture your design intent and their requirements.

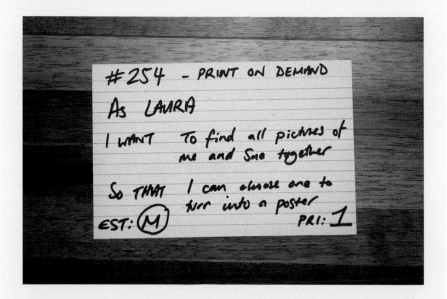

*Figure 7.2: User Story card showing number, title, story written with persona Laura as the actor, estimate (how difficult it is to make), and priority (how important it is). (Photo credit: Martina Hodges-Schell.)*

- A hot tip is to use the personas you have created to describe the different user roles when you write the user stories, not just "the user." This avoids creating a dreaded "elastic user" who is pulled in all directions by team members and is stretched beyond recognition of a real person's needs into a one-size-fits-all representation of "everyone." Make the personas visible to the development team so that they empathize with and understand the persona's capabilities.

- Write concisely and in plain language.

- Ensure that the scenarios and acceptance criteria match what is shown in the wireframes and mockups, so developers and QA are not confused over which aspect of the story has primacy.

- Remember that the card is not the whole story. Ron Jeffries's[3] "3 Cs" formula reminds us to use the Card to give physical form to, and track the history of, Conversations that we have around the feature, and the Confirmation we reach when we're happy with the outcomes.

## What to avoid

- Task descriptions that are too vague or too long. Break the flow apart into simpler tasks instead.

- Writing stories from your own perspective ("As a designer, I want").

- Writing too many stories from the perspective of the business, especially when there a user interaction is involved ("As a business, I want tracking metrics so I can respond to market preferences" is great, but "As a business, I want users to leave comments so that they create a community" should be rewritten to show the benefit to the end user).

- Writing stories without business value or user benefit in the *so that*. These sometimes repeat the *I want*; for example, "As a user, I want to log in so that I can log in." Dig deeper to understand the benefit of delivering this story.

- Writing stories that don't include clear acceptance criteria. Without these, it is unclear to developers and QA what success looks like for the story.

Using cards will get you started, help you establish the right length of user story, and also help with prioritizing workload. Physical cards also have the benefit of being persistently visible in the project space, so team members and outside interests can quickly get an overview of progress by glancing at the story wall. Of course, there are many digital user story management systems, such as Jira or Pivotal Tracker. These are great for mirroring a physical wall and adding in extra detail, or even assets like wireframes or scans of sketches to stories. We don't recommend using them in place of the physical wall unless your team is geographically distributed or has developed enough discipline to know to check the virtual wall frequently.

Remember that, when it comes to bandwidth, the only thing that beats the interactivity of a conversation is the interactivity of a conversation *with collaborative sketching*. Talking through your solution, sketching each step of the way – and ideally using the business vocabulary of the other party, is one of the most powerful tools you have for ensuring the proper transmission of understanding. If you need to justify this to a planner, find ways of demonstrating this power within a project context they'll understand. Can you sketch and tweak the project life cycle with them as though it was a user journey, for example? Can you tell a story about the project that lodges in their brain?

There are roles in every project team that are antagonistic toward each other – not outright hostile, but there to protect contradictory aspects of the business of building things. Project managers are there to ensure the project stays on time and within budget, but this naturally makes them antagonistic to roles that focus primarily on scope or product quality – for example, a Scrum Master or a UXer. This is perfectly OK – it's why we work in teams! The planners aren't wrong for seeking measurable and foreseeable efficiencies, but we know that, in reality, human brains don't work that way – they're messy and irrational. We can't let planners think we're wrong for seeking efficient ways of co-creating that embrace this messiness and irrationality.

Be aware of the focus of the role of people who challenge your process, and look for the levers you can pull which reassure them that their concerns are being met, just in ways they aren't necessarily expecting.

*"The society based on production is only productive, not creative."*

—*Albert Camus*[4]

## Find a shared rhythm

Change is often a stressful experience for human beings and organizations. Much has been written about integrating Agile and Lean UX, for example. Take steps toward working together more. Be explicit about how you would like to work with others and what benefits this would have for them and you. You don't have to be in perfect sync with the pace of other teams, but it is very useful to establish a shared rhythm that lets your workflow and theirs coincide in a productive way.

For example, James once found himself at a company where the product development was being driven by a very strict two-week sprint process, leading the product team to act in a way that was only responding to the sprint at the last minute. Products were being built in a stack-feature-on-top-of-feature way, and were handed, fully specified, to the design team at any point in sprint $n$ for inclusion in sprint $n+1$. Naturally, as the designers finalized the solutions, they found they had to solve unexpected problems, resulting in a nightmare of feedback and rework, usually right up against the wire of sprint planning.

James drew up a sprint rhythm that established a requirements-gathering session on the first day of sprint $n$ to feed the design for sprint $n+1$. This changed the conversation about how the team planned the sprint, allowing UX and design to discuss the requirement rather than accept a specification. It also put a stick in the sand about *when* the design team could accept requirements – while they still had enough time to work on them properly. To keep them responsive to business needs, they kept a process available for work to be injected later in the sprint if it was necessary, but the need for that fell away after a few sprints.

The designers' solutions were then played back early in the first week in a scribble session, where the product team was invited to review, comment, and contribute. Then, a few days before sprint planning, the final designs were reviewed, agreed on, and attached to stories.

The improvement was dramatic. Within a couple of sprints, the requirements-gathering sessions were able to look three to four sprints ahead, which improved the cohesion of the product. The design was taking half as much time to complete because feedback was arriving earlier, and at a level of fidelity that had low cost of change. The designers were happier because they had more influence, and the product team was happier because they saw that the solutions were better for the

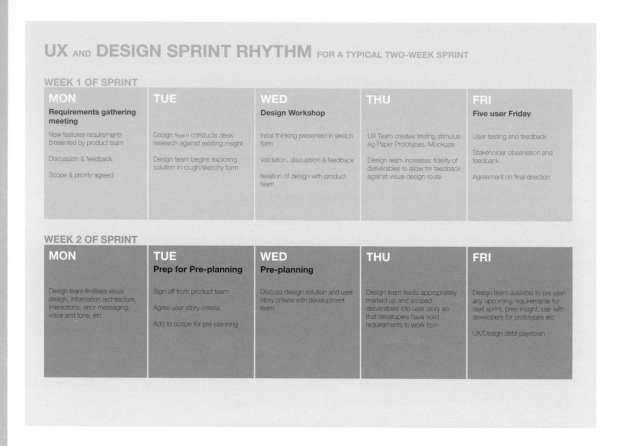

**UX** AND **DESIGN SPRINT RHYTHM** FOR A TYPICAL TWO-WEEK SPRINT

WEEK 1 OF SPRINT

| MON | TUE | WED | THU | FRI |
|---|---|---|---|---|
| **Requirements gathering meeting** | | **Design Workshop** | | **Five user Friday** |
| New features requirements presented by product team | Design team conducts desk research against existing insight | Initial thinking presented in sketch form | UX Team creates testing stimulus eg Paper Prototypes, Mockups | User testing and feedback |
| Discussion & feedback | Design team begins exploring solution in rough/sketchy form | Validation, discussion & feedback | Design team increases fidelity of deliverables to allow for feedback against visual design route | Stakeholder observation and feedback |
| Scope & priority agreed | | Iteration of design with product team | | Agreement on final direction |

WEEK 2 OF SPRINT

| MON | TUE | WED | THU | FRI |
|---|---|---|---|---|
| | **Prep for Pre-planning** | **Pre-planning** | | |
| Design team finalises visual design, information architecture, interactions, error messaging, voice and tone, etc | Sign off from product team | Discuss design solution and user story criteria with development team | Design team feeds appropriately marked up and scoped deliverables into user story so that developers have solid requirements to work from | Design team available to pre-plan any upcoming requirements for next sprint, prep insight, pair with developers for prototypes etc |
| | Agree user story criteria | | | UX/Design debt paydown |
| | Add to scope for pre-planning | | | |

*Figure 7.3: Example of a sprint rhythm. (Photo credit: James O'Brien.)*

designers' input. The extra capacity opened up the opportunity for the design team to begin contributing to, and illustrating, the overall product strategy.

## Collaborate across the project timeline

Teams are distributed in many different scenarios: perhaps you work for the same company, but not in the same office, in the same time zone, or with a shared mother tongue. As an external agency, you often get invited to do a slice of the work, but your client doesn't always encourage collaboration with the other stakeholders, they are not appointed yet, the team taking over isn't hired yet, or they are busy on a different project.

Throughout this chapter, we've shown you ways of making the case for involvement with the rest of the team. When an extra block exists to doing so, like location or language, it's even more important to use these techniques to make the case for collaboration to those running the project. You may have to use several, or campaign hard to get the company to spend money on a technical solution that overcomes distance.

Be interested in the rest of the process. Instead of accepting that some collaboration solution "can't be done" and returning to your desk to think it over in private, stick with the other party and build a shared understanding of the intention, the blocker, and a solution that serves everyone.

Be in the team. Make yourself available for standups, planning sessions, and retrospectives. Show a commitment in terms of time and attention to the team. Treat planning sessions and retrospectives with respect – participate in the discussions and activities, and don't be in the room but concentrating on your phone.

New collaboration technologies – for example, voice chat, screen sharing, and collaborative editors – arise all the time. Try out what works best for your team, and keep an ear open for others that might solve the problem better. Simple efforts like having a Skype video (or Google Hangout) screen open, pointing at your team so others can virtually "drop in" to catch up can make a huge difference.

Extend your efforts to socializing and consider a virtual happy hour. Sharing insights and experiences over a beer can be a great trust builder.

Make an extra (visual) effort with your communication if other teams' first language isn't the same as yours.

## Deliver awesome products

As with all the other anti-patterns we are discussing in this book, we encourage you to challenge the way you work to make more awesome products, to see your ideas get out there into the world, and to work together more collaboratively with the rest of the delivery team to make this happen.

## Summary

To UXers, our deliverables feel like the finished product, but they are only a blueprint. We have to explain them to the people receiving them as effectively as possible. And we have to be available throughout the making of the product or service to help solve unforeseen UX challenges. Only then can we hope to see a project go live that we recognize and can be proud of.

## The "Throwing Deliverables Over The Fence" anti-pattern

The job of Experience Design is not complete when we hand over our wireframes. The product design lifecycle is fraught with assumptions and guesses which, when tested, may require changes and compromises. If we throw our work over the fence and make ourselves unavailable to deal with any changes or compromises that arise during the later stages of development, these will be addressed by people who have priorities outside the lens of user-centric design.

## You know you're in it when...

- You don't know who is going to receive or implement your deliverables.
- You don't know how many audiences will be using your deliverables (development? brand? business? investors? ...).
- You rarely speak to anyone involved in the product development process outside your work group.
- You're concentrating more on sign-off than the outcome of the developers' implementation (which is where our work becomes *an experience*).
- You and the developers don't discuss features before the story is played in development.
- The developers don't know you're available for conversations.
- The developers aren't discussing the design with you, and it's coming out wrong in the product.

## Patterns

### Take the battle to the planners

Push back on project plans that force the creative roles into silos and leave aspects of the final product without a champion during the implementation phase. Identify the planners' thinking processes behind project structure and find ways to explain your process that align with their objectives. Ensure that, even if you do move on to a different project, there's still time built into your schedule for ongoing contact with the team.

## Make the value proposition obvious

Encourage planners to buy into the benefit of de-siloing the team by exposing the efficiencies that result from coworking. Compare the ongoing cost of dedicating a small amount of your time to shepherding the experience to the cost of reworking just one major feature. Expressed this way, your involvement becomes a safeguard against implementation risks and is much more attractive to a planning mindset.

Look for ways to reveal the value proposition: it's far better to talk in terms of what *more* you can add in terms of expertise, quality, or efficiency than to talk about *needing* or *deserving* to have a seat at the table, even if the latter is true.

Look for small shifts you can make that will bring the planners into the creative process – for example, in the sprint rhythm, James initially sold the requirements-gathering session as an opportunity to ensure that the designers had the time and context to work up the solution optimally. The planners agreed because they wanted the promised benefit, and they liked the structured approach. When the benefits were proven, the product team became much more involved with other, more ambitious suggestions for improving the creative process. This small success opened the door for much wider cooperation at all levels and with all groups across the organization.

## Meet and greet

If you find yourself in a situation where you don't know the different parties involved in working with your design deliverables (e.g., in a design agency setup), insist on meeting all partners at design reviews. Get to know them; facilitate workshop formats to get their voices heard. Insist with your client that meeting the production partner is vital to a successful UX delivery. (See the Stakeholder Safari pattern in Chapter 1 for some helpful ideas to make this work)

## Breaking down the fence

Don't let the developers get comfortable with your absence. Walk around, check in, be visible and available, and make sure they won't *let* you throw things over the fence at them.

Be friendly with the whole team. This makes it easier if you have to gatecrash stand-ups or retrospectives. We recommend learning techniques for facilitating retrospectives so you can offer to be involved when these events are seen as "developer-only" (although you should work to change that perception, too). Offer – and keep repeating the offer – to do design handovers whenever a card is picked up. Offering to bring QA into the handover so there's a shared understanding of the aim of the story across the development cycle – that can sway a developer who doesn't see the value. Every developer has argued the fine points of a card with QA at some point in their career.

Remember how Martina met her husband – in a literal common space that developers and designers both used, but not for meetings. Look for these places and use them as opportunities to get to know the team. It always helps to open the conversation with a compliment or acknowledgment of some favor the other party has done for you recently: "Hey, thanks for accepting that story late in the last sprint, you saved my bacon. If you have any suggestions about how we can make stories quicker to write, why don't we have a coffee and talk it through some time?" The meeting before the meeting and the meeting after the meeting from Chapter 1 are other opportunities to find these spaces.

## Be the champion of design

*"You need to know whether the design work is meeting the business goals of the project. You say 'design,' and clients hear 'art,' and now everyone's uncomfortable. Act like the design expert the client hired; remind them – if need be – that they hired a design expert, and their job is to be the business experts."*

— *Mike Monteiro*, Design Is a Job[5]

Let businesses own the business expertise and designers own the design expertise. Always be open and willing to sell the business on a better creative process for the sake of the product. Share your experience in a friendly and approachable way so people throughout the business know they can come to you for advice without feeling intimidated. Equally, avoid overriding product strategy decisions on the basis of design. Show the business you can be businesslike.

## Bring your defense

Stakeholders can be just as bad at throwing down requirements without explaining the business logic behind them. But we don't design experiences if we only implement decisions that have been made without true consideration of the user. That makes it our job to push back on predesigned requirements without context and get a greater understanding of what value underlies the requirement and how we can best use our expertise to serve it. The more often you can invite stakeholders into your requirement-solving process and show them the wide range of experience and insight you apply in solving it, the more value they'll apply to the UX process and the easier it becomes to justify more user-centric design.

## Sharing a rhythm

You don't need to force yourself into a working pattern of other teams that actively stops you from getting your work done. We encourage you to find a pattern in which you and your fellow team members find ways to work with each other that make sense and give each of you the input and output you need to do your work well. Remember that most businesses don't have the wide view of design needs and techniques that we as designers have. It's part of our job to sell them on better ways to be creative.

## Track inefficiencies

When rework does come up, it's often so far removed from the original cause that the link is not obvious. Trace the cause and make it visible, so the hidden cost of siloing communication is obvious for the next project. Make sure this learning is part of the project memory that is written in retrospectives.

## What to do if others throw deliverables over the fence to you

- Insist on opening a dialogue with them.
- Suggest that you become a liaison between teams.
- Invite people to co-design sessions and workshops to get involved in your design process.

## Terminology explained

User stories

Agile

Planners and doers

Project rhythm

Hidden efficiencies and hidden inefficiencies

Antagonistic roles

### REFERENCES

1. Gothelf J, Seiden J. Lean UX: Applying Lean Principles to Improve User Experience. O'Reilly; 2013. ISBN 978-1449311650.
2. Agile, Principles behind the Agile Manifesto. <http://agilemanifesto.org/principles.html.> [accessed 4.1.15].
3. Jeffries R. Essential XP: Card, Conversation, Confirmation. <http://xprogramming.com/articles/expcardconversationconfirmation/> [accessed 4.1.15].
4. Camus A. The Rebel. 1951.
5. Monteiro M. Design is a Job. A Book Apart; 2012. ISBN 978-1937557041.

# TAKEAWAYS

1.  Look beyond your team boundaries. Who else is involved in creating this product or service?

2.  Understand who will use your work to implement your UX solutions and how you communicate with them. If there is no obvious collaboration between your team and theirs, make it your responsibility to be the go-between.

3.  Understand the different goals for *planners* and *doers* on the project to address their needs and concerns. Use co-design sessions to bring planners and doers into the same mindset.

4.  Stay involved throughout the delivery process to ensure that assumptions in your problem solutions are evolved with new insights.

5.  Code quality is a UX concern. We don't expect you to write production quality code; instead, we encourage you to be involved in QA reviews to ensure the design is implemented correctly.

6.  Help to write good *user stories* to translate your design intent into useful development tasks. Include personas as actors instead of the "elastic" user, to avoid room for broad interpretation of who the user is and what they want.

7.  Find a shared rhythm with the other parties involved in the product development process. Reach out to be involved in the process throughout as best as possible.

# CHAPTER 8

## Living in the deliverables

"The only thing is that the map, the map is not the territory." —Ronin (1998)[1]

UXers have a strange relationship with deliverables. We want to do the best possible job, but if we don't keep sight of the fact that the end purpose is to build a product, we can get too deep into creating the most polished deliverable rather than the best explanation of the design intent.

Chapter 5 talked about "Being in the Room, but not Present." That is one way of shutting yourself off from collaborating closely with your team and developing your ideas. This chapter looks at another facet of missing crucial collaboration opportunities with your team.

## Best-in-show deliverables

Early in the days of UX as a formal discipline, Martina was at a conference where the team was still figuring out how to communicate experiences. The group made a deliverables wall to share what they had crafted, compare their experiences, and learn as a community. There was huge interest in this wall and it sparked lots of conversations about how beautiful and glossy some of the examples were. She ended up winning second prize in the Best Deliverables contest. It makes her cringe a little bit to remember that – in hindsight, she thinks they got sidetracked into drooling over these deliverables as though they were beautiful photography or sculpture and forgot what deliverables are about: making our thinking visible to facilitate a conversation.

The craft of UX has taken many of its cues from the visual design world – indeed, UX has been the natural career progression for many visual designers. It's great that we have taken on the ethos of providing quality to businesses in the form of our deliverables, but there are many kinds of quality. All design should communicate its rationale and context, but the way this is expressed is different for different purposes.

If we show an inappropriate level of fidelity in our deliverables, we close off important opportunities for feedback and collaboration, and can even make it harder to make our own point. For example, not every stakeholder can read a wireframe properly – although most stakeholders think they can – so they miss aspects of the page layout until they see a full mock-up. By this point, more money has been spent, more interrelated decisions may have been made, and less time is available to rework. A sketch may take less time to make than a wireframe, but it can have exactly the same amount of thinking behind it, and it is presented in a way that is easier for some stakeholders to grasp. Feedback on a sketch happens at the right level, targets the right subjects (e.g., have we got the flow right?), and arrives while the cost of change is still minimal.

What are we trying to do with our deliverables? They aren't the end goal; they are a step between the process of discovery and the process of delivery. They need to embody our thinking in the most appropriate way to enable the next step to happen. This doesn't mean that high fidelity is the enemy: when a product concept is being presented to the board, board members may only buy in if they can see the shine on the end vision. When an experience is being user-tested, the emotional aspects of the experience will only come through when the correct visual cues are present. But earlier in the process, putting too much fidelity into our deliverables can affect discovery by giving stakeholders the impression that conclusions have already been made, or aren't worth challenging because the cost of change is too high.

Recently, James was working with a more junior UXer to prepare assets for the discovery phase of a site redesign. The junior UXer was keen to demonstrate his commitment to the project and spent extra hours on polishing the audited site map, and his recommendations for restructuring the navigation, as an infographic in OmniGraffle. It was one of the most beautiful UX deliverables James had ever seen, but it failed to make the case. The product owner (PO) commented that she felt "the job of thinking it through has already been done, and I have no input into it." The PO didn't feel confident about moving forward without having the right involvement with decisions that had been made, and the project was at risk of stalling. A reset workshop, where the PO was empowered to collaborate in a card-sort using sticky notes on a whiteboard, solved the issue. The PO felt she had a far better understanding of the rationale behind the new navigational structure and could agree on it with the UXer. Now that she had confidence and ownership, she was able to sell the wider business on its benefits.

Communicating our thinking is about understanding the audience: their needs and desires, their capabilities, and their engagement with the product. Deliverables must fit a purpose that drives the project forward – enabling conversations that lead to decisions, supporting testing to gain actionable insight, or selling a vision to mark the spot on the horizon that the team is aiming toward. All of these factors call for different types of deliverables at different levels of fidelity. If we forget this, and create deliverables that are too intricate for anyone but a UXer to understand, or too polished for a stakeholder to feel comfortable about critiquing, or that don't embody enough of the experience to make testing meaningful, we don't serve the product need.

You can quickly get mired in this anti-pattern when stakeholders demand pixel-perfect mockups before they'll sign off. When stakeholders have this expectation, they won't see the value you add to the product development process as better experiences; they'll see the output as polished documents.

## Conversations, not lectures

We all know that a picture paints a thousand words. But a picture is a lecture, not a conversation. As social animals, we have evolved to find conversation and story to be far higher bandwidth and much more memorable.

If you spend forever polishing your deliverables, then you see changes as unwelcome destruction of your hard work, rather than testing a hypothesis. Highly polished deliverables leave fewer cracks for stakeholders to tease at and can leave them feeling that their only choices are to accept or reject the whole piece. Worse, all that time spent carefully honing the deliverable was time spent out of communication with the business and, as you "add definition" to your work, you're really adding new, unvalidated assumptions – and increasing risk by building assumption on top of assumption.

Don't assume deliverables can do the whole job of communicating your idea. If a deliverable could perfectly communicate the experience that needs to be built, it would *be* the experience. It's important to make room for discussion with the team as much as the intended users. Conversations bring interactivity to testing assumptions, as well as foreknowledge. In conversation, we can easily gauge which parts to skip over that the team already understands, tease out what they don't understand, and elaborate on that to create a shared understanding of the design intent.

## The increasing difficulty of documenting digital experiences

How do you document intricate behaviors on static paper?

The experiences we create in the digital world are no longer static documents where interactivity is limited to links between documents. Increasingly, the kinds of experiences we build are modular, flexible; treating the screen as a fluid canvas, not a rigid grid. Interactions happen in place, using animation to convey personality or hint at capabilities. Content strategies demand multirole capabilities for content areas, able to hold text, an image gallery, video, or a mix of all three.

Traditional static deliverables are, at best, guesses and, at worst, a brake on the kind of flexible thinking that modern interfaces demand. If a deliverable could completely encapsulate every behavior of a product, it would *be* the product – and it would take as long to produce. That's not where we need to be, especially not in an iterative test-and-learn environment.

## Beware the IKEA effect

People assign disproportionate value to things they put effort into making themselves (Norton, M.I., Mochon, D., Ariely, D., *Journal of Consumer Psychology*, July 2012).[2]

*Figure 8.1: The IKEA effect. (Photo credit: James O'Brien (with apologies to IKEA))*

# EFFËKT

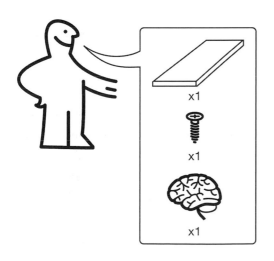

And the more effort invested, the greater the disproportionality of the value they assign, much like the disproportionate value we place on our creation efforts, such as IKEA flat-pack furniture we have heroically assembled without even reading the instructions. This is a great customer experience principle to be aware of – and also a potentially destructive anti-pattern to avoid!

It's inevitable that our thinking will contain some assumptions. Part of the process of building a product involves testing those assumptions and seeing which can be proved and which need to be discarded, which makes change inevitable. The IKEA effect bites when we polish the deliverables to too high a level, which makes us reluctant to undo all that work if a stakeholder or developer needs changes. That reluctance can be misinterpreted as defensiveness or stubbornness, when really we should be responsive to change for the shared goal of creating the best possible product. Failing to respond to the need for change makes us seem obtrusive and arrogant. (We'll talk about some of the other problems the IKEA effect can provoke in Chapter 11.)

When we talk about quality in our deliverables, we're talking about how the underlying thinking is made visible. Making sure everything is correctly spelled, using real copy and data, and adding imagery where it serves to illustrate an interaction: these all contribute to the conversation with your client by not distracting from the feedback, demonstrating understanding of the product, and illuminating your thinking respectively. Lorem ipsum or "Greek" placeholder (fake) text and other assumptive ways of indicating content can muddy the water. Is this block of lorem ipsum in the middle of the wireframe the body copy, or just a really long legal disclaimer? Unless the material appears concrete with realistic content, two different observers could come to two different conclusions about what it represents. Be especially aware of any assumptions you add and include opportunities to expose and discuss them in your deliverables.

It's important to set the expectations of those who will receive your work – whether on your team or on the client side – so they understand why you are delivering at the level of fidelity you choose. Explain that it keeps the decision making flexible: it saves time and money by keeping rework easy and cost of change low, and it gives everyone involved in the process the opportunity to contribute. Remember, it's about the right fidelity at the right time: today, when you're exploring a hypothesis with the team, sketches are great. Tomorrow, when it's time to present to the client, it may be appropriate to move to a higher level of fidelity. If clients are uneasy with sketching, you can explain that it's only the initial step. Each set of ideas should evolve from low to high.

## Collaborate, collaborate, collaborate

*"UX designers should also encourage, support[,] and facilitate collaboration. This can be done through different techniques, like design studios, brainstorming sessions, conversations, collaborative discovery, user testing and observation, customer interviews[,] and allowing everyone in the team to participate in the design process, for example[,] through sketching sessions."—Alexis Brion*[3]

Championing the experience doesn't mean having sole ownership of its definition. Everybody on the team has a stake in the success of the project and product – and often, the more senior the stakeholder, the greater the risk they assume. They have

*Figure 8.2: Collaborative design session. (Photo by: Martina Hodges-Schell.)*

to believe in the solution we present because they have the power to put the brakes on if they don't feel reassured about the level of risk involved.

One way to increase their confidence is to give them a level of ownership in the definition. By opening up the creative process and becoming more of a guide and facilitator, we can involve the rest of the team in a way that gives them an emotional investment when it comes to delivering the best product. Not only will they understand the solution better, they'll fight for it when challenges arise.

Facilitating creativity is a different skillset from being creative on one's own, or collaborating with people who have creative roles. People whose job titles are not traditionally creative may see the process as impenetrable magic, or feel that their contributions will be seen as inferior by the "professionals" running the session. Push participants' boundaries to help them see that they can break out of their self-assigned roles.

We love encouraging people to sketch, but it's not the only way to encourage them to take a more creative position. Grouping mood boards together, writing bullet points into a pen portrait, or shuffling around elements of cut-up printouts are all great contributions to the design process and are all things that can be done without an art school qualification. The more they contribute, the greater the quality of their contributions will (usually) get.

Guidance in sessions like these means handling terrible ideas sensitively just as much as it means encouraging good ideas. The Positive Disagreement patterns we introduce in Chapter 12 are great ways of gently reshaping turkeys into eagles.

There are lots of resources on the web for different ways of running collaborative sessions. We recommend you explore a few and see which resonate with your individual creative instincts, the audience, and the task at hand.

## Make space for collaboration

You can't *make* people be creative; you can only set up a relaxed and enjoyable environment that lowers the stakes and makes them feel encouraged to contribute. Creative spaces feel very different from traditional desk-and-chair work environments or meeting rooms and help to break participants out of their self-assigned roles and expectations.

We recognize that a full restructuring of your working environment is unlikely to happen, but you can make large gains without calling in the builders. As with many other aspects of changing the creative process in an organization, it often helps to start small and demonstrate the value of setting up a simple, cheap creative space as a way of opening up the possibility of bigger gains later on. It doesn't take an architect and six months of building work to make a creative space – just reconfiguring a room by pushing all the tables against the walls and taking out the chairs can enable creativity, by encouraging people to stand next to the whiteboard instead of sitting and passively watching someone else draw on it.

Design studios are great at creative space reconfiguration with plenty of white-wall space. If you don't have walls that are easy to use, make some! Foam-backed board is lightweight, easy to move around, and perfect for attaching sketches and sticky notes.

Try to keep your team's workspaces within each others' eyelines. Rather than have two pods of four, where people are sitting with their backs to each other, can you have a single pod of eight, all facing inward?

Everything is a potential surface for displaying ideas. Dry Erase paint can turn a wall or tabletop into a wipe-clean sketching surface. Liquid chalk markers turn windows into backlit notice boards. String and bulldog clips, pinned discreetly high on a wall or hanging from overhead conduits, can be used to display printouts when poster putty or pins are verboten.

Breakout spaces should feel different from desk areas. Ensure that you sit lower than chair level – on sofas, beanbags, or cushions – to encourage relaxation and freer composition and expression of ideas. A change of color also helps separate the areas and reset the brains of participants into a new mode.

When your sessions require more creativity and participation, don't let your participants settle into low-energy postures such as sitting or slouching. Keep their energy high by encouraging them to stand and perch, so the barrier to participation is simply straightening their legs rather than levering themselves out of comfortable chairs.

Use the social power of the kitchen. Making tea or coffee for others is a powerful social ritual that bonds teams and builds trust. It's also an opportunity to have quieter, more informal chats away from the formality of the desk area. Extend these powers over time by adding a café-type ambience and facilities to a breakout area.

## Leaner, meaner... UX

Organizations are increasingly recognizing that the Agile practice of Build – Measure – Learn has value in the entirety of the product life cycle, and embracing lean product development. Assumptions become hypotheses and are tested at the lowest possible cost with a minimum viable product (MVP). Learnings from the MVP are fed back into the product development cycle, which is built up iteratively. The Build – Measure – Learn loop is great for UX, as it incorporates ongoing testing and user insight right into the product roadmap, but it can mean changing how we make deliverables to support it.

### *Getting out of the deliverables business*

Jeff Gothelf and Josh Seiden[4] captured the essence of this rethinking of how we add value as designers to product and service development. They urged us to focus on outcomes (immediate results) and impact (long-term results) of the design work we do, not the deliverables (those pixel-perfect documents).

**Getting out of the deliverables business**
*What is it?*
Lean UX refocuses the design process away from the documents the team is creating to the outcomes the team is achieving. With increased cross-functional collaboration, stakeholder conversation becomes less about which artifact is being created and more about which outcome is being achieved.

*Why do it?*
Documents don't solve customer problems – good products do. The team's focus should be on learning which features have the biggest impact on their customers. The artifacts the team uses to gain that knowledge are irrelevant. All that matters is the quality of the product, as measured by the market's reaction to it.

**Shared understanding**

*What is it?*

Shared understanding is the collective knowledge of the team that builds up over time as the team works together. It's a rich understanding of the space, the product, and the customers. You'll know you have shared understanding when there are artifacts on the walls to communicate it, and when the team has built a solid dialect about the project.

*Why do it?*

Shared understanding is the currency of Lean UX. The more a team collectively understands what it's doing and why, the less it has to depend on secondhand reports and detailed documents to continue its work.

These are only two of the core principles underpinning Jeff Gothelf and Josh Seiden's[3] book, *Lean UX*. The book contains a wealth of useful patterns and techniques.

## Prototyping

We believe in creating the right deliverable at the right time for the right purpose. While sketches are great for early explorations and strategic agreement, sometimes to really explain your point or sell your concept, only a working prototype will do. Again, it's not about building the whole product; it's about communicating ideas and expanding on them.

The goal is to show, not tell. Lots of tools now exist to produce interactive prototypes without needing to know how to code in depth. They don't take long to learn, and it doesn't matter if the code isn't of production quality as long as it gets the intent across – it's about showing the intended experience. We advocate designers having code literacy (an understanding of how things are built and how that affects product development), not full-stack developer skills. (Unless that's your thing.)

If it works for your project, and you're comfortable with it, you can design and create a prototype directly in the browser with any of a growing number of libraries and frameworks. You can quickly create interactive "sketches" of your ideas this way, and they easily lend themselves to gathering feedback from users. At the same time, you get instant feedback on your interaction ideas and can make more confident design choices (e.g., that swipe action seemed really neat in theory, but you notice it gets distracting and annoying very quickly when you have to do it repetitively to accomplish a common task). For example, Martina recently tried out the Bootstrap prototyping library on a project. It took her a day to learn to work with the framework, but it gave her the ability to test core functionality for a new service across different platforms.

If designing in the browser is right for you and your project, a whole world of tools is emerging. We can't recommend one single prototyping setup for you here. Due to the nature of a printed book and the rapid advancement of tools and frameworks, we can only provide a snapshot into ways to help you move from a high-fidelity spec deliverable to quick and iterative testing of design hypotheses. We found this comparison of prototyping tools by Emily Schwartzman really helpful: http://www.cooper.com/journal/2013/07/designers-toolkit-proto-testing-for-prototypes

We are keeping a collection up to date at http://www.communicatingtheuxvision.com/tools and would love to get your input.

Depending on your own development skill set this is a great opportunity to pair with a developer (or sometimes a prototyper or creative technologist, depending on your workplace role mix). Pairing with a developer gives you a much broader opportunity to explore how to make your ideas interactive and possibly plug in live data to try out functionality where this is advantageous. And often, together you will come up with new ideas on how to tackle a design challenge that you didn't think of by yourself.

A note on getting stuck on tools and other gimmicks: we get quite frustrated with all the noise about tools, when exploring the quality of the design thinking would be more productive. It's akin to a photography debate over what camera and lens and filter you use – your equipment doesn't make you a great photographer (or designer, in this case). It's about framing the idea.

And a prototype is only a prototype when users interact with it and you can gather understanding of whether your design ideas work for the intended audience. Otherwise, you are simply creating interactive demos.

## What if you work in an agency?

Working in an agency adds an extra challenge to combating this anti-pattern. The traditional agency model doesn't just erect a fence between designers and stakeholders; it digs a moat. Clients want to see value for money and, because they only have occasional contact with the design team, it is harder to express the value of thinking. The statement of work that defines the agency's responsibilities may specify exactly what deliverables will be created. All of these factors reduce the flexibility available to UXers to drive change in the way deliverables are created.

However, the agency model is open to change. As clients begin to ask agencies to create more complex products, the limits of the agency model relative to these demands are beginning to show. There are opportunities for UXers to drive this change. Conversations with client services can lead to new ways of writing the statement of work that leaves room for flexibility in what we deliver. Setting client expectations properly and explaining the rationale for appropriate fidelity (and presenting in context, as we describe in Chapter 4) can add some push from the client side to adopt leaner ways of working. Ultimately, the agency is not selling the client the deliverables themselves – it is selling better product or campaign outcomes. Encouraging client services to set up a conversation that explores more efficient ways of working is in everyone's interest.

We don't claim that changing the agency model is easy, or that it is an overnight process. But to stay competitive in a market where disruption is the norm and speed of change only ever seems to accelerate, the agencies that don't adapt their processes are the ones that will be swamped by change. UX can be at the heart of enabling that adaptation.

## Collect user feedback

Feedback from real users is vital, and needs to happen on a frequent and regular basis – ideally weekly. Bake it into your team process and into your culture. Get everyone involved.

If you need pointers on how to collect qualitative feedback for design research, we recommend *A Pocket Guide to Interviewing for Research* by Andrew Travers.[5]

This is the best way to get out of the deliverables and into crafting more meaningful experiences, as you can be confident that your ideas resonate with your audience and you can influence your team to put emphasis on the solving design problems and away from pixel perfection. You get through a lot more testing with users if you keep to the lowest fidelity you can possibly get away with. A sketch with some sticky notes? Great! Ten pages beautifully worked up in Photoshop? Just ate up the time we had for testing and iterating.

A paper prototype can change and evolve in-situ in response to a user's reactions, while a full-fidelity mockup or prototype can't. On the other hand, users may respond to calls to action very differently depending on the final visual treatment they receive. Low fidelity helps gather great feedback because it doesn't look finished, and it helps you not to feel too invested in the idea to make changes. High fidelity helps validate which colors, imagery, and fine-tuned layout will work with the users. Think first about which hypothesis you want to test, and then decide what level of fidelity is most appropriate for the session.

You can be proactive about this anti-pattern by reframing your understanding of the role of deliverables. See them as enough, and no more, to get the product through to the next stage. Recognize that conversations use a much higher bandwidth than documents, and have the added benefit of increasing trust.

Dialing down to 90% can be a difficult and scary experience. If we still see our deliverables as the final output of this project, not the built product or service, it's hard to let go.

You may need to find new ways to approach sign-off, so the deliverables become proposals rather than promises.

Take the time at a project kick-off to explain your process and what outcomes should be expected from the UX team. Show examples and demonstrate how you will use these tools and processes throughout the project to avoid mismatched expectations and stakeholder feedback.

## Summary

Focus on outcomes and impact, not outputs. Our documentation tools don't allow for capturing the intricacies of crafting digital experiences and beyond. Review your set of deliverables and pick the right tools at the right depth from your UX toolbox to communicate and test your ideas. Remember that your real deliverable is agreement and understanding, and do the right things to foster that. In our experience, it's a balance between conversation and demonstration.

## The "Living in the Deliverables" anti-pattern

An experience is not an experience while it exists only as a wireframe or mockup. Our deliverables are just steps on the road to creating a product, not the final product itself. Spending time on perfectly polished deliverables makes rework expensive and unwelcome, and can intimidate stakeholders into feeling they cannot offer input about a design that is already "decided." When this happens, our deliverables are not doing their job of explaining, encouraging conversation, prompting decisions, or testing assumptions.

## You know you're in it when...

- Every request for change seems as if it will take forever.

- Design value gets measured by the number of documents created, not the quality of problem solving and communication with stakeholders.

- You write endless specs.

- You're crafting documents, not experiences.

- Your job is to wireframe, and nothing else.

- You're more concerned about the document than the product.

- You get frustrated by interruptions from team members.

- You find yourself pushing back on fair but minor requests because of the number of times they'll have to be replicated in the deliverables.

## Patterns

### Dead Poet Society pattern

In the film "Dead Poets Society," Robin Williams's character encourages his students to stand on their desks to get a different perspective on the world. We invite you to do the same. Step back, examine – are you communicating your ideas effectively or are you getting stuck in anguishing over document details?

The question to ask yourself around this pattern is, What is the right deliverable to get the right response, right now? There are three parts to this question, which are best approached in reverse.

*Right now*: As your project evolves through different stages, different levels of decision have to be made. Don't waste time polishing call-to-action text when the business still needs to validate core experience principles. What's the right depth of decision today to get you to the next stage?

*Right response*: What do you need to move on to the next step of delivering this product? If it's a decision from a key stakeholder, what is going to drive that decision? If it's broadening stakeholders' minds to possibilities, what is going to make them reconsider their position? If it's communicating the experience to a UI developer, what is going to enable them to implement it in the best way? All of these scenarios call for their own techniques and deliverables, and are sensitive to the individual(s) receiving the deliverable.

*Right deliverable*: With the time and response in mind, what's the most efficient thing to create? What goes into the right level of depth and explains the thinking behind your decisions completely enough to get the response? Remember that even within a class of deliverable such as a wireframe, there are many possibilities in terms of fidelity and time to create, from sketch through Axure all the way up to a Photoshop comp.

It's OK to agree on the level of fidelity with the recipient of the deliverables: "Will an annotated sketch work for us here, or should I take this into Axure?"

Understand your strengths and play to them. If you have the gift of gab, you may be able to get more of the buy-in you need from low-fidelity deliverables and engaging explanations. If you have substantial experience with HTML or Flash, you may move to prototyping or paired in-browser design with a stakeholder sooner.

## Embrace the creativity of everyone

Co-design sessions have several benefits for the design process. By bringing "non-creatives" in at our ideation stage and encouraging them to contribute, we demystify our process and give stakeholders a sense of ownership of the ideas. A demystified process leads, in the long term, to better requirements and feedback, as stakeholders learn what works for us. Ownership of the ideas gives stakeholders more impetus to comprehend and internalize the thinking behind design decisions, and leads stakeholders to defend those decisions when they are challenged.

Encouraging creativity is about giving permission and encouragement. *Permission* is usually about convincing participants that the workshop counts as actual productive work, and that their contributions will not infringe on anyone else's role. *Encouragement* is about convincing participants that co-design workshops aren't about creating high art. Often, some participants in a workshop will refuse to engage unless shown that even we designers will only be producing scribbles at this stage. James calls his co-design workshops "scribble sessions" for this reason. (As an aside, these reluctant participants often turn out to be amazing sketch artists who are just overly self-critical.)

Each team is different, and you will need to spend time working out which encouragement techniques work for your individual participants. However, the general process is to avoid flat-out disagreeing with assertions your participants make, such as "I can't draw" or "This is pointless." Disagreeing just opens up opportunities for your reluctant participant to argue, thereby "proving" their point. Instead, *positively disagree* with them. "I'll tell you a secret, nor can I! Take a look at my sketches – if your boxes and arrows look worse than mine, I'll be astonished!" or "Well, go with it anyway – there's an outside chance we might come up with something brilliant, and that chance is worth spending an hour on."

Co-design workshops are about starting the process or gaining consensus on a creative direction to solve an individual problem. Once the workshop is complete, you can collect all the outputs and use them to inform your work, sieving out the ideas that don't work and honing the ones that do. As long as you can tell the story of this process, stakeholders will usually see the bones of their ideas in your final solution, and will get that vital sense of pride about it.

We talk more about positive disagreement in Chapter 12. For a full guide to different workshop formats, see Chapter 15.

## Spring clean

If your deliverables ever reach the point where you're too invested to throw them out, then your ability to respond to change has been compromised.

Unfortunately, change is a fact of life when designing and building software products. Assumptions get tested and proven incorrect, or a competitor launches a disruptor product squarely into your target market. At these times, a reluctance to view your solution with a critical eye and see what must be made anew will lead you to defend your solution in the face of reality.

We don't mean that you should literally throw out your work, or start it again – rejected ideas from the past can be very good at sparking new creative solutions on future projects. But you should be prepared to abandon your attachment to work you may have spent considerable time to create. As William Faulkner said about writing, "You must kill your darlings" for the sake of the end product.

Retain focus by remembering that design is a march to a city on the horizon that will only come into sharp focus when you get close. If, at any point, you have to change your route, or you get a different hint about what the city looks like, you're still making progress toward it, and now with a more realistic idea of what awaits you. Consider your work to be a hypothesis until it is tested.

## Fast feedback

You only know whether your experience works when someone interacts with it. The more often you can validate whether it works in this way, the lower you keep the financial and psychological costs of change. Try to test with real users at least once a sprint/agile delivery cycle (or weekly, if you are in some form of continuous delivery), whether in-person or using a remote testing solution. "Five-user Friday" or "Test Tuesday" are good ways of creating a rhythm and setting expectations in the business about the need for testing. Remind the business that the longer they spend without testing, the more risk they are stacking up.

User feedback is most valuable when the rest of the business can see it, so invite them to (silently and unobtrusively, or remotely) observe the sessions, or find ways to bring the key findings to life. If you use an app that records the user's facial reactions, such as Silverback, show stakeholders the five top reactions to the test scenario. As well as being entertaining, these human reactions create a powerful drive to fix the issues that have been identified – or amplify the sense of success when a great feature is accepted by the users.

## Toolbox bonanza

Never tie yourself to one software package or way of doing things. Being able to pick the right deliverable for the right response at the right time gets a lot easier if you can choose from several methods of accomplishing each class of deliverable. For example, it's easy to make a wireframe look like pencil sketches in Illustrator, so you can print agreed parts of a page and sketch variations at the same fidelity in the unfinished part, but it's hard to keep a set of modular wireframes for a whole site in sync, which is where specialized Information Architecture (IA) tools like Axure shine.

Having a broad toolkit at your disposal also helps the quality of your thinking. In accordance with the saying that "when all you have is a hammer, everything looks like a nail," when your wireframing tool makes certain interface patterns as easy as drag-and-drop, everything looks like an opportunity to add a carousel.

Keeping up with the evolution of existing tools and the emergence of new tools is part of the craft of UX, but also remember to explore what already exists and find the toolkit that fits you.

One last thought on this pattern: *invest in your tools*. The saying "a poor workman blames his tools" is as much about the fact that a poor worker will buy tools of poor quality that break easily or make it hard to finish the job well. Obviously it is your employer's responsibility to make the equipment available that you need to do your job, but putting some of your own money into (or expensing, if you can) a set of alcohol-based markers, pigment Fineliners, or a new sketching app is a worthwhile investment if it helps you get better results. Plus, it sends a valuable message to your team that you are a professional who uses quality tools to get quality results.

### Push the changes upward

Ensure that the business understands the benefits of this approach and structures its expectations (and statements of work!) accordingly. Otherwise, you may find yourself still having to crystallize your thinking into wireframes, or other unnecessary deliverables, to meet arbitrary milestones.

## If others inflict this anti-pattern on you

### Ask how it works

Break the ice by starting a conversation.

### Suggest gathering some quick user feedback

Validate your assumptions early and often. No glossy deliverables are needed.

### Sketch on the wall

Assure your stakeholders that you'll reach the high-fidelity stage, but you want to be certain you're moving in the right direction before you commit to the time, effort, and risk involved in creating high-fidelity work. Always take photos of your work at the end of a session – for socializing and presenting the work in context later.

### If stakeholders demand pixel-perfect mockups before they'll sign off

Bring the conversation back to the level of documentation of ideas the team needs to make progress. Make a case for spending time on quality of problem solving versus deliverable making and agree with the whole production team on what level of fidelity is needed to move ahead in a timely manner.

### If the quality of the design is measured in the deliverable, not the problem solution

Discuss quality of thinking and problem solving over time spent on quality of deliverables. Focus on spending design time on better design outcomes rather than design deliverables.

## If procurement is buying documents, not design solutions

Sometimes it's not the immediate project team that is challenged by measuring value in outcomes (problems solved and design goals achieved), rather than deliverables (time-intensive documents that can only capture the thinking of a moment in the product development process, not iteratively improve on initial hypotheses). Get involved in selling and setting up your project. Show examples of the artifacts your design process is likely to produce. Focus on validating hypotheses (design's best guesses tested with users and verified or modified) and spending more time on problem solving, less time on unnecessary deliverables. Agree with the whole team on what is necessary to progress.

## Detailed discussions about the documents procured, not the project outcomes

You can tell the vision of the project delivery is shifting toward a deliverable focus when the team is spending way too much time discussing what documents will be "handed over" instead of what design problems will be solved; "Have you done those wireframes?" over "Have you found a solution to the poor sign-up numbers?"

## CASE STUDY

Aline Baeck, lead UX designer, Global Products at eBay Europe

*Figure 8.3: Aline Baeck. (Photo by: Aline Baeck.)*

I know just how comforting living in the deliverables can be. I spent several years working on a software product with millions of users and, during my first few years, design was a fairly new function in that company. So we leaned into the engineering culture, which at the time was defined by deliverables. Our personas, task flows, and design specs were the focus; our success was judged by our ability to deliver these documents within a waterfall process. Of course, there was collaboration with Product Management (PM) and engineering, which was highly valued by the company, but that collaboration became intertwined with these documents, and the majority of collaboration was done through document reviews, in three- to four-hour review meetings where we hashed out every detail within the context of the detailed design specification.

As a design team, we recognized how dangerous this practice was. Not only did the emphasis on documentation devalue our design practice, since our true value lies in our way of thinking, not in what we produce, but it reduced our relationship with our PM and engineering partners to focus on the tactical rather than the strategic, and reinforced role barriers by constraining how each function interacted with the others – the structure of the documents and review meetings defined our relationships.

We made a conscious effort to change the way we operated as a design team. Our first simple change was in our project plans; instead of listing the document deliverables with a due date, we defined our project in phases, with the activities and end result rather than the document. So instead of "personas, due xx/xx/xx," we would list "define the customer," with open questions we wanted to answer, such as "Can our current customer segments be used or is this for new customer group(s)?" 'What do these users care about?" "How much do these users value being able to do this? " etc., with a time interval. This simple change served several purposes: it opened the design "black box" and educated our partners on how we work and why we do certain activities. It invited participation from them by making them curious enough to help us answer those questions. And it uncovered overlap with other groups that might need some of the same answers, inspiring a natural collaboration within the team.

This incredibly simple change had a profound effect on the design team and our partners, and promoted a much more collaborative environment where there was co-ownership of these questions and in finding the answers. The burden was no longer on the design team, whose answers then might be questioned by those who did not participate; instead, we found much less friction between the functions as we collaborated more, rather than deliverables being thrown "over the wall."

Within a year or so, we were operating in a completely different environment, where the cross-functional team had embraced responsibility for all deliverables within the team, where engineers were also held accountable when design didn't deliver and vice versa, and where arduous meetings reviewing design documents were no longer held – instead, lightweight wireframes were used to promote discussion within the team, and designers sat with engineers to work out design details. And it all started with our recognition that focusing on deliverables was hurting us more than anyone, and our simple change to our project plan.

## Terminology explained

Lean UX

Design studio

Co-design

Prototyping

Code quality

Code literacy

Qualitative user research

## Additional resources

1. Gray D, Brown S, Macanufo J. Gamestorming: A Playbook for Innovators, Rulebreakers, and Changemakers. Cambridge: O'Reilly Media; 2010.
2. Humble J, O'Reilly B, Molesky J. The Lean Enterprise. Cambridge: O'Reilly; 2013.
3. Klein L. UX for Lean Startups. Cambridge: O'Reilly; 2013.
4. Schwartzmann E. Designer's Toolkit: Road Testing Prototype Tools 2013. <http://www.cooper.com/journal/2013/07/designers-toolkit-proto-testing-for-prototypes> [accessed 25.1.15].
5. Sherwin D. Creative Workshop: 80 Challenges to Sharpen Your Design Skills, Cincinatti. 2010. F+W.

## REFERENCES

1. Frankenheimer J, Mamet D, Zeik JD. Ronin. MGM UA; 1998.
2. Norton MI, Mochon D, Ariely D. The IKEA Effect: When Labor Leads to Love. J Consumer Psychol 2012.
3. Brion A. The Lean UX Designer. <http://www.designvsart.com/blog/2013/06/30/the-lean-ux-designer/> [accessed 13.11.14].
4. Gothelf J, Seiden J. Lean UX: Applying Lean Principles to Improve User Experience. New York: O'Reilly Media; 2013. ISBN: 978-1449311650.
5. Travers A. A Pocket Guide to Interviewing for Research (Kindle edition). Cardiff: Five Simple Steps; 2013. ASIN B00EPOXTJ6.

# TAKEAWAYS

1. Design deliverables are not the finished product. It's not an experience unless the intended audience is interacting with it.

2. Deliverables and documentation never manage to communicate the full experience intended by design. You need to talk to the recipients of your deliverables.

3. The goal of our work is to communicate design intent as clearly as possible and elicit feedback on our assumptions, not to make the "shiniest" spec possible.

4. Communication is most efficiently achieved by finding the right deliverable to elicit the right response at the right time.

5. The role of the designer is shifting from individual "rockstar" creator to group facilitator.

6. Collaborative sketching and ideation sessions improve team understanding much better than annotated wireframes.

7. Flat specs and static deliverables aren't good at communicating the kind of rich experiences we design for modern digital products.

8. Used at the right point in the process, prototypes can be incredibly powerful at getting your interaction aims across.

# CHAPTER 9

## Assuming others don't get design

"Every child is an artist, the problem is staying an artist when you grow up." —Pablo Picasso

## A note from the authors

*In this chapter, we'd like to cast our net a little wider than our usual focus on UX design and talk about the broader context of creativity across the whole product design life cycle. This means we'll be considering service and process design, UX, UI, and visual design all under the same umbrella of "design." We feel that all of these elements are so tied up with the user's experience of the product that any discussion of this anti-pattern has to encompass the whole creative process of product development.*

## Creating design and understanding design

Design is a wonderful and curious animal. It's not quite art, not quite science, but has a foot in both camps. It has no hard rules, except the unwritten rules that we enjoy breaking from time to time. The corollary is that sometimes you can only tell what works by having the taste to know what not to do. What we shorthand as "taste" and "experience" are the result of years of learning to develop an understanding of those unwritten rules, and even longer in learning how to communicate them in ways that commercial minds feel comfortable with.

But the challenge of this long, detailed study of creating design is that we can forget that, to have an understanding of design, one doesn't necessarily need to understand the technicalities of creating it. When we believe that, we can all too easily place ourselves in ivory towers, creating a division between our work and the rest of the organization.

## Pretentious little jerks

Martina studied for her master's degree at the top floor of Central Saint Martins, a famous design school in London. When we originally prepared this topic as a conference talk, she was looking for pictures of ivory towers to act as a visual metaphor. It quickly dawned on her that the building she studied in looked very much like her own design school ivory tower.

Recently Martina visited their new campus and found a piece of artwork (Fig 9.1) on the wall that provided the perfect illustration.

Back in Chapter 2, we discussed self-imposed success metrics – our intrinsic motivation as designers to do a great job. We strive for products and services that are easy to use and delightful experiences for their intended audiences. But often, we find ourselves exasperated by working with people who don't have our design schooling and experience. We easily fall into a pattern of telling ourselves a story of stakeholder committees that

*Figure 9.1: Pretentious Little Shits, as seen at Central Saint Martin's School of Art and Design. (Photo credit: Martina Hodges-Schell.)*

destroy our ideas, and make ourselves the lone force standing between the marketing department and the user.

But if that's true, what does that make us? The *hero designer,* the ill-tempered genius locked away in their studio scribbling down their big idea, chasing perfection for perfection's sake. There was a time when design was practiced in isolation, locked away from stakeholders and clients until the reveal of a shiny artifact. While it's a guilty pleasure of ours to follow Don Draper & Co. on TV in the hit series "Mad Men," the reality of working in the design industry has (thankfully) evolved since the 1960s. We've discovered the need to move away from creative elitism that inevitably dictated a waterfall process of working, toward a collaborative and more transparent process that embraces the ever-evolving digital technology landscape.

In a world of rapid delivery, incredible complexity, and distributed teams, it's more important than ever to challenge this reputation for aloofness and elitism. Of course it feels great to be the hero – just witness the number of job ads calling for "rockstars," "gurus," and "ninjas" – but heroes by definition work on their own. Product design is, by its nature, the opposite of ivory-tower separation. For a product to succeed, its design has to be appreciated by everyone, not just designers.

### Hero designer

In his book *Designing for Interaction*, Dan Saffer[1] describes the hero designer as the kind of practitioner who relies heavily on their intuition and experience to design, rarely engaging in user research or cross-team collaboration to develop their design work.

## Pitchslapped

*"Everything that's wrong with design today is your fault. That's a great opportunity. You have the power to change things. Fix it."* —Mike Monteiro, Design is a Job

When we rail against the myth of the hero designer, there is one particular kind of business that must stand up and take its brickbats: the creative agency. Agencies win work by pitching: responding to a client brief with a glossy, pixel-perfect solution, based in design effort, just to *win* the contract to work with the client. This, despite the fact that during a pitch, with its time and budget limitations, it's not possible to properly unpack or understand the problem space, let alone the customers. This culture, which elevates design into a business-winning dark art, has made us feel infallible. It's also taught us that our opinions trump real-world learnings, and that our shiny ideas are what bring customers to us.

The problem is that it's a working model that falls apart when the brief explores an area of significant uncertainty or complexity. In essence, the pitch process restricts good UX process by making the client fall in love with a glossy but incomplete solution. Why pay for research when they've already chosen the "best" solution? Why maintain a channel of communication between the design team and the delivery team, when that would only compromise the design vision?

Clients and stakeholders don't understand our process, so they focus on the tangible things we create for them. As designers, we evaluate the quality of our problem solving with design thinking, while the recipients of our work can often only understand what we do in the deliverables we produce. To be able to put great products into the world, we need to work as a team with those recipients to help them understand the process and include them in it.

## We live in a designed world

When we work with others, the line between professional authority and being patronizing can be thin and hard to see. However, the best way to ensure you frequently end up on the wrong side of this line is to assume that you're the only person in the room who "gets" design.

Try this: next time you're around a table with a cross-section of stakeholders, take just a second to observe the things they've brought – their phones, pens, and books. Look particularly carefully at the things people value so much that they keep them on their person at all times – jewelry, eyeglasses, watches, shoes, accessories, and even body art. We guarantee you that every person in that meeting has made careful, calculated choices about those items, not just at the time of purchase but every time they put their clothes on in the morning. There may not be anyone but you around that table who knows leading from kerning, you may or may not agree with their taste, but everyone around that table *understands* design and its social implications.

In Dieter Rams's words: "good design is honest and understandable." If it isn't understandable to nondesigners, then it fails its purpose. Stakeholders may not be able to articulate design in technical terms, but, from everyday interactions with a designed world, they certainly understand it.[2]

When we don't acknowledge colleagues' or clients' ability to appreciate design, we exclude their feedback from anything more than the most basic level of response – which is almost certainly not what the other party intended. It leads us to offer superficial responses without really engaging with what the feedback is getting at. And the people whose feedback is not being fully appreciated will see us as elitist and arrogant, which erodes trust in us and our work.

## "Creative" isn't a noun

Neuroscientists are beginning to understand that creativity as a superpower is a myth. Those flashes of genius quite often come from people outside the domain, as they literally think "outside the box." Be sure not to throw out criticism or a suggestion from other areas of the business without testing its validity in the wider picture first.

Listen to the input from everyone on the team. You simply never know where the best idea or problem solution is coming from. A fellow UX consultant shared an anecdote of the cleaning lady coming up with the winning copy on a multivariate test to improve online conversion on a website.

## How can you make sharing easier?

You can create a lot of resistance against your design by not opening up your process to the rest of the team. A very simple, and effective approach to getting the team on the same page is to collaborate throughout your design process with your stakeholders, business, developers and marketers alike to avoid *us-versus-them* dynamics.

## The not-invented-here bias

Research has shown that, as humans, we prefer our own ideas. We fall in love with our own ideas. Love is a strong emotion, and rarely brought into the context of the workplace. We believe we are quite rational in our decision-making and think we have picked the logical "best choice."

We are inclined not to like the ideas of others. That, in turn, means other people's ideas are never quite as interesting or convincing as our own.

Knowing this can motivate us to share our practice and help us create a collaborative work process to give our stakeholders a stake in the design process. You can harness the "not invented here bias" to your advantage – you can create group buy-in on your design by letting them have a stake in it. Dan Ariely,[3,4] an Israeli-American professor of psychology and behavioral economics, explains that even a small token in the ideation process, as simple as arranging a line of text from pre-printed words, makes us feel enough ownership of an idea to feel it's ours. By turning the not-invented-here bias on its head, we can benefit from its flipside, the "I-invented-this" bias.

You can read more on this research and insights into human nature in Ariely's books, *Predictably Irrational*[3] and *The Upside of Irrationality*.[4]

### The toothbrush theory

*The Toothbrush Theory: Ideas are just like our relationship with toothbrushes. We all want, need, have one, but we don't like using anybody else's.*

—Dan Ariely[3,4]

### Pair design

You can help yourself, your ideas, and your stakeholders by bringing them into your design process.

We have adopted one very effective way of sharing skills and collaborating from the programming community: pairing. That is, two people working together on the same task with one set of artifacts (e.g., working on the same single file on the same computer). It's great for getting to solutions faster and sharing knowledge on the project but also sharing skills with the team.

Pairing is an easier sell when you're part of an in-house team or in a consultancy relationship, but in an agency context, you can suggest this as a "working meeting" or "co-design workshop" to ease client buy-in.

## Feeding back

You can be proactive about this anti-pattern by internally recasting your own statements about design into everyday language. We dedicated the whole of Chapter 1 to bridging the gap between your stakeholders' language and your own, because it is vital to get to a shared understanding.

This will also help because correcting stakeholders with accurate design vocabulary is often counterproductive to creating a solid working relationship. Probe feedback to understand what your colleagues are trying to explain, and remember that sometimes, even stakeholders who do have a strong design vocabulary will still recast their feedback in lay terms for the sake of others in the meeting.

## Well-intended suggestions

Design criticism from people who aren't designers is absolutely valid. Admittedly, the degree of its validity can be affected by the critic's level of domain knowledge, their assumptions about users, and many other factors. But you already have skills to synthesize this feedback and align it to project goals and professional experience from working with user feedback. Not all suggestions are practical, as they may not take design limitations, budget, or time constraints into account.

Hear out feedback from all kinds of subject matter experts. Having all this knowledge available to tap into makes your life as a designer so much easier. You can glean fruitful insights that spark design ideas or help understand design limitations before you explore a route unnecessarily. *It's possible to get that data? You can do what now with the new API?* Questions like these can lead to incredibly enriching insights for your design work.

If you are faced with well-intended, but poor "design advice," make a synthesis of all the good design ideas that are raised by nondesigners, without making the originators of the bad ideas feel as if they're being ignored or belittled. Often, you can incorporate your response to bad ideas into the response to a better idea and show inclusiveness that way – we'll show you how to do this in the Positive Disagreement group of patterns in Chapter 12. Another powerful technique is to cast your feedback as we demonstrated in Chapter 4, re-rolling a suggestion presented in the form of a design solution into a workable business aim that design can respond to.

If your stakeholder is persistent with their well-intended idea, you can consider adding this option to the next round of user testing or A/B testing to gather customer feedback (which may demonstrate it doesn't work, or may show that it improves the product).

## Get the HiPPO on board

It's valuable to understand how your clients decide on what ideas to move forward. Is their decision based on merit, or based on the status of the decision maker? Everyone knows about the elephant in the room, but every meeting also contains a HiPPO: the Highest Paid Person's Opinion. According to Andrew McAfee of the MIT Center for Digital Business, many organizations still operate by giving the HiPPO the decision-making power. Work with your group to create an environment where everyone's ideas are heard and considered.[5]

## Some people view creativity as risk

Sometimes the disconnect in the team stems from different views of *uncertainty*. Traditional business processes interpret uncertainty as risk and try to minimize it wherever possible. But innovation is a phenomenon that can't happen without new ideas, and new ideas can't be fully formed and fairly tested without some uncertainty. As designers, we are trained to deal with much uncertainty – to create order from unknowns and chaos. Sometimes it's easy to forget, and difficult to put into words, that uncertainty is an integral part of the process and usually diminishes over the course of a design project.

We celebrate innovation and creativity as a culture, but we should remember that organizations and education largely prefer certainty, people who play within the rules, and people who don't challenge the status quo. It's important to help stakeholders who are concerned with risk to understand the need for uncertainty, and also that we recognize its boundaries and won't steer the whole project into muddled waters.

## The "Assuming Others Don't Get Design" anti-pattern

Creating design is a learned skill that grows with experience. But consuming design is something we all learn as part of our aesthetic and cultural upbringings. When we forget that a nondesigner's views of design are valid, we set ourselves up to dismiss their feedback as trivial or unconcerned with the "right" values. This response makes stakeholders feel they're not being listened to, which drives a wedge between designers and other team members, and hurts the ultimate experience that the user will have.

### You know you're in it when...

- You roll your eyes a lot when stakeholders contribute.
- You prefer to keep the client away from your design process and to share work in "the big reveal" at carefully curated intervals. The later, the better.
- There's a palpable disconnect between the design team and the rest of the group.
- You refuse to collaborate with nondesigners.

## Patterns – making sharing easier

In this chapter, we focus on patterns to help you share your working processes and create buy in for your design. For in-depth guides on applying many of these co-working practices, see Chapter 16, Guide to Group Design Techniques.

### Collaborative workshops

Collaborative workshops with low barriers to entry of artistic skill work best to get everyone contributing. Make it easy for everyone to feel welcome and able to contribute. Collaboration also has the wonderful effect of promoting ownership bias of ideas, so stakeholders who feel involved in the ideation process will work harder to make their visions come true.

Dan Ariely[3,4] has proved that I-invented-this bias can be created from as simple an action as rearranging a scrambled sentence to form a solution – even when only one arrangement made sense, participants in his study still exhibited attachment to the solution. Use this information wisely: we would never suggest that you should structure a collaborative workshop to lead stakeholders to think that your own predetermined solution was their idea. *Never*.

## Sketching

Help your nondesign colleagues articulate themselves visually. We have heard many excuses from stakeholders for not wanting to participate, but sketching is about getting your idea externalized, not artistic skill. A simple trick to encourage skeptics: ask them to explain what a cat is to someone who doesn't speak the same language as they do. Chances are they will be able to get their point across, even if they feel they are not a master of Renaissance-like realism.

## Storyboarding

Help the team understand the goals for the product from the user's perspective. Storyboard out a task flow from the customer's perspective. What goals do they have? Then you can brainstorm ideas together for how you can help your customers achieve those goals.

## Moodboards

Moodboards are another great leveling activity. Bringing magazines, scissors, and glue to a session lowers boundaries and helps everyone contribute. Creating moodboards for personas is a great introduction for the team to viewing the project/product through the eyes of their users.

## Paper mockups

Remove the need for any proprietary software knowledge by mocking things up on paper, with Sharpie markers and sticky notes. Stickies are easily repositioned, rephrased, or removed as you layer on complexity. You may have much more experience with page hierarchy than your stakeholders, but this is a great way to help them understand the need to prioritize and to carefully consider what's most important for users to achieve their goals.

## Word association

Help your team extend the brainstorming session beyond what's already in your collective minds. Introduce nonrelated objects to each group and give them a worksheet with thirty to fifty blank spaces to write down word associations for the object. Don't restrict yourself to sensible words that fit with the project at hand. In step two, get everyone to pick one of these associations and a design problem, and come up with different ideas to solve the problem. This generates a much broader set of solutions.

## Dot voting

In this technique, each team member gets three dots (or chocolates, in Martina's office) to vote on their preferred ideas/solutions. Agree on how many of the most popular ones you will pick to move forward with.

## Design the box

If your team has difficulty with articulating or prioritizing what your product is and what problem it solves for your users, get them to design the packaging for a fictitious future product. Give it a name, a strapline, a couple of bullet points. This exercise helps everyone focus on what's really the most important thing, not to themselves, but to their customers, who need to be convinced to pick this thing over the competition.

## Role-playing

To completely change out of the design exercise context, consider role-playing the user experience with the team. It helps them understand how customers interact with your service, and how, as human beings, those customers want to be treated.

## I-invented-this pattern

Devise workshop formats that let your team participate in creating your concept. Bring artifacts of your insights (for example, an empathy map would be an artifact of insight gained from a scenario mapping exercise) and goals. Shepherd the thinking in positive directions rather than steering it toward a known solution.

## Kate Rutter's skills map

A great way to understand unarticulated skills across your stakeholders and multi-disciplinary team is a simple mapping exercise that Kate Rutter introduced us to. For each team member, print out the spider map on a transparency and fill in with a permanent marker. One sheet per person. You won't just discover great skills that will help the project, but you are also able to overlay all maps to see where you have strong skill representation and where your group may have skill gaps.[6]

## Patterns – principles to strive for
## Transparency

Make your design process transparent by explaining your process, artifacts, decision making, and language.

## Respect

Extend respect to everyone on your team. It's easy to dismiss other people's ideas or input because they think differently from you or have a different cultural background. See this as a great source of inspiration, not a hindrance.

## Use everyday language

It's also easy to forget that the words we use to describe our work are familiar and precise to us, but can cause much misunderstanding and bewilderment with our audience. Be proactive by internally recasting your own statements about design into everyday language. This helps your audience to not feel "stupid."

## Frame of reference

Explain your frame of reference to the group, to demystify how you make design decisions and prioritize work. This is also a good way to explain design principles such whitespace, leading, and other less-tangible aspects of our craft.

## Facilitation magic

As UX design is developing as a practice, one skill has been emphasized like no other: the designer as facilitator for the group. This may not have been your idea of a core competency when you chose to pursue a career in UX, but it has become vital to take the lead in client, stakeholder, and team facilitation. Devise hands-on formats for the group to share insights and develop ideas.

## Pairing for design and development

Pair with nondesigners and designers alike to double up on getting to the best design outcomes, knowledge sharing, and skills transfer.

## Empower the nondesigners

Some stakeholders will shut down at the mention of design and refuse to participate for fear of making themselves look stupid. One way to draw them out is to co-design through sketching with them. Encourage them to believe that everyone can sketch, even if it's just boxes and lines. Often you'll find they're considerably more capable than that and are just self-critical of their skills. Show them terrible sketches of your own to help them understand that communicating the idea is more important than creating a work of art.

## If others inflict this anti-pattern on you

Sometimes you might find yourself in the position where other team members don't expect you to have a valuable contribution for their domain, whether it's creative, development, or business.

- Invite yourself to meetings.
- Contribute meaningfully.

- Facilitate the team.
- Get into the feedback loop (review work before it's deemed "done").
- Define success criteria from a UX perspective.

## Terminology explained

Not-invented-here bias

Hero designer

Collaboration

Bias against uncertainty

Pair design

# CASE STUDY

Chris Nodder, Interface Tamer at Chris Nodder Consulting LLC, and blogger at questionablemethods.com

*Figure 9.2: Chris Nodder. (Photo credit: Chris Nodder.)*

### Design consulting

I work primarily with agile teams in large enterprises. Even if they have access to a design resource, that designer is normally spread over several teams and so can only devote a portion of their time to each project.

I meet with a variety of responses from these designers, ranging from relief because they now have contract help to finish their Photoshop mockups, through attempts to get me removed from the team because I'm seen as a threat to their dominance. The truth is, I'm neither of those things. I don't do Photoshop and I definitely don't do dominance. What I do is facilitate user-centered, team-led product creation.

### Designers belong inside the team

Designers who try to hoard all the design work on a project are perpetuating the myth of the lone wolf expert and making life extra hard for themselves. This type of behavior shows contempt for teammates' skills, makes it harder to integrate with co-workers, and means it's unlikely that anyone on the team will be able to do their best work. It also shows a level of insecurity; it suggests that the designer is not sufficiently sure of his or her own skills to open their methods up to inspection and criticism.

It takes a distinct lack of humility for a designer to think that he or she knows best when it comes to building an application or site. Even the most tech-centric team member's role affects the UX, because design has many components and isn't a thing that designers do in isolation. It's possible that designers have more expertise in one small area of the process than do others on the team, but even then, it's better to feed off many diverse ideas and observations, and to understand the technical limitations of the platform before producing a visually ideal but functionally untenable solution that subsequently gets compromised to the point that it neither looks good nor works well.

### Integrating design into the whole team

My engagements occur at the beginning of a project and require the whole team to work together in the same room for one week with no external interruptions. This means developers, testers, business managers, marketers, system architects, project managers, tech writers, subject matter experts, and designers. I get a lot of pushback about the time commitments in leading up to this week, but after it's over, everyone involved comments on how productive and refreshing it is to be able to focus on nothing but the task at hand, and not to be held up by scheduling sequential meetings with each of the interested parties, which can take weeks during which the project languishes.

Working with the whole team during the early stages of product exploration and prototype design has many benefits. As a group, you identify issues that an individual wouldn't have noticed, because different team members have different sensibilities and are attuned to different parts of the interaction. You spend less time "selling" the design idea to team members who don't "get it." Team members buy into the solution because they helped to create it, rather than having had it presented to them in pixel-perfect comps. Because representatives from all disciplines are present, this work produces well-rounded solutions that incorporate business and end-user needs in a way that IT folks can actually build, implement, and support.

What about all the different factions that will be fighting for dominance in the room? The answer is to focus on the needs of the users of the system. By gathering user data rather than team member opinions, you can turn that data into a design, using a set of methods where each step feeds data into the next step, from initial observation through user-tested prototype and finally an implementation plan.

### Research is the key

We spend the week as a whole team first observing users in their own environment, then building an experience map of our observations and deciding on the largest pain points that need to be fixed. Everyone on the team participates in ideation sessions, and then creates scenarios and storyboards. The storyboards feed into team-built paper prototypes, which we then test for usability and use as the basis of a planning exercise to set the priority and schedule for building the product. It's an intense week, but at any stage, any team member can point to the resources pinned up on the wall and say what each one is for, what it means for subsequent stages, and how each relates to the original pain points observed during user sessions.

### The whole team needs to be user-centric

My aim is to leave each team feeling empowered to perform user-centered design themselves in subsequent stages of their project and on future projects they are involved with. There are no more black boxes where "design magic" happens. There is still a lot of room for design skills, though. Someone typically has to play the facilitation role on the team, and this falls easily into the designer's realm. Because they are facilitating cooperative work and driving the interpretation of the whole team's ideas, this type of work allows designers to demonstrate a broader architect skillset, which is normally a great opportunity for career progression and also a more fulfilling role.

## Additional resources

1. Dickerson G. Avoiding the "Client as Enemy" Black Hole. Available from: <http://giles-dickerson.com/2010/06/08/avoid-the-client-as-enemy-competitor-as-friend/>; 2010 [accessed 9.1.15].
2. Gallagher D. The Decline of the HPPO (Highest Paid Person's Opinion) Available from: <http://sloanreview.mit.edu/improvisations/2012/04/01/the-decline-of-the-hppo-highest-paid-persons-opinion/?utm_source=twitter&utm_medium=social&utm_campaign=sm-direct#.T3jXdzG8aKc>; 2012 [accessed 9.1.15].
3. Lee T. What Clients Don't Know (...And Why It's Your Fault). Available from: <http://muledesign.com/2012/05/what-clients-dont-know-and-why-its-your-fault/>; 2012 [accessed 9.1.15].
4. McCoy T. Studio Time and the Road to Pair Designing. Available from: <http://pivotal-labs.com/studio-time-and-the-road-to-pair-designing/>; 2013 [accessed 9.1.15].
5. Olien J. Inside the Box – People Don't Actually like Creativity. Available from: http://www.slate.com/articles/health_and_science/science/2013/12/creativity_is_rejected_teachers_and_bosses_don_t_value_out_of_the_box_thinking.html; 2013 [accessed 9.1.15].
6. Wroblewski L. Writings. Available from: <http://www.lukew.com/ff/entry.asp?1704>; 2014 [accessed 9.1.15].

## REFERENCES

1. Saffer D. Designing for Interaction: Creating Innovative Applications and Devices. San Francisco, CA: New Riders/Peachpit/Pearson; 2009.
2. Rams D. 10 Principles for Good Design. Available from: https://www.vitsoe.com/gb/about/good-design [accessed 9.1.15].
3. Ariely Dan. Predictably Irrational: The Hidden Forces that Shape Our Decisions. HarperCollins; 2009.
4. Ariely Dan. The Upside of Irrationality: The Unexpected Benefits of Defying Logic at Work and at Home. Harper; 2011.
5. McAfee A. Big Data: The Management Revolution. Available from: https://hbr.org/2012/10/big-data-the-management-revolution [accessed 9.1.15].
6. Rutter K. Skills Map Workshop, Balanced Team Conference, San Francisco, Nov. 2, 2013.

# TAKEAWAYS

1.  Designers are not the only people who consume design. Your product can only be successful if its design also appeals to nondesigners.

2.  Everyone on the team can contribute meaningfully. Respect their contribution and understand their language and comfort zone to share more successfully.

3.  Heroes work on their own, but design is a team sport.

4.  Harness the not-invented-here bias to sell your idea to your team.

5.  Be transparent. Not everyone understands the design process.

# CHAPTER 10

## Insisting on perfection

"Simplicity – the art of maximizing the amount of work not done – is essential."
—Agile Manifesto[1]

## Delivering on your vision

Of course, if you are living in the deliverables, you'll expect every aspect of the product to match your specification perfectly because you spent so much time and effort carefully perfecting your vision of the product. Even if this is not our intention, we get very attached to the model of the product we build in our minds and, naturally, we want reality to live up to this dream.

But that's not always possible, for a variety of reasons. While we can and should push for quality of ideas, design, and delivery, there comes a point when it's damaging to the product to carry on designing it instead of getting it out into the hands of users. "Better is the enemy of done," a popular saying in software development, is just as true in design as it is in code. You learn more about the quality of your design from people using it than from trying to perfect it over time, in your own space, without real-life usage learnings.

Every designer, at some time or another, has to strike a balance between adding more polish and delivering the solution. However, sometimes it can be seductive to carry on working far past the point where the solution is fit for a purpose and the extra effort is rapidly running into the law of diminishing returns. When we get stuck in this mindset, we must remind ourselves of what design is defined to achieve: "Designing is finding the best solution to a problem within a given set of circumstances".[2]

### Defining objectivity

Subjectivity is a challenge in design. Code successfully runs, or not; business makes money, or not; but design evaluation seems to be a more subjective topic that makes it harder to define what *good*, or *done*, looks like.

UX, as an emotional and empathetic discipline, requires us to be passionate and self-critical artists, not just keen craftspeople. While we may be working in the best interests of a user very different from ourselves, the work we produce is personal – exposing a piece of ourselves – and hardly feels objective. But this can make design critique into a painful process, one that feels more like criticism of ourselves than an objective measurement of the success of a design solution we have produced. In this context, it is hardly surprising to develop a perfectionist streak. Finessing the work a little more before you want to share it or hand it off feels like the magic ingredient that will get it through the critique without requiring any painful compromises.

In traditional design-centric working environments, the emphasis has been on winning work with glossy, perfected answers to barely explored questions in pitches. But this is the point – at the beginning of a working engagement – where we haven't had the opportunity to fully explore and understand what the problem is we are asked to solve. Thus, this way of working encourages glitz and polish over solid thinking and deep understanding of needs – the recipe for a broken experience.

Unfortunately, this way of working has also led clients and other consumers of design to interpret *polish* as *value*. If you have ever had a client who insisted they couldn't critique a wireframe or sketch without seeing the finished design, you've experienced this anti-pattern being externally imposed upon you. But polished design, as the final iteration of a long discovery process, is expensive to change and often requires extensive rework in other deliverables to keep the design system consistent.

Our working practices have bred designers to be seen as (or feel like) infallible answerers of woolly, sticky, difficult to define problems, with little else to go by than our creative experience and expertise. Without data and understanding, we fall back on (educated) opinion and best-guess – emotional responses that are easy to become too attached to. Wanting to get it right the first time is a very human response to this setup of expectations, but it leads to the care and work we lavish on unfounded assumptions making change expensive and painful.

## Setting expectations

Before getting stuck into the design process and laboring over a design solution to finesse it to perfection, there is a more deceptive form of *insisting on perfection* that happens earlier on. And that's designing the ideal without setting stakeholder expectations about the reality of what is achievable. To help us avoid getting stuck in our perfectionism, it's critical to set expectations with the team at the beginning of our engagement with them. We have the desire to work toward a harmonious end point so we can avoid damaging reworks of the UX. To designers, that is a job well done, but in doing it, we have to ensure that we communicate the state of reality now, at the next release, and at the mythical future point of *done*. Even (especially!) in Agile projects.

Designing without a shared vision can damage the end product. A product is more than a collection of loosely bound features. It requires coherence in design and interaction, and must allow user learnings from one aspect to be taken to another and produce related outcomes. Without these principles in play, users will find the product impossible to model mentally, and will never engage with it.

The vision doesn't have to be a perfect encapsulation of everything the product will ever be, but it needs to look far enough into the future to allow the team building it to make smart decisions about what they build today without requiring major mental model changes or architectural rework when tomorrow's requirements are being built. But a vision must also be socialized within the team, and put in a form of record that doesn't shift with individual interpretations or fallible memories. That usually means paper on walls.

However, when you have ambitious end goals on the wall, people naturally get excited about the possibilities and start to want to play with their favorite feature. This is a recipe for feature creep, so expectations must be firmly set about what's coming when. Early on in your project, you need – as a team – to sit down together and work out a grammar that lets you talk freely about any goals and intermediate stages for your project. As well as allowing for a holistic view of the end product, the aim is to save time and effort by not needing to create intermediate deliverables, as well as the functional product.

## Introducing a functional grammar

Here's an example of a functional grammar from a recent project. We used it to set expectations appropriately with our clients to clarify what they would see in the first release of an ambitious photography product they asked us to design and develop on a challenging timescale.

Along with functional requirements, we also needed to develop an interaction grammar that suited this extremely visual medium, and to deliver micro-interactions that fulfilled product principles based on engineering prowess, longevity, and supporting both beginners and prosumers.

An initial problem that arose was that, despite the tight timescales attached to the initial release, the primary stakeholder loved many of the ideas we explored so much that he took them as commitments and added them to the release schedule. While being a nice problem to have, this also led to damaged expectations when the stakeholder had to be repeatedly disappointed about what the developers could realistically deliver in time. However, we couldn't work in a scenario where it was impossible to explore the holistic view of the product with the client – that would have led to wildly diverging visions of the product.

To solve this issue, we agreed with the stakeholders and the client that everything we discussed, sketched, workshopped, or prototyped would fall into one of four labeled buckets:

1. **Baseline** – Everything that needed to be delivered in the first release to let users achieve a minimum set of goals in a minimum viable product (MVP). This included raw capabilities (what a typical project might define as a feature), and what aspects of the interaction grammar were necessary to set up the user's mental model of how to do things in the product.

2. **Optimistic** – The features and aspects of the interaction grammar that moved beyond outright capabilities and added to the concept of minimum viable wow (also known as a minimum delightful product). Because of the progressive nature of the interaction grammar, many of this bucket's contents were of the nature of adding delight rather than functionality. It was understood that once the baseline bucket had been served, any remaining development capacity for the initial launch would be dedicated to delivering this bucket.

3. **Vision** – A long-term view of what the product would evolve *toward* (not necessarily *into*). This allowed us to make smart decisions, such as restricting the use of a particular gesture, knowing that it would be better suited to a feature being released some iterations down the line. *Vision* deliverables were often used with the wider stakeholder group to explain and justify decisions being taken at the time of the initial release.

4.  **Thinking out loud** – to be used if a requirement didn't have one of the other three labels on it. In this bucket, along with potential future features, we were able to explore delighters, micro-interactions, gestures, language, interface concepts, and a host of other valuable experience differentiators. The project team agreed that we understood that this bucket did not represent any commitment to deliver an eventual feature or interaction, but, if agreed to have value and fit scope, it could be added into one of the other three buckets. It gave us a space for new, interesting, unexpected ideas to be captured, but managed expectations to not have these amazing new ideas built in the same time we estimated for the baseline of the first release.

Using this bucket system also allowed us, as designers, to uncouple our vision of the perfect product from the limited early capabilities that had to be delivered by the deadline. The required pace for delivering the baseline and optimistic views kept the focus on the realm of the possible, while still allowing us enough time to explore the future, but the balance of time made sure we never got so deeply into the details of the end vision that we became resistant to change. Even after the initial release, keeping the buckets in place let us put the right amount of focus on the next iteration while still having a long-term vision to validate against.

Bucket systems can be very flexible and powerful when it comes to setting expectations. Be the facilitator of this technique and develop a bucket system that works for your needs. You can keep it on the wall with index cards, or in a shareable online spreadsheet. Make sure to capture ideas and categorize them.

When questions arise about what is *in* or *out* of the first release, use the buckets to review the list. And *always* have a bucket for in-progress, half-baked, or far-future ideas and set the expectation that anything not labeled as being in one of the other buckets is in this one.

This is also a great tool for creating a roadmap. A roadmap is a long-term vision for your product/service that documents all the ideas that didn't make it into this version due to current time and budget constraints, but are anticipated to be developed at a structured later time.

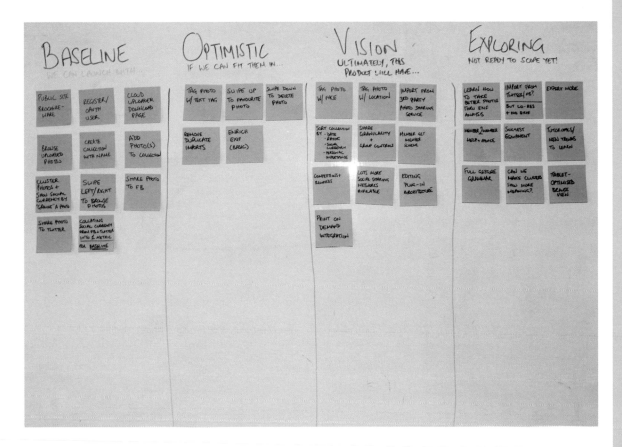

*Figure 10.1: Example of a Functional Grammar. (Photo credit: James O'Brien.)*

## Trade-offs

These trade-offs have to be made on all projects. We simply don't have limitless time, money, or people to work on developing software.

As the popular adage goes, "Fast, Cheap, Good. Pick two." You can't (over-) deliver on all three. We use this triangle to steer project goals all the time. Quite naturally, stakeholders and clients are keen to get everything they can, as quickly as possible, as cheaply as possible. Unfortunately, that is just not realistic.

Set expectations with the team for what it means to cut down on time, add to the *critical* function bucket, or limit UX staff on the team unrealistically. It is your responsibility to communicate when you see a discrepancy between expectations and realistic delivery. We often experience designers who promise much more than can be optimistically achieved in a given timeframe.

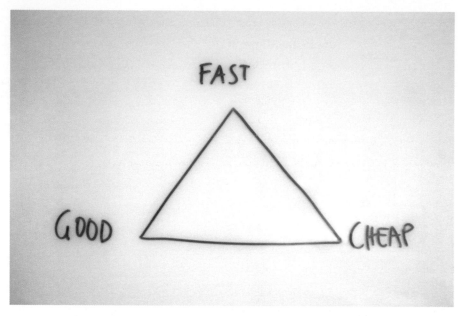

Figure 10.2: "Fast, Cheap, Good. Pick two." (Photo credit: Martina Hodges-Schell.)

## Sustainable pace

Getting your perfectionism in check also means being realistic about what you can do in a given timeframe. Many design environments we experience have fostered a culture of night-time heroes: the only way you could possibly get your work done to the level of quality you expect is to work long beyond healthy office hours. If you recognize yourself here, you are not doing yourself or your team any favors.

Collaborating with the broader team stresses the importance of finding a sustainable design pace that falls into rhythm with the development and other teams that rely on your interaction. This is often a pain point when UX initially integrates with development, but you don't have to work at the same speed, which may be impossible anyhow when tackling differently sized tasks. You need to find a way for the workflow to reach a pattern that makes interaction with each other possible.

Sustainable pace is all about being smart about what you deliver and how – *the art of maximizing the work not done*, as the Agile Manifesto[1] puts it. If a stakeholder can sign off on a sketch and a developer can work from a sketch plus a conversation, why go to the bother of creating a fully specified wireframe? The ultimate expression of this smarter style of working is when a developer and designer pair up together and the only deliverables are a conversation and the final product, but the authors caution that this may not work for every team or product. Have the conversations with the rest of the team to see what your colleagues are capable of and comfortable working with, and focus on those things. Let the other possible deliverables be part of the *work not done*.

These conversations should be ongoing, even down to the level of each individual user story. The working process also needs to work for you – if a developer thinks they can work from a sketch but they don't interpret it correctly, you'll need to find some way to add context so the right outcome is reached next time.

## UX debt

If you need to cut down on the workload that can be tackled right now, borrow a technique from the development community. Ward Cunningham coined the phrase "technical debt" to describe "those internal things that you choose not to do now, but which will impede future development if left undone"[3] in software projects.

Similarly, you can introduce UX debt to the product development to park and mark important pieces of the user experience that can't be worked on because of time or other constraints now, but need to be addressed within the context of developing this product or service to create a successful experience for your audience.

## Knowing when you're done

It can be incredibly difficult to know when you're done. In continuous delivery environments, it can feel like you are never done. With a cantankerous stakeholder blocking sign-off, it can equally seem as if you are stuck in an endless iteration loop.

Break the work down into chunks. Can your users successfully achieve their goals? Does the visual design convey the brand goals? Is feedback positive? Use user and business goals to drive design decision making, not whether individuals *like* or *dislike* your idea. Equally, be honest with yourself and agree that you've achieved your goals, and any further work at this time would result in diminishing returns for the time you spend on it. Spending another week to make things 5% more amazing? Usually not a luxury we'd recommend. For personal projects without commercial constraints, this is obviously different.

We believe that keeping our inner perfectionist in check does not mean that you ever deliver sloppy work. We want you to deliver very good work before you damage its effect by overworking it and underdelivering to the rest of the team.

## Take inspiration from start-up entrepreneurs

There is a great quote we remind ourselves of when we are struggling with our perfectionist designer hats on: "If you are not embarrassed by the first launch of your product, you've waited too long." Jeffrey Veen[4] has said this in the context of bringing new products to market, but we remind ourselves of this when we struggle to let go on any design project, and agree that our work is done.

A product is only ever truly tested when it reaches the market. Say your traditional design process to build a fully featured perfect product takes eighteen months. Now think of a competitor who can put a MVP live in three, and spend the next fifteen months learning and iterating toward a full-featured product. When your product reaches its release, who knows more about how the market really uses products of this type? Who already has an embedded user base? Who has already set expectations about how a product of this type should work? Who has been able to react to changes in the digital landscape and user demands over the last fifteen months and add support for that hot new third-party service that's not on your radar yet? Never mind that the original MVP wasn't the best thing in the world; it's almost certainly a better product by the time the traditional competitor arrives.

The trend is *faster*. The market moves faster; other people claim their space in your niche; in mobile, a whole generation of devices is eclipsed by the time a traditional design project gets to market.

## Launch your idea in 3 hours, 24 hours, a weekend

A whole generation of budding digital entrepreneurs is being taught how to get their ideas to market in hours, or at most a weekend. With the tools at our disposal, our work becomes much more focused on testing our hypotheses quickly, with as little impact on resources as possible to understand whether the idea works.

As start-up culture and Lean practice are influencing how we design digital products, it becomes even more essential to embrace the *perpetual beta* mentality – the low-fidelity prototypes that become MVPs. Big design upfront, and our obsessive perfectionism that goes with making the whole thing, the right way, the first time, is becoming outdated – fast. It's up to us to adapt and become more nimble, less glossy, and less perfectionist. Knowing when to draw the line is vital.

## Summary

"Better is the enemy of done." While we all want to produce the optimum possible product, we need to retain perspective with regard to how closely it approaches a platonic design ideal. At every stage, we need to ask ourselves whether design and development effort is being expended on worthwhile features, or simply adding extra polish at an inappropriate time. We need to remain realistic with regard to the media we work in and remember that our deliverables have to respond to the possible and the unforeseen.

## The "Living in the Deliverables" anti-pattern

We want to do the best job, but when we keep working beyond the point where the ideal solution has been achieved, we damage delivery by being inefficient with our time and we damage the project by setting unrealistic expectations with shareholders and clients. Perfectionism is what makes jobs expand to fill the time available, but in today's software development world, time is the ultimate luxury, and it's one that our competitors won't allow themselves. We have to compete by finding efficiencies in our process. We have to recognize that doing the best job means knowing when we're no longer adding value by adding effort.

## You know you're in this anti-pattern when...

- Velocity on the project falls off.
- Nothing seems to be making it through design QA.
- The project manager is threatening to override you and just release as is.
- You are frustrated that you are not given enough time to make things just right.
- You push extra hours to add more polish.
- You're exhausted and you feel you can't sustain this pace.
- You toy with the idea of offering to work for free to finish your work the way you want it.

## Patterns

### Checking in with yourself

Honesty is one of the most important qualities in feedback, but it begins with being honest with yourself. Take a critical look at your own approach, with a focus on objective measures such as outcomes. Are there moments where you overworked a good idea too far? Do you often end up working nights to meet your own standards? Identify your tendencies toward perfectionism and be open with yourself about how much of it is about the product and how much is about self-validation.

This pattern is brutal to begin with, but it is a vital part of maturing your outlook. Using internal feedback to gain honest visibility of your own assumptions and approach will help you view external feedback in a more objective and less emotional way. It will also help you articulate your solution more clearly, and aid with getting outside your own viewpoint when you need empathy.

There are useful techniques for approaching this pattern in Chapter 14, Spotting and Fixing Your Own Anti-Patterns.

## Design/UX debt

When delivery is moving fast, and particularly in Lean-style environments, the creation of a rounded experience often ends up taking a back seat to simply shipping workable features. UX debt can be used to ensure that the business makes the time to refocus on the experience before so many dependencies build up that you're "stuck" with a sub-optimal experience throughout.

Raising UX debt has two functions. First, it tracks the existence of the debt so it doesn't get overlooked as development progresses. Second, it makes it highly visible to the business as a product risk. "Product risk" tends to be taken a lot more seriously than "suboptimal design."

How should you raise UX debt? Take a lesson from the way your development team tracks technical debt. This tends to happen in the same place as other user stories – for example, a Kanban board, which often uses card colors that indicate *danger* or *warning*, such as yellow or red. Some teams even give debt its own swim lane so everyone can track the volume of debt as it builds up. We recommend that you raise UX debt in *exactly* the same way – in fact, even in the same place. Draw an equivalency between the two so the business learns to treat UX debt with equal urgency.

Lastly, *what* should you raise as UX debt? We recommend you exercise restraint in raising UX debt, at least until your team sees the value of paying it down and trusts the concept. Don't use it for chasing perfection – that will rapidly devalue it. Use it for those moments where the experience has been measurably compromised for the sake of delivery or experimentation, and the "true" solution is well-defined and ready to be implemented as soon as the story is picked up.

## Divide form and function

Split high-fidelity visual design from low-fidelity interaction design and create a modular toolkit to help you focus your deliverables. Visual design can be developed in a living style guide, perhaps in a shareable online format so it can evolve easily over time.

## Sketch + code

Moving straight from sketching ideas on paper/ at the whiteboard to prototyping in code can be a liberating experience and save a lot of valuable time. Pair with some-one who can prototype in code if that's not your forte, and cut out the labor-intensive, pixel-perfect design comp phase in static tools like Adobe Photoshop or Illustrator (or your weapon of choice). You get time to focus on solving more design problems instead of illustrating a few to a higher fidelity.

## Pairing with developers

Understanding the limitations of the medium helps to identify the places where further focus won't bring any results. Pair with your developers to gain a better un-derstanding of these technical limitations. Added bonus: you pre-empt any frustra-tions later on in the development process, when the team has to break the bad news to you that your idea is not implementable.

## 90% rule

If you know that you have perfectionist tendencies that lead to late nights, head-aches, and the project getting delayed, apply the 90% rule. Simply put, ship your design at a point where you would consider it to be only 90% finished. This can be difficult at first, but benefits the product development, the team, and your sanity in the long run.

## If others inflict this anti-pattern on you

- Stakeholders who have a defined idea of perfection may push back against what they see as a lack of polish, so it's important to set their expectations early on. Introduce a modular design approach that demonstrates the look and feel separately from the interaction of the whole system, without the time-intensive, pixel-perfect detail given to every screen and element.

- Pairing with developers works to educate the development team as well. Help them understand why you consider certain things critically important over other nice-to-have elements of your user experience design and give them tools to prioritize design goals.

## Terminology explained

Functional grammar

UX debt

Design debt

Technical debt

Sustainable pace

Roadmap

# CASE STUDY

Jonathan Berger is Associate Director for Product Design at Pivotal Labs New York

*Figure 10.3: Jonathan Berger.[5] (Photo credit: Jonathan Berger.)*

### Is design objective or subjective?

There's a long-running argument about whether design can be objectively called "good." But what are we judging? We tend not to distinguish between the types of design that are highly objective and the types of design that are highly subjective (e.g., marketing and branding design has a high degree of subjectivity to it, while UI design may be better if judged objectively). When designing a brand, a professional designer may advise the client on design fundamentals like color and form, but ultimately, the design cannot be successful if the client doesn't feel good about it. Conversely, designing a usable user interface is much more objective: patterns exist, solutions can be tested, and we can often state with a high degree of confidence that one solution is (objectively) better than another.

This is a problem. Even among professionals, we tend not to distinguish between different types of design when discussing work. More importantly, when scoping design work, we confuse the meaning of "done" across various types of design. Designing a new logo and brand? It makes sense to plan for several iterations of client approval. Designing a signup form? "Done" can simply mean "a user can complete their goal."

To subject this to the approval of a nondesigner client is akin to demanding client approval from your dentist or surgeon. When the stakes are high, it may be prudent to seek a second opinion, but it's ill-advised to say, "I just don't like your diagnosis. Can you come back to me with three alternatives by next week?"

### A strategy for articulating objective and subjective design

How can we address this problem?

- by crafting better stories for nondesigners, explaining which parts of design benefit greatly from subjective feedback and which don't

- by starting a conversation about a taxonomy of design types and the level of subjectivity for each. Here, I'll start.

### A provisional taxonomy of design types

If we agree that subjective reactions to design have varying degrees of utility, based on the type of design in question, how do we talk about it? A strict taxonomic hierarchy isn't useful. A rough scale, aimed at helping to guide conversation, is. From most subjective to most objective, here's a first try:

### MOST SUBJECTIVE

Visual Design (Marketing/Communication) – "How should we design our brand?"

Product Design – "What problem should we try to solve?"

Visual Design (Graphic Design) – "Does this color scheme effectively direct the user's attention?"

User Experience Design – "Is this product a compelling way for users to accomplish their goal?"

User Interface Design – "Does this interface help the user do what they need to?"

Information Architecture – "Does this IA help the user model the world we're building?"

**MOST OBJECTIVE**

**TL;DR (Too Long; Didn't Read)**

The utility of objective and subjective judgment varies by type of design, and we don't do a good job of speaking clearly about this. If we, as a design community, can educate clients about the spectrum of subjectivity vs. type-of-design, we can save ourselves tons of pain – and save clients megatons of money.

*Jonathan Berger is a designer, developer, and technologist who has been active in the New York City technology scene since around 2005, building products, speaking, and organizing events. As a consultant, he's worked on about thirty projects in the past six or so years, but his product the whole time has been building an Agile design practice. He makes it a point of honor to include Comic Sans in every design project.*

## REFERENCES

1. Agile Manifesto. Available from: <http://agilemanifesto.org/> [accessed 10.1.15].
2. Kizer M. Teaching Lessons in Scenic Design: Art from Nothing. Available from: <http://broadwayeducators.com/?p=904>; 2013 [accessed 10.1.15].
3. Cunningham W (last edited). Technical Debt. Available from: <http://www.c2.com/cgi/wiki?TechnicalDebt>; 2014 [accessed 10.1.15].
4. Veen J. How the Web Works, UX Week 2010. San Francisco. Available from: <https://www.youtube.com/watch?v=1apQS-VgK9w>; 2013 [accessed 10.1.15].
5. Berger JP. Sustainable Pace, Balanced Team 2013. San Francisco. Available from: <https://www.youtube.com/watch?v=1apQS-VgK9w> [accessed 10.1.15].

# TAKEAWAYS

1. Perfectionism doesn't create exceptional design.

2. Create a functional grammar to manage team expectations for what "done" looks like.

3. Create a sustainable working pace. Burning the midnight oil in search of perfection isn't viable long term.

4. Introduce UX/design debt to mark up design work for further exploration later on.

5. "If you are not embarrassed by the first launch of your product, you've waited to long." (Jeffrey Veen.)[4]

# CHAPTER 11

## Responding to tone, not content

"How many wars have been precipitated by firebrands! How many misunderstandings which led to wars could have been removed by temporizing!" —Winston Churchill, 1985, Vol I

In earlier chapters, we talked about how important it is for everyone on a team to have the same understanding of the words the team uses. But even when you have an ideal vocabulary, another aspect of communication leads people to misinterpret your meaning or motive: tone. Even a tiny change in tone – emphasizing one word over another in a sentence, for example – can result in a very different message coming across to the other party.

A classic sentence that illustrates this point is "I didn't say he took my money." Putting a simple stress on each word in this sentence in turn gives it a different subtext:

| | |
|---|---|
| *I* didn't say he took my money. | But someone said it. |
| I *didn't* say he took my money. | No, really, I didn't say that; that isn't what I said. |
| I didn't *say* he took my money. | But it's implied. |
| I didn't say *he* took my money. | But someone took it. |
| I didn't say he *took* my money. | But he got it somehow. |
| I didn't say he took *my* money. | But he took someone's. |
| I didn't say he took my *money*. | But he took something else of mine. |

See how some of the interpretations are completely opposed, notably the second and third ones, which appear to exonerate or incriminate "him" respectively. Even though the words haven't changed, the whole meaning of the sentence has been turned around. Try it for yourself with the phrase "I'm not saying we should drop this feature."

These examples show a simple verbal stress applied to a single sentence of just a few words. Now imagine the huge variety of tones that a voice can carry, from a mellow whisper to an enraged shriek, applied to the vast number of conversations that occur in bringing a product to market. If you misunderstand someone else's tone, or someone else misunderstands your tone, there are a lot of opportunities for trouble to arise.

## Nonverbal, not unimportant

We perceive that we're constantly aware of our surroundings, but, in truth, that's an illusion that arises from the brain's amazing ability to fill in the gaps in our perception. A wide swathe of what we think we observe is actually a series of educated guesses. However, this can also mean that we jump to conclusions about what we *think* we're observing. Albert Mehrabian found that "the verbal component of a face-to-face conversation is less than 35% and that over 65% of communication is done non-verbally".[1]

Think back to the last time you were only half-listening to someone in a conversation: weren't you following along based on their tone, observing their posture out of the corner of your eye, nodding at all the right times, without comprehending the content? Despite a lack of conscious awareness, our minds are constantly observing and evaluating the nonverbal cues of every interaction, but they're filtering through that guess-making ability, based on prior experiences, snap judgments, and extrapolations from half-seen cues such as posture, expression, and sightlines.

And unfortunately, they're not always getting it right.

We don't get any formal lessons about how to communicate when we're children; we learn by doing, by discovering the limits and being corrected when we exceed them. By the time we go to school, the foundations of how we communicate are set, and social interactions with our peers define how they will grow. In this way, our style of interacting grows incrementally, built as much from negative as positive reinforcement, subject to the distorting lens of all sorts of social pressures.

The mix of personalities in a typical product development team often leads to a mismatch in expectations of tone. Some members will be people-focused, some more task-focused. Some will wear their passions on their sleeves, others will rely on a more rational approach. There is also always a power dynamic at play whenever there is any kind of hierarchy, even when all the right steps are taken to minimize it.

## Tone varies with culture

Our work is becoming truly global, and it's rare these days for all members of a team to be from a homogenous cultural background. This can cause huge gulfs in expectation of tone. Even within the US, there are differences in tone between normal communication on the east and west coasts. Cross the Atlantic to the UK, where there is a minefield of class differences to add to the equation, and things become more complicated. When parties don't share a native tongue or as many cultural parallels as the US and UK, things get more difficult still. All cultures have inbuilt assumptions and limits, and it can be remarkably easy to sail past these in a haze of enthusiasm or frustration, without picking up novel nonverbal cues from the other parties.

## Caveat

The authors are not immune from the cultural expression of tone. Our experience encompasses working in the UK, the US, and parts of mainland Europe; it is our experience that shapes the examples and advice we present in this chapter. In cultures outside of these areas, a heated tone may be part and parcel of normal communication, or interactions may not carry weight unless an audience is present. We recommend that you make a careful study of the "normal" tone of the culture you work in and use it as a lens to interpret this chapter.

## Gaps in understanding

All of these factors can mean that it's easy to ascribe meaning to someone's tone that was never intended on their part – or miss meaning that was. That could translate into failing to pick up on an important concern, passing up an opportunity to solve a problem before it becomes a crisis, or, at worst, souring your interaction by prompting one of the parties into an emotional reaction.

For the record, we don't think it's a bad thing to be emotional about your work. We are in the business of crafting experiences, and there is no experience without emotion. If we approached the craft coldly and without empathy, we wouldn't be able to champion the user. However, a significant portion of the craft of UX, at least at the time the authors are writing this book, is to explain the value that UX brings to a business. Many businesses, unused to user-centric product design, are still on a journey of understanding the return on investment from soft inputs like UX. These businesses need to see a balance between emotion and rationality when dealing with UXers. If we don't find the right balance of passion and logic during this educational process, we risk UX being perceived as a subjective discipline – and, by implication, one that doesn't understand business realities. Once enough people in an organization believe this, the agenda tends to shift toward UX as "nice-to-have" rather than essential, and the time, budget, and support we need to craft the best experiences diminish rapidly. Raising your voice might get the right result today, but the debate might not even reach you next week.

Of course, as we discussed in Chapter 3, there's also the risk of sending negative signals to your colleagues. The same response can be a passionate defense or an argumentative rant, depending on who the recipient is. Knowing your colleagues' preferences and styles of communication is vital to getting the message across in the most effective way. Signaling your own mood also helps set expectations about what your tone really means. One of the authors' colleagues makes sure everyone in the office know when he has his "grumpy pants" on so they don't take a gruff tone personally.

Remember also that the presence of an audience has an effect on perceived tone. Audiences have the effect of amplifying hierarchical or factional structures, and can embarrass involved parties simply by having others present to witness their involvement. An exchange that might be just a bit of frustration-tinged problem solving between two people could look like a public dressing-down when there are observers in the room.

The worst-case scenario is that your passionate disagreement provokes the response of an even-more-passionate disagreement from your colleague, and the two (or more) of you end up locked in an arms race of volume and tone over something that shouldn't have been a disagreement in the first place. Recognizing the rising tone and agreeing to park the matter for later examination with cooler heads is a better way to respond.

If you are tempted to respond in a heated manner, make sure you observe this one simple rule: Always separate point of view from personality of the person you are having an argument with. Disagreeing passionately with someone's opinion can be a delicate matter; trying to fix a broken interpersonal relationship can take years.

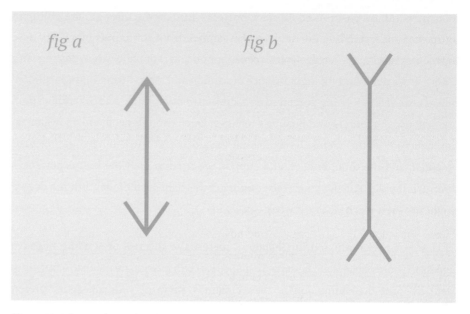

*fig a*          *fig b*

Figure 11.1: Perception and reality can differ: both vertical lines are the same length. (Photo credit: Martina Hodges-Schell.)

## Who you are and who you're perceived to be

One of the most difficult things to master is seeing yourself through the eyes of others. What makes this most difficult is that people naturally begin to make judgments about each other on first sight. Even before you've opened your mouth, people will look at your hairstyle, your posture, your clothing, and form an early opinion of what they expect from you. Often, this leads to a clash between their expectations and your reality.

For instance, James speaks with an English accent, which leads most people to think he's English or "a Brit." Although he was born and works in London, his family is Irish – a culture that settles interpersonal disputes in a manner that is more florid and passionate than the generally calmer English way. He's found that he gets the best reception from British colleagues when he tamps down the fiery side of his nature because, in an English person, that would be seen as aggression. However, in a Spanish person, or someone with a strong Dublin accent, Brits would be more likely to accept that fire as natural passion.

Martina is German and, after nineteen years of living in the UK, is still coming to terms with the fact that Londoners take her dry sense of humor extremely seriously. Surely this is just a bad stereotypical joke?

Understanding the first impression you make and the expectations it sets is vital to communicating effectively. This doesn't mean you have to fit perfectly into the role someone assigns you on first glance – but understanding that initial perception gives you a roadmap to changing that impression into something that more accurately represents the real you.

Informal social occasions are the perfect opportunity to canvas people who have known you awhile to probe whether and how you surprised them with how different you are from their first impression. Make it a fun chat rather than a detailed questionnaire. This advice will be too specific to you for us to make a recommendation here on how to act on it, but, in general, you have two choices.

You can *change the first impression* by working on your openings and small talk, making different clothing choices at work, changing your posture, and so on. Of course, none of us wants to be a corporate bore, so we recommend you only go as far as your own personal style can stretch. For example, the authors' colleague Richard Wand is a huge fan of body art and has fifty-six individual body piercings. This can make his first impression seem intimidating, so, for new business meetings and introductions, he removes some of the more attention-grabbing fittings and replaces others with less-obvious studs. As time goes on and he gains more familiarity with the other parties, he reintroduces the "real" fittings he normally wears.

Alternatively, you can *reset the expectations* by directly challenging them while they are still fresh in the other parties' minds. A gently self-depreciating joke about some surprising aspect of yourself always helps (with Brits at least) to soften hard edges. A straight-up disclaimer before a presentation can help reset skewed cultural expectations. Subtly highlighting some unexpected area of your life – an unusual hobby, a curious dwelling-place or some bizarre family history – can swing people away from a set impression and reopen them to understanding who you are. Richard uses this technique, too. The introductory slide for his external presentations is a carefully crafted montage of him playing with his two children and other family scenes, which tells more of the story than just his physical appearance.

## The IKEA effect strikes again

In Chapter 8, we talked about the way the IKEA effect causes people to place more value on the work they've invested their time into. When this comes into play, the more confrontational the (perceived) tone of the challenge, the greater the affront to our value system appears, "justifying" a more robust response.

Compounding this is the previously discussed tendency of stakeholders to respond to our proposals with a complete solution of their own. This comes as a challenge to our process and assumptions, whereas the insight that underlies the stakeholder's solution probably would not.[*] If you can connect the solution to the point where the insight becomes apparent, then you can make real progress. But this process of working back requires careful moderation of tone to avoid seeming defensive. The patterns we present in this chapter, and the next two chapters, can help you find the right tone for these moments.

## Respondent fatigue

Respondent fatigue is a well-known effect in user research, where a subject reaches a certain threshold and then ceases to engage (Lavrakas, 2008).[2] The quality of feedback drops and the subject loses interest in answering more questions. If pushed, the person can become snappy and sarcastic in his or her responses. As the person at the front of the room during a feedback session, you're highly susceptible to respondent fatigue, especially if things don't seem to be going well. You can proactively avoid it by structuring your workshops and review sessions to include variety and breaks. If you feel respondent fatigue setting in during a session, use the Break It Up pattern to give yourself some recovery time.

## Summary

Despite our best intentions to be rational and controlled, every person involved in building a product is human and flawed. Giving people the benefit of the doubt and backing down from emotional flashpoints can do more to win trust and deliver a better product than winning the battle through force of will there and then. Be

---

[*]This works in the other direction, too. If stakeholders look blank when you present your elegant solution, you'll find answers in Chapter 4, "Presenting without contextualizing."

aware of your own emotional state and ready to change things up if you feel yourself becoming combative.

## The "Responding to Tone, Not Content" anti-pattern

Tone can completely change the meaning of a sentence, but it can be easy to misinterpret another party's tone and misconstrue their meaning. At its worst, this leads to a downward spiral into an argument, leading to ill-will and lost trust. We need to be aware of how our own first impressions and personal styles of expression lead others to interpret our tone. And we need to recognize that it is often better to give others the benefit of the doubt, rather than assume their tone carries a message they may not intend.

## The patterns

### Set expectations

If the opportunity arises to address your presentational style, drop in a sentence along the lines of "If you find me getting loud and animated, I promise it's just my passion for the product coming to surface." This can buy you a surprising amount of goodwill.

### Paraphrased playback pattern

This is a fast but powerful way of testing your assumptions about tone. Put what you understood of the question into your own words and play it back: "So when you say you want the text in Comic Sans ... is that about giving the site a more playful tone?" Paraphrasing encourages the other party to put their response in different terms, too, rather than simply repeat what they said the first time. Paraphrased Playback is also a great way of getting to the root of the insight when feedback comes in the form of ready-made solutions; you can use it to open a discussion of where the solution came from, and reveal your own insights in a way that doesn't come across as dismissive. Another benefit of Paraphrased Playback is that it is a form of *reflective listening*, an active listening technique that builds rapport by demonstrating engagement and understanding.

## Yes, and... pattern

Your interlocutor will begin judging your response within the first couple of words, so keep those words positive to maintain their engagement. Nobody likes to be disagreed with, so if you start with "No," the other person will spend the rest of your response looking for reasons to shoot it down. In improvisational theater, the actors literally *can't* say no to a proposal in a scene, because it shuts the scene down. They also can't *just* say yes, because that takes the scene nowhere. To stay in the game and move things on, they have to say "*Yes, and ...*" as a springboard to add a new idea that goes somewhere. This can be a great way to embrace and redirect a suggestion in a more workable direction. The stakeholder wants the logo to be bigger? "Yes, and maybe we should be looking at the overall role of branding to ensure everything's in balance."

If you're forced to flat-out disagree, you can still moderate your language and tone to avoid starting on a negative note. One trick we often use is to lead with facts first, so the rebuttal starts with context that cushions the negation. For example, if a stakeholder suggests an inappropriate technology choice based on a cool website they've seen, rather than saying "No, because ...," we would say, "Because ..., therefore no":

"So, when we looked at the results from the survey, what it told us very clearly was that users expected to use the site on their mobile devices. Which means, unfortunately, that Flash isn't going to be a suitable solution here." (Some people have a stylistic problem with starting a sentence with "So ..." but this, or some other fill-word of your choice, really does help to soften the hard facts that usually follow.)

You can, of course, frame your response with a personal pronoun; "I think ...," "I'm not sure ...," "What I heard from the requirement was ..." This is still much better than an outright negative response, but it can open the doors to a conversation based on your opinion versus the stakeholders'. If it is your only line of defense, it may well be that the discussion is identifying something that would be best resolved by testing or more research – which is an excellent way to resolve the discussion and move forward.

## The power of silence

This is often recommended as a tool in user research: don't respond immediately after the other person stops talking. Jumping in compels you to respond to your initial perception of their tone, rather than making a reflective response. Moreover, if you leave a gap, they will often be compelled to fill it, which can give you valuable understanding of their intentions and assumptions. You can prompt the same kind of effect from a recalcitrant voice by using the magic words, "Tell me more about that." You'll even find that some apparently troublesome stakeholders who propose crazy ideas are just thinking out loud and will talk themselves out of those notions in the next sentence (or with a little gentle guidance).

Beware of looking disengaged while you're silent. You can indicate that you're capturing the feedback, raise an eyebrow to indicate interest, or just nod and look expectant.

## Mind-body considerations

Be aware of your physiological reactions to the situation. If you find yourself sliding down in your chair or your shoulders coming up around your ears, you're not just looking defensive; you're putting yourself into a posture that makes you *even more* defensive. If you find yourself in an aggressive posture – shoulders forward, arms folded, muscles tight, eyes squinting – remember that your body is preparing you chemically for confrontation and that will affect your responses. And, of course, you're sending loud, flashing nonverbal signs to the rest of the room. Shift out of these postures to something neutral and open – torso unobstructed by your arms, shoulders and muscles relaxed, eyes open and clear – and you'll be amazed at how your mindset changes, too.

## Break it up

If you find yourself beginning to shift into a difficult place tonally, do whatever you can to change things up. Call a break from the meeting for around 30 seconds to reset moods and mindsets. Shift from sitting to standing or vice versa, stop and take a drink of water, encourage someone else to talk, or even propose a longer break so you can make a cup of tea (we both work in British companies and have never known this last option to fail). Anything that offers a physical and mental break from where you were previously will help your tone. And a few moments to digest what's been said will help your understanding, too.

*Figure 11.2: Coffee break. (Photo credit: Martina Hodges-Schell.)*

When you use this pattern, it can be useful to outright state that you're going to pause for the sake of a tonal refresh: "I think we're getting a bit heated, so why don't we take five minutes for a break and see if we can come back feeling refreshed?"

## Mirror, mirror pattern

It's part of human nature to like people we think are like us, and a powerful way to get into someone's good books is to mirror their phrasing and actions. You probably already shift your accent subconsciously when you're talking to different types of people – one way for a police officer, another for your auto mechanic – and that is one way of mirroring. Adopting a stakeholder's terminology and idiom (provided it can be done in a way that's not obvious flattery or mimicry) extends this principle, shows understanding, and taps into that subconscious sense of tribe.

## The meeting before the meeting and the meeting after the meeting

Meetings are special places with their own rules and decorum. That means a great opportunity to short-circuit many of the anti-patterns that show up in meetings is to use the time immediately before and after the official meeting to discuss things in a more informal manner. Before the meeting is a good opportunity to build rapport or tease out where stakeholders' concerns lie so you can be mindful of addressing them (or avoid stepping on a land mine!) in the meeting itself.

After the meeting is a great opportunity to gently clear up any misconceptions of individual stakeholders without the risk of making them feel uncomfortable in front of everyone, or discuss implementation or co-working aims. However, do be careful not to undo the consensus of the meeting by changing the outcome at this moment.

The meeting after the meeting is an excellent opportunity to set up an informal review and working time with stakeholders who "solutionize" excessively. It gives them a chance to get their ideas out without disrupting the next feedback session or design review, and it lets you gently feed in enough context to make their input as useful as possible.

## Encourage feedback at natural breaks

Clients and stakeholders don't go through Feedback 101, so they rarely learn to give feedback in any structured form. It helps to invite them to give their feedback at natural breaks in the presentation. Otherwise, you may find that they miss the more subtle pauses and cues, and reach a point where all all of their reactions tumble out at once, leaving you feeling bruised and defensive. Sometimes it helps to set expectations that you'll do a full run-through of the journeys involved, then return for a detailed look at each stage, which is when you'll collect feedback. This helps avoid stakeholders questioning apparent omissions that are actually dealt with in later stages of the journey.

We talk more about managing feedback in these situations in Chapter 4, "Presenting without contextualizing."

### Subvert the script

Sometimes the best thing to do in these situations is the exact opposite of what the other party expects. When a conversation is escalating into an argument, one of the quickest ways to take the heat out of it is simply to agree with the other party so effusively that they can no longer hold their anger. When this bubble collapses, they may even spontaneously re-examine their attachment to their position.

### You'll know when you have encountered this anti-pattern, because ...

- Your co-workers seem to avoid looking to you for input and, when they're forced to, they seem scared and defensive right from the start.

- Stakeholders always seem to have the knives out for you, and come prepared to knock down your arguments.

- Stakeholders are doing end-runs around you rather than discussing the work.

- You often find yourself making up defenses for decisions you hadn't considered important at the time.

- Your colleagues describe you as "confrontational," "in-your-face," or "scary."

## What to do when someone is being confrontational or misunderstanding your tone

When you're sure someone is deliberately being confrontational with you, the best thing to do is *change the power dynamic.* You can do this by shifting activities into something more collaborative, where voices need to be heard equally. This isn't always possible in a feedback meeting, so change what you can – using some of the techniques described in "Break it up" – and then slow down your own responses. Let the confrontational person push until they run out of steam, and then take a second to collect yourself before responding calmly and patiently, with a pleasant and open expression. Remember that people associate deeper voices with authority, so, if you have the ability to do so, shift down an octave.

Remember the cardinal rule of UX: *When in doubt, tell stories.* Respond to aggressive challenges by zooming out to the *who, what,* and *why* of your reasoning, and telling a story about the subject of the discussion, and your passion for it. Putting a human narrative behind feature decisions can help with buy-in; the act of telling the story, and removing a direct response to the aggression, can diffuse the tensions in the conversation. Casting the story from the perspective of a persona (if possible) helps by making the story a step removed from your own experience.

When someone is misunderstanding your tone, it can be hard to revert back without sounding more defensive, or even passive-aggressive. Instead, use an impersonal statement like "We're all pushing to make the best possible product, so it's OK if we get passionate about it." Again, you can halt the meeting and, before resuming, take the opportunity to re-address tone, or set ground rules for communication. If this seems like it could be a persistent problem, then *the meeting after the meeting* is an ideal place to catch the ear of the disruptive person and say something like "Hey, I think maybe we were a bit at cross-purposes in there. I'm sorry if my passion sometimes comes across as defensiveness. What can we do in future to make sure we get the best communication in our meetings?"

## Tips

People associate deeper voices with authority. You'll find that, if you make a conscious effort to speak more slowly, your voice naturally becomes a bit deeper. Breathing into your belly helps with improving your voice. Practice your calm, reasonable voice so you can make a conscious effort to shift into it when you need to.

Schedule and structure your meetings with cognitive fatigue in mind. Try to chunk them out so you can address one theme per chunk and take recharge breaks of a few minutes between. Standing up increases blood flow to the brain and gives you the chance to reset your mind-body relationship with movement.

Be aware of cultural differences. "Normal" in some cultures means fiery and passionate, while in others, it's taboo to challenge anything said by an authority figure. Learn about your audience wherever possible – from friends and colleagues who have worked with the group or culture, or even by finding out yourself with a stakeholder safari. Moderate your own style to respond to the expectations of the audience.

Don't write off people who challenge aggressively. If they feel they have ownership of ideas, they can become powerful allies in defending your work. Try setting up a couple of co-design sessions with them, so they can explore ideas collaboratively in a less formal setting. In the next review, the IKEA effect will work in your favor.

## Terminology explained

ROI

IKEA effect

Tone of voice

Cultural differences

Social styles

### REFERENCES

1. Mehrabian A. Silent Messages. 1st ed. Belmont, CA: Wadsworth; 1971. ISBN 0-534-00910-7
2. Lavrakas PJ. Available from: http://srmo.sagepub.com/view/encyclopedia-of-survey-research-methods/n480.xml;2008 [accessed 11.01.15].

# TAKEAWAYS

1. It's easier to head off developing conflict in a meeting by moderating your own responses than to recover from it by trying to affect someone else's.

2. Know your audience and tailor your tone to them. For stakeholders, getting to know them and their style should be an integral part of the knowledge safari we discussed in Chapter 1, "Speaking different languages."

3. When things go downhill, don't be afraid to take a break and reset the meeting. It's more effective than trying to argue your way out of a problem.

4. These tips are aimed at preventing misunderstandings, but if someone is deliberately intimidating you and doesn't respond when you reach out, take it up with their manager or HR. No workplace should support aggressive behavior or bullying.

# CHAPTER 12

Defending too hard

It's tempting to believe that every disagreement with team members and stakeholders is a battle. And that every design battle can be won – even more so, that every design battle *should* be won. We've heard designers sigh wistfully at the freedom they perceive someone like Jony Ive, director of Design at Apple, to have, believing that when they move up to the next level of seniority, they'll face less questioning, not more. Unfortunately, any director of design can tell you the reality is the opposite. With more seniority comes more direct responsibility for a project's budget and success, and with that responsibility come harder questions from people who themselves are more senior.

However, that's not to say feedback is inevitable for every designer. Many clients, stakeholders, and team members see a division between design and other factors of the product creation process. Often, they feel comfortable with measurable, provable aspects of business like cash flow and supply chain. However, design has a whole different set of rules that aren't always evident to other kinds of thinkers. Faced with someone who knows these rules, they can be afraid to lose face by suggesting something that might be seen as naïve or tasteless. They will offer complete creative freedom – except, as we established in Chapter 9, they aren't as design-illiterate as they think they are.

Other collaborators' unconscious design literacy usually ends in a messy explosion of difficult-to-implement feedback right at the end of the project. Or worse, they simply decide never to re-engage with you, because what they got was not what they had in mind – no matter how much they insisted they didn't have anything in mind at all. This lack of feedback is, in many ways, worse, because it removes the opportunity for you to learn and grow, not only by finding out what didn't work, but by seeing what aspects did work. This lack of quantifiability can be disastrous for your self-image in the long term and is far worse than any pain that an honest feedback session may cause.

## Spotting this type of client

Clients like this usually telegraph their uncertainty by saying things like:

- "I'll know it when I see it."

- "I'll handle the business side, you've got carte blanche when it comes to the design."

- "I don't know much about design."

- "Can you make it pretty?"

It's important with these clients to help them understand that design needs to be an integral part of the product development process to succeed. We like to refer back to a quote from Steve Jobs: "People think it's this veneer – that the designers are handed this box and told, 'Make it look good!' That's not what we think design is. It's not just what it looks like and feels like."[1]

We've discussed lots of ways of introducing design to clients over the course of the book. When clients have this particular mindset, be prepared to use more strategy and patience in explaining it to them, and remember to be positive in your presentation: they *do* know more about design than they think, and there *are* objective benefits they can measure.

We have feedback for a reason – the same reason that developers have code demos and project teams have stand-ups: humans, and human communication, are fallible and predicting the future is impossible. We use feedback to make sure that everyone involved with a project is pulling in the same direction. Feedback isn't there to allow the untrained to meddle with our designs; it's there to stop us from creating a perfect piece of art that can't be implemented or doesn't fulfill the business requirements once it is. Feedback can be perceived as painful, but it is vital to creating the best product.

But if all the participants in the process can be assumed to have the best intentions, why is feedback so often such a pain? Think back to your persuasive design techniques: the best way to make a user commit wholeheartedly to a decision is to get them to make an initial investment in it. As we discussed in Chapter 8, the most powerful persuasive design techniques are known to make people stick to a decision even when it becomes irrational to do so.

Now think back to the amount of investment the average design job takes in terms of your time, your thinking, and your effort to create deliverables. That investment is concrete, visible, and present, to the degree that we'll do almost anything to protect it. We end up accidentally using those persuasive design techniques on ourselves! Meanwhile, the inexact assumptions, missed nuances, and changed business realities to which we were working are invisible. Except, that is, to the stakeholder who raises them, for whom they are concrete and immediate. For this stakeholder, if these concerns appear to be brushed off or treated as unimportant, the discussion can rapidly begin to feel like a collision between their real business needs and what they perceive to be subjective aesthetic considerations.

This would be a difficult enough situation without an extra complicating factor: stakeholders usually don't express business concerns in pure form. Instead, for a variety of reasons, they tend to present their concerns in a way that appears to put a foot into UX territory. Mismatches over the accuracy of a persona behavior or comfort level become "Will the user understand that?" – a question that often has an easy yes-or-no answer to a seasoned UX, or leads us to suggest usability testing rather than engage with the question properly. Worse, when a design doesn't meet a given business need, our experience is that many stakeholders will identify the need by proposing a design solution that they think addresses it, not by articulating the need. Without that vital foundation stone, we can't judge the quality of their solution effectively, so we end up defending a solution to the wrong problem against a solution to a problem we can't see. No wonder it creates friction.

With all this in mind, can every design battle be won? Absolutely. But if you want to learn how to do it, put down this book and take up an apprenticeship with someone who sells bridges to gullible investors, because winning every design battle means convincing people of the magic power of your design solution to overcome the inherent messiness of human communication. But winning every design disagreement is strategically and ethically the wrong thing to do, and doesn't serve user needs and better product outcomes. And that's an anti-pattern.

## The hidden cost

There is a real danger to defending too hard: the better a project is run, the faster it will route around bottlenecks. If people find that it's too difficult to get your agreement on things, they'll find ways to make an end run around you instead. Excessive defending also encourages others to find reasons for your intractability – it's the quickest way to reinforce their perception that design is subjective and can be dismissed if the "arty" people become too much of a problem. The rework in these cases will still fall to you, but now you'll be disempowered because the project governance will have been reshaped by people who "understand the business realities" better.

In UX design, it's useful to imagine that users have a "bucket" of goodwill that slowly empties as they have issues in working with a website. When the bucket runs dry, they'll give up in frustration and serve their need a different way. This same bucket of goodwill exists in stakeholders at feedback meetings, and needs to be conserved with just as much care. We borrow this mindful approach to positive experiences and goodwill (overcoming negative experiences) from psychologist John Gottman, Ph.D., whose research points to a positive interaction ratio of 5:1 to keep relationships happy.[2]

As human beings, we have a bias toward remembering the most critical situations (both good and bad). In terms of this discussion, that means if a stakeholder walks away from a meeting with an almost-empty bucket, the bucket won't be much more full next time they come back. You can, of course, refill the bucket by creating a positive interaction with your stakeholders. Keep in mind the useful rule of thumb of having five times as many positive interactions as negative ones, and that a more generous gesture is a more memorable outlier for day-to-day team interactions. This is something to do whenever possible, not just at a critical disagreement, because you never know when you need to rely on your team's bucket of goodwill.

## Business theater

An important way of conserving goodwill is to telegraph your intentions when you introduce your argument. We like to refer to this as *Business Theater*, because, like pantomime or Kabuki, it has its own specialized and exaggerated stylization of performance, and it works because the audience is literate in this mode of communication. You're probably already well versed in it without realizing – it comes into the language and structures that form the culture of your company. Ways of presenting feedback, the more formal language of business, the ritual of greeting and saying goodbye to clients when they visit – these are all forms of Business Theater.

For our purposes, we need to zoom in on the area of Business Theater that relies on *polite fiction*. Polite fictions are a form of social glue that save individuals or groups from embarrassment by agreeing to believe a convenient untruth, half-truth, or bent truth. For example, everyone at a party may know that Alan and Barbara's marriage is on the rocks, but they all pretend to believe that Barbara really does have a stomach bug that prevented her from attending. In Business Theater, polite fictions are generally used to allow stakeholders to maintain face in front of colleagues or third parties, and take the form of restating how their feedback is a clever (but flawed) interpretation of the product goals or user behaviors, or warmly making it clear to all present that a stakeholder's misinterpretation is entirely understandable, so your response is a way of "getting us all back on the same page." For example, Stephen Spielberg employed this tactic to resolve a terrible suggestion for changing the name of the "Back to the Future" movie by offering the executive who posed the suggestion a simple and face-saving way out – that the group thought he was making a joke. The executive could agree and drop his idea without embarrassment.[3]

Polite fictions can go astray, especially if they are patterns that become well-known. One of the most discredited techniques in Business Theater is the "s**t sandwich" technique of framing critical feedback between two pieces of complimentary or positive feedback. It has become so common that recipients of this compliment/ critique combination have come to disregard the thinly veiled positive feedback that is intended to soften the impact of the criticism it is supposed to deliver. A ratio of positive to negative feedback of 2:1 is quite far removed from the 5:1 ratio that lets us expect to feel OK about working with the criticism. The polite fiction in this case is that all three pieces of feedback are of equal importance; in fact, usually only the central, negative piece is intended to be taken on board.

Reversing this to situations where you need to respond to someone giving feedback, your polite fictions have to flatter the giver of feedback without being overly obvious to make them authentic. This is naturally easier if you have some pre-established rapport with the person giving feedback. Business Theater can help you establish this rapport with stakeholders.

Active listening is another form of Business Theater. It involves not just listening, but giving nonverbal cues of engagement to the speaker to demonstrate your understanding and desire for them to continue. Nodding, making eye contact, vocalizing assent, and note-taking are all great signs of active listening.

It may seem from this brief introduction that Business Theater is the art of being false with stakeholders, but we urge you not to take this interpretation. Like any kind of theatre, it only really works when it comes from genuine intentions combined with deliberate presentation. At its heart, Business Theater is about amping up and projecting the goodwill you feel toward the project and the people you're working with. Goodwill projected outward will result in goodwill being reflected back onto you and your thinking.

## Summary

It's natural to feel pride in our work, but criticism is inevitable, so every response to criticism has to be considered in the wider context of whether it moves the project forward with good design, or makes design the enemy of progress. For design to maintain its seat at the table, designers have to find ways to win the important battles without seeming intractable or difficult to deal with. Developing this skill is one of the most important parts of leveling up as a designer.

## The "Defending Too Hard" anti-pattern

It's natural to become attached to our work and to know that we have the moral authority to do what's best for the user. But we need to retain perspective and know when to re-evaluate our point of view. We need to maintain empathy with our stakeholders as much as our users and we need to know when our cognitive biases are shaping our judgment. Defending too hard erodes trust and credibility, making it more difficult in the long run to deliver great experiences for our users.

## You'll know you're in it when ...

- The project's approach is shifting to one that cuts you out of the loop on more occasions.

- Stakeholders are reluctant to give you feedback in person, and send it by e-mail – often directly to your superiors rather than you.

- People attending reviews look as though giving feedback is painful, and speak as though they're expecting or trying to avoid a fight.

- You get told you're "combative," "defensive," or "inflexible."

- Your rationale frequently is overruled by authority rather than reason.

## The patterns

The patterns we'll demonstrate in this chapter fall into two types: *Choosing your battles* helps you understand which things to let go of. *Positive disagreement* shows you how to reshape your response into a form that embraces the challenge to your design rather than dismissing it. Successfully negotiating this anti-pattern requires both of these skills – positive disagreement might sound like a panacea to all design challenges but, when overused, it quickly becomes obvious.

If you are not sure which of these patterns to choose and when, Chapter 13 contains useful advice about judging the situations where they can be used.

### Choosing your battles: Don't get attached

As we explain in Chapter 8, one of the main reasons not to live in the deliverables is that increased polish requires increased investment. Increased investment makes rework appear to be a bigger waste of that investment. In truth, *every* stage of design is a slightly more refined guess at what the final product will look like. Rework goes with the territory, so embrace it. Structure your design assets in such a way that they're easy to reproduce, modify, and remix. For instance, if you're sketching, photocopy your first sketch so you have a version you can chop up, shift around, and rework without having to redraw it several times. If you would feel bad about tearing up your asset and starting again from scratch, you've invested too much in it already.

### Choosing your battles: Let the silence speak

One of the trickiest aspects of feedback is that some people will think aloud in feedback sessions. It's tempting to jump on any negative assertions they make, but often the thing to do is to hold back and think. Not only does this give you space to formulate your response, but you will often find that any others present will do the job for you, or at least agree to such a degree that it becomes clear there really is an underlying problem that has to be addressed. In some cases, the person thinking out loud will even talk themselves around, leaving some valuable goodwill in your pocket for later use.

## Choosing your battles: Concede gracefully

When you decide something's not worth fighting over, you can eke out a little goodwill by simply accepting the change. Recognize it as a positive input for your understanding, be energetic about capturing it, and expand on it as a springboard for further discussion. This shows the stakeholders that you're embracing their input, which has a powerful effect on their goodwill reservoirs. A simple "Thank you for your input. That is really helpful. We can [insert how the feedback can be incorporated and build on it]" sets the scene.

## Choosing your battles: Tactical retreat

As you prepare assets for feedback, keep clear in your own mind those aspects of the design that are crucial to meeting the UX requirements, and those that are beneficial but not crucial. This gives you a measure of where to draw the line in the sand. Explain every feature before conceding, but only go to battle over the crucial stuff. You can always add more and different beneficial aspects during the rework, but you won't be able to patch up an idea that's had the core removed from it.

## Positive disagreement: Get to the why

Few things are worse, or more counter-productive, than arguing a point that the other party wasn't making. Engage fully with the criticism and make sure you get to the root of the other party's concern before arguing your side. If defending is still the right thing, you've shown respect and understanding of the opposing position (and the party holding it) and you'll be better placed to make a solid argument. If you need to draw a stakeholder out on their reasons, try the Paraphrased Playback pattern from Chapter 6, or Five Whys from Chapter 13.

### Positive disagreement: Embrace and extend

Adopt the feedback as a positive suggestion, and then, without disagreeing or turning it around, broaden the discussion to include new options. You can do this by adding behavioral aspects or user goals that the feature should serve. This accepts that a new solution has to be found, but retains the importance of meeting UX goals rather than solely serving the needs of the challenging stakeholder. You can work with the stakeholder in the session to expand on the ideas, or capture your expansion of the feedback to work on after the session. If you do the latter, it's worth checking in with the stakeholder in question before the next feedback session so they can see the solution beforehand. If they still disagree at this point, you can have a deeper discussion without derailing a feedback session.

### Positive disagreement: Get them to expand

Work with the opposing party to expand on the idea, guiding them into fitting it into the rest of the solution. The more areas it touches, the more opportunities you will have to note conflicts with other functionality or UX goals. For maximum benefit, ensure that the conflicts are identified not negatively, but simply as subsequently resulting effects of the proposal. "OK, we could definitely rethink the page structure if we bring that element up above the fold" makes the scale of impact clear without being a disagreement. If the end scope of changes is unachievable, you have a solid basis for challenging a good, but sadly too-expensive suggestion. If you can't formulate any conflicts as the stakeholder expands, then ta-da! They have just helped you design a better product.

## What to do when someone keeps repeating the same objection

This is one of the more painful anti-patterns to have used against you. It's draining and demoralizing to have to repeatedly find new justifications for a design decision. And, of course, your own goodwill is vital to the project.

Get to the why. Try to ascertain the reason for the other party's defensiveness. Are they protecting their sphere of business from perceived competition, cannibalization (invasion of their domain), or being sidelined? Are they struggling to communicate some deeper misgiving through the medium of surface details? Are they simply a particularly willful individual, who needs their input validated in depth before accepting a different route?

Embrace their concerns. Ask for a conversation (a shift of context to a coffee shop or more casual space is a huge help here) and be quite open about wanting to find a better way to work. "I wanted to have a chat because it seems the work isn't really clicking with you, so I wanted to unpack that and see if we need to change things up." Use active listening as they unpack and reveal their concerns. Treat the conversation like a user research session and drill down into their reasons until you understand their core worries. Once you've identified these, work with the stakeholder to find some suggested solutions – for example, if they fear their business area is being sidelined, suggest that the two of you could speak to the product owner together about a change of strategy.

If the stakeholder is on the willful end of the spectrum, focus on the disruption to the project. Express concern that, although you're all working toward the best outcome, you seem to be pulling in different directions and it's becoming acutely clear that the time taken to gain agreement is hurting progress. If you can, task the stakeholder with a particular area of control (or focus on an area they already control) so they still feel able to project vision into the project. Work with the stakeholder to define that area in some design workshops so they will fight with you, not against you, when it comes to review.

## Tips

If your cultural context allows, let a little of your personality show through when engaging in Business Theater. That helps uncover your goodwill and lets the other party see the human side.

When in doubt, take things offline for further investigation, and have a more intensive session on the feedback with the stakeholder(s) in question at a later date.

Beware of sinking cost into your solutions and deliverables. When you feel yourself getting too attached, call for an interim feedback session as soon as possible or park it and work on something else for awhile, if possible.

Be proactive in getting buy-in. It's far better to ask for confirmation and expand on matters to people who seem reluctant to give it than to assume its existence and be surprised by a broadside of criticism.

## Terminology explained

Active listening

Business Theater

Polite fiction

## CASE STUDY

Sophie Freiermuth, UX Consultant at Baguette UX

*Figure 12.1: Sophie Freiermuth (Image credit: Sophie Freiermuth.)*

I've walked out of many meetings feeling demoralized, because I hadn't managed to sell in a workshop, testing, or research, or to deflect the conversation from features to benefits, or to impart how working with users and not against was simply a benefit to the business, even if it took more effort to build or a never-tried before approach. I long thought it was because I was too junior, yet, when my job title became "Lead," that didn't change. I sometimes thought it was because I was female (I have an excellent anecdote about being superbly ignored in a meeting and all UX questions asked to the – male – project manager) however that's a hard one to prove. Now, I've come to realize it maybe was because I was one voice amongst many, and a voice who hadn't acquired enough weight on the table to be balanced with that of others, better known and understood.

I was on a project where discovery had been done by another agency, and resulting creative was gospel. For weeks, all my requests for real data, access to users, even how decisions had been taken and what the rationale was, were denied by a very clever business owner, who was confident that having buy-in from the business was all he needed and had refined the art of deflecting to a high shine. I had even taken to starting practically every sentence with "I believe there is value in," which, by the way, is incredibly powerful a statement. However, that was also overruled with arguments such as "I know what the stakeholders want" or "That's how I did it before and it worked."

Understanding that his future rested not in the hands of the users but in those of the stakeholders, I started instead using the process we had committed to, and focused on the big batch of testing we would do with users at the release of the first build – a long way before the full product was built. Basically, I chose to go with the given direction and shoddy data, letting functionalities go through build, then fail or succeed with test participants. Strategy, you see, is a long game. The testing gave me a golden opportunity to spend time with stakeholders; interview users; and get test features, functionalities, and designs.

The result was that I had priceless video stills of users looking very puzzled when looking at some screens, quotes of users telling us what we had been wondering about for months, and – last but not least – a bit of traction and credibility at the discussion table. The test report I produced highlighted multiple issues that would need to be fixed and, although the cost of getting these insights was considerable to the business in terms of time and money, I had gained sufficient credibility that it was circulated to the team for action.

I'm not the most patient of people, but I know a losing battle when I see one, and that's from having been through so many, and having heard more than I wanted to gems such as "we don't care what users want, that's what we want," "well, your tests showed that it doesn't work but we think it will with more people." So now my approach to defending users hard is to do it not in a meeting when presenting, not in corridor conversations when I casually happen onto a client, not even in sly e-mails sent without difficult stakeholders cc-ed in. These are losing tactics in my book. Instead, I treat the entire length of the project as the opportunity I have to build positive relationships and a rapport of trust and confidence between me and, basically, everyone else. I don't expect big wins, and I come in at every step prepared to sell my solutions.

My earlier career in sales and marketing has helped me a lot in learning that you sell best when you sell specifically, and it all comes down to the big question that's almost never asked: "What's in it for me?". When I present an idea, I do my best to ensure that I give a 360-view of the benefits for all participants at the table. Even what's for the benefit of users gets taken to the next level: what it means for the business. A poorly designed form doesn't make users go away; it makes the business lose hot leads that cost them a considerable amount of money between advertising, marketing, and even building the pages that failed. And I focus on being an asset rather than an obstacle, choosing to let go of some requests if it means acquiring support and credibility in exchange. And some of these times, I even see that, after all, what's not a benefit is not necessarily a harm: it'll just add a pinch to the already considerable amount of user-value-less fodder on all sites and apps.

As you can see, I approach serving the interest of users throughout the time and length of projects, focusing on what I can do with the leverage I have right now. It's part of my job to defend the users, and it's also part of my job to work well with others, for my own career's sake as well as for the benefit of my discipline, so that the people at the table see UX as an asset, not a troublemaker. My slow and steady approach has borne results I'm proud of, with stakeholders surprising me with agreement when I expected resistance, with my words being used by others as their own (I don't mind – users win that one), and with a day-to-day work atmosphere that goes from strength to strength. Making my life better and serving, truly, the users in the long term while building trust into the discipline of user experience – now that's a good day's work in my book.

*Sophie Freiermuth (@wickedgeekie) is a UX designer, trained through years of agency work on some of the world's biggest brands, who realized she had a lot to give beyond her UX deliverables and skills in leading workshops. She currently focuses on mentoring, teaching, coaching, and training individuals and teams at the crossroads of UX, Lean Startup, Agile, and product design. She helps foster a strong sense of users, of purpose, and of vision in teams focused on working collaboratively on valuable products and propositions.*

## REFERENCES

1. Design is How it Works. Available from: http://www.nytimes.com/2003/11/30/magazine/the-guts-of-a-new-machine.html [accessed 10.01.15].
2. Gottman J. The Magic Ratio is 5. Available from: http://www.psychologytoday.com/articles/200403/marriage-math;   http://www.gottmanblog.com/sound-relationship-house/2014/10/28/the-positive-perspective-dr-gottmans-magic-ratio [accessed 9.01.15].
3. http://en.wikipedia.org/wiki/Back_to_the_Future [accessed 9.01.15].

# TAKEAWAYS

1. We want to be proud of our work, but an excess of pride can lead to us having reduced influence over the process and outcome.

2. Remember the bucket of goodwill and, whenever possible, err on the side of filling rather than spilling it.

3. Choose your battles carefully and argue your point in a way that is inclusive to other viewpoints.

4. Use Business Theater to telegraph your goodwill and positive intentions, which will build goodwill in other participants.

5. When it's the right thing to defend yourself or your design element, do it in a way that is not psychologically or emotionally draining to the other party.

# CHAPTER 13

## Not defending hard enough

Over the last 12 chapters, we've made the case that what we design isn't an experience until a user is experiencing it. We've provided better interpersonal patterns and ways to keep discussions on track. We have shown you how to harness testing and user feedback to tighten feedback loops and make better product decisions as a team. But sometimes, you'll still be challenged by stakeholders and colleagues and, if you back down on the most important aspects of your design for the wrong reasons, you still won't deliver the experience your users deserve. In this chapter, we'll show you the right reasons to defend your decisions.

## Everyone's a critic

Collaboration, cooperation, and co-design are all fundamental tools in identifying and understanding business processes and stakeholder intentions. But you – you in particular – are in the room for a reason. It's vital not to lose sight of the specialist knowledge and experience that you bring to the process of product development. You are there to ensure that the business processes are reconciled with the user's aims, and that often means protecting their interests against people with skewed or outright antagonistic views of those interests.

One of the drawbacks of being highly collaborative is that it makes it hard to draw demarcation lines around the things that *we* do as a group and the things that *you/I* do as a specialist. People who have been empowered by involvement at the business discovery stage can't be expected to get back in the box once you begin refining the user experience. They will continue to give feedback at the level they got accustomed to previously. Naturally, some of this will be of great value. However, some of it will be unsuitable for implementation.

For example, James once worked with a product owner who announced that he'd wireframed the easiest interface ever. The wireframe had some 200 controls laid out in a column on the page. In the (very analytical) stakeholder's mind, the key metric for usability was clicks-to-target, so making everything one click away was the easiest thing possible. Needless to say, James gave this stakeholder some support in understanding broader UX principles and goals.

People who don't do UX as their primary occupation get odd ideas about which metrics count, about the ways users behave, and frequently even about the role of UX, limiting it to the domain of User Interface Design (UID). We are in the room to ensure that the right metrics are chosen, users behaviors are well understood, and we get to bring the whole of the job into making the right product.

That's why it's critical to be able to defend the right decisions, at the right times, in the right ways. We hope that, in the previous chapters, we have shown you the patterns that help you defend the right *way*. This chapter is all about identifying the right *decisions* and choosing the right *times*.

## Explaining UX

User experience is a very elastic term, encompassing almost everything to do with developing the front end of a (digital) product or service, from formative and evaluative user research and synthesis to strategy and product definition through to information architecture, interaction design, and even visual design. This is a positive: UX return is maximized when all of these aspects are considered for their effect on the user. However, it does mean that many people only encounter a part of the UX process, and mistake that for *all* of UX. Most often this means interaction design and information architecture, so for many people, *UX* equals *wireframes*.

It's important not to let this misconception persist in your organization. One option is to ban the term "UX" in relation to the work you do. James worked in one company where everybody involved in the creative side of development was called a product designer (specializing in *x*). At one of his workplaces, the department deliberately uses the term *customer experience* rather than *user experience* to highlight the expansion of role beyond simple UI design and to encompass whole people ("customers") rather than a narrow range of online behaviors ("users").

Alternatively, use the term "UX" to embrace *everything* the company does. This was a route some of Martina's design consultancy workplaces took, renaming the UX design team as interaction design to acknowledge that all designers (visual and interaction), as well as insights and development teams, play a part in delivering the user experience.

Whichever route you take, or context you find yourself in, strive toward communicating the notion of a balanced product team that brings together a core group of practitioners that can cover design, product management, and development competencies. This does not necessarily mean three people representing a discipline each, but a small number of cross-disciplinary collaborators who cover knowledge in all domains.

Treat your job as though it were a product: how would you persuade people of its value and get them to engage with it more? Here are some ideas that have worked for us.

- Brown bag sessions – lunch talks about what UX can deliver and how we like to work

- Departmental presentations, especially as part of onboarding new hands or ramping up for new projects

- All-hands introductions to UX, standing in front of as many people as possible and presenting what we do

- Advice booth, where people from around the business can bring UX challenges to get the team's advice

- Turning the UX department into a "pub" on a regular basis – putting the work up on the walls and inviting the whole business into the space to see what we were up to, with refreshments on tap

- Using the departmental space for passive engagement – creating a huge UX Wall about who we are, what we're up to, and what we want to do better as a department

- Inviting colleagues into UX activities such as research, focus groups, and testing – the value becomes much easier to understand when it comes from users' mouths

- Socializing deliverables and outcomes – for example, showing the marketing team how personas are useful for their needs

- Getting social – having an elevator pitch about UX ready for when people around the business, at the coffee machine, in elevators, etc., ask what you do.

## What is the right decision?

The right decision is one where the UX value is clear, the UX value is high, and the business rationale behind the challenge is not clear or of high value.

For (an admittedly contrived) example, let's take this message, which contains a social proof metric.

"Last summer, 600,000 people trusted us for their holiday insurance."

"What about people who bought the insurance on behalf of someone else?" objects a stakeholder.

In this case, the value of persuasion arising from social proof is clear and high, but the business value of serving the edge case (a scenario that the system is not intended for, and only a small proportion of potential users would be served by) is neither clear nor high.

Technically, the challenge is correct: there may be users who didn't use the service for their *own* holidays. But *a* holiday was still covered.

However:

- Will that section of the audience that buys for other people have a literal interpretation of the phrase, or will they interpret it to include them anyway?

- If they don't feel included by it, will that negatively affect their conversion rate (do they feel excluded from this company by reading the message)?

- If conversion *is* affected, is it affected at a rate great enough to offset the uplift for the proportion of the audience that is directly engaged?

- How many people are affected by this edge case anyway?

- What's the risk of accommodating this concern?

Let's accommodate this edge case (we don't know the exact number, so we'll add a disclaimer instead) and see.

"Last summer, 600,000 people trusted us with insurance for a holiday taken either by them or someone they bought insurance for."

If a persuasive strapline (that short and snappy brand expression accompanying the product logo) is rewritten to be arbitrarily applicable to 100% of all possible readers, it ends up including so many sub-clauses and disclaimers that it loses its flow, its memorability, and its power. Plus, it will fail any kind of copywriting step and end up being massaged into something with no social proof power, like,

"Last summer, a lot of people trusted us for insurance."

Of course, we can construct perfectly viable reasons for this message to be challenged.

- "That's commercially sensitive information."

- "Those numbers don't stand up to scrutiny."

- "That's a smaller number than our very visible competitor is using."

In these cases, the business value is both clear and high enough to agree that the message should change. But what about those times when a stakeholder has a valid business reason for their challenge, but isn't expressing it well? How do you know when *Defending too hard* and *Not defending hard enough* are in conflict?

The first step is to employ some of the patterns we've introduced throughout this book to understand the challenge first.

- Step back, use the power of silence, and let the stakeholder talk their way through their thinking.

- Use paraphrased playback to ensure you both have the same understanding of the challenge.

- Use positive disagreement to explore the problem space. Once you understand the challenge, you should understand the business value and know whether or not it's in conflict with the UX value.

## Using the Five Whys to understand business value

The Five Whys,[1] originally developed by Sakichi Toyoda at Toyota, traditionally are used in the engineering domain to understand the causes of failure. Looking at the outcome of a failure and following it up the chain of causes by asking "Why did that happen?" at each step will help us get to the root or systematic cause that led to the failure. Most times, the root cause is arrived at within five layers of investigation.

You might have used this technique in user interviews to get to the root of a belief or a behavior.

We can also use the Five Whys to revert from solutions or outcomes back to business value, but it should be employed with great care. Simply asking a stakeholder "Why's that?" five times will come across as annoying at best and downright rude at worst. To make the Five Whys effective in this context, we need to frame them appropriately and use persuasive language.

### Framing the Five Whys

Introducing the technique as something that's beneficial to the whole team is extremely important, so phrases such as "I'd like to unpack that, so I'm going to ask a few questions to uncover the root" or "Just to really get to the core of that question, I'd like to run through a quick validation exercise ..." help to set your audience's expectations that this is a business discovery tool rather than a pedantic drill-down.

It may also help to introduce the technique's history, mentioning that it was developed as part of Toyota's famed Six Sigma quality assurance process. Some development teams (particularly in the Lean sphere) are already familiar with the Five Whys, so, in these cases, just mentioning the name can help.

Finally, give a condensed version of what to expect. "We're going to focus for a little while on uncovering the cause. It might get a little repetitive, but we hope this will validate some of our assumptions."

## Asking the Five Whys persuasively

*Figure 13.1: The Fishbone diagram illustrates how to apply Five Why questions to explore a topic in more depth. (Illustration by: Martina Hodges-Schell.)*

You can begin with a first question that is quite open. For example, "How does that tie back to business value," or "What's the expectation behind that?" This sets the direction of the investigation and also gives the stakeholder room to explore any assumptions or validated reasoning behind their suggestion. One or more key pieces of reasoning should be revealed by this first answer, and those are the pieces to pursue with the next line of questions. If no key reasoning arises, you can pursue the next line in a more general sense, or rephrase the first question, making it clearer that you're still seeking to understand the business value.

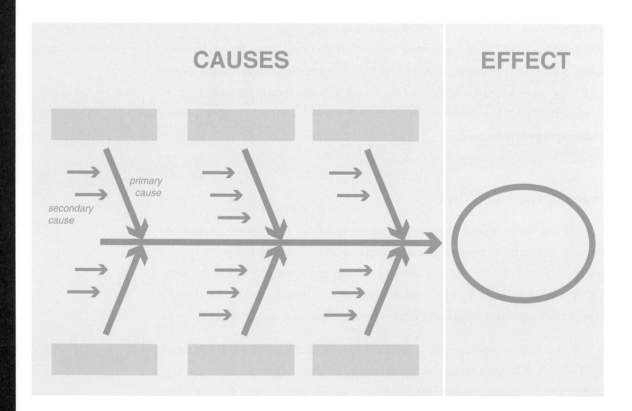

Remember that, as domain specialists, some types of business value may not always be intuitively obvious to us, and there may be times that we don't recognize extant business value and need it explained better.

Your second line of questioning can be more focused, using phrases like:

- "Tell me more about *x*."

- "What does the company get from that?"

- "How is the *business objective* served by that?"

- "Is there a research source for, or prior experience of, that?"

- "Are there any assumptions driving that?"

- "How does that touch the business model?"

- "The value of that isn't obvious to me – can you elaborate?"

- "Help me understand why that's a benefit for us."

Using these second-line questions in combination will allow you to progress to a level where the root cause (or lack of same) should be clear.

## Closing the Five Whys

Close by restating the root business value that has been identified, and reiterate how it relates to the challenge. This demonstrates your understanding and buy-in of the question, shows the value of the technique you've run through so people don't feel their time was wasted, and frames things in common language for the further discussion.

"OK, so what we've determined is that we don't feel this feature fulfills the key business need of ..."

If no root business value was identified, close by asking the group whether the challenge has identified a new business value and whether it should be pursued or not.

"This sounds like an area that our current requirements don't touch. Are we happy with leaving this out of the scope, or do we want to reconsider it?"

## UX Value vs Business Value

UX Value is, of course, a form of business value. We've separated them here because, in many stakeholders' minds, there is a very clear distinction between the two. For these stakeholders, business value means those features that directly drive conversions or other measurable activities. Areas of UX value can fall outside this definition, and solid customer experience aims such as loyalty, goodwill, and brand perception are much harder to measure. This leads these stakeholders to consider UX value to be "soft," as it resides largely in potential.

The long-term value of UX is something that you should aim to communicate to the business through your wider UX initiatives, as described in "Explaining UX" in this chapter. However, that's a perception change that takes time and reinforcement, and it may not always be possible to create that shift in the environment of a feedback session. However, even if it's not possible to draw that link, it should be possible to argue from the position that it is still a desirable outcome to have the best possible experience. This is a weaker position, but it's also the difference that makes a pro*ject* into a pro*duct*.

Now that you know the UX value and the business value, the question is whether to defend, and how to do it effectively. And that's something that's easy to plot on a square graph:

## Quadrant A: High business value, low UX value

*Concede*. Let the business value win. Accept the challenge and reshape your solution around it.

## Quadrant B: High business value, high UX value

*Flex*. Both outcomes have to be respected, so you need to reach agreement about a solution that maintains the UX value but encompasses the business value as well.

## Quadrant C: Low business value, low UX value

*Withdraw*. Unless the cost of change would be disruptive to progress, accept that the value is too low to waste time arguing about it. You're better off earning goodwill by accepting the challenge.

*Figure 13.2: Decision-making Matrix. If you're not sure whether to fight or concede for a particular decision, refer to this matrix to understand the balance between UX value and business value to make a better decision. (Illustration by: Martina Hodges-Schell.)*

## Quadrant D: Low business value, high UX value

*Defend.* Low business value may equate to low return on investment for changes to the solution, plus the cost of losing the UX benefit. Now is the time to be the user's champion. Delighters, in particular, will usually fall under this category.

## Shortcut: Always defend user research

If there is one aspect of the UX process that we would always, unquestioningly, fight for, it's a valid and well-grounded understanding of the user – their needs, goals, and behaviors. So many businesses see this as an optional part of the process because "we know our users" or "we know what works," and baulk at the upfront cost of having what they "already know" "confirmed."

In terms of our UX graph, user research is hard against the right-hand side, offering higher UX value than almost anything else. It should be high on the business value axis, too. If the business doesn't see this, find out why. Is there existing research about the users that they're using for insight, and can you get access to it? Is there a large amount of embedded knowledge about the market in the team (careful here: experience is not always the same as insight)? Is the business too inward-looking and not able to recognize that consumers might take a different view?

Part of the problem is the difference in perception between present concrete costs and future potential costs. If a stakeholder is even willing to concede that a lack of user understanding might cause the product to fail and need rework or a pivot, it's only a (far less scary) potential at this point, even if the pivot might cost a hundred times the research bill. At root, this makes user research a risk management proposition. The longer a deficiency exists, the more it costs to eventually fix it. The more areas a deficiency touches, the more it costs to eventually fix. These two factors multiply together, so a lack of user research – which touches your entire interface! – can be a very costly omission if it comes to light later down the road. Framing things this way makes the link between small user testing costs now and the *avoidance* of the more expensive pivot far more obvious.

On the other hand, once you manage to get research into a project, the Sunk Cost Fallacy works to your benefit. Sunk Cost Fallacy describes an organization's bias toward carrying on with something they have already invested money in, despite not necessarily believing that it will deliver the right result. In this case, the investment in research becomes a touchstone that the business will seek to grow. It's also a great opportunity to get non-UX colleagues immersed in the value of what we do by inviting them to observe sessions.[2]

Even if you can't win the full-scale research plan you originally proposed, fight for whatever remnant you can justify. In the same way that you can get good usability testing results with only a few users, you can get great insight from only a handful of well-chosen subjects.

## Summary

Cooperation and goodwill are vital to the creation of a working product, but we don't do our jobs effectively if we don't ensure that our specialist knowledge makes a difference where it counts. Being able to take a strategic view and understand where the difference is of most value allows us to maintain the working relationship with our colleagues, while ensuring that we can push on the most important things when we need to.

## The "Not Defending Hard Enough" anti-pattern

Consensus is a key part of our mission as UXers, but we always face a challenge in balancing business requirements and user needs. Shying away from necessary hard conversations doesn't deliver on the user needs side of this equation. We must find ways to challenge incorrect assumptions or redress imbalances. Not speaking up for user needs and yielding to stakeholder pressure without making the case for a better product experience is the anti-pattern.

## You know you're in it when ...

- Everyone seems happy with progress, but no one (especially not you) seems happy with the level of quality.

- You always seem to be conceding ground, even where there's no gain for anyone in doing so.

- Your colleagues or reviews say you should be more assertive or take more ownership of UX.

## The patterns

Note: The patterns you learned in the previous chapter are just as applicable here. These are a few extra ones, aimed at helping you express the value of your design when defense is the correct response.

### Arrive via MoSCoW

Before you enter the feedback arena, have a clear understanding of which elements of your work are Vital, Important, Nice, or Incidental to UX value or, as the acronym would class these categories: Must do, Should do, Could do and Would be nice to do. Remember, we're treating UX value as distinct from business value, so delightful experience elements may have higher UX value. You need to know this so they can be slotted into the decision-making framework shown above.

## Beginning, middle, and end

For every element of your design, be ready to tell a story about how it relates to business value. This pattern works better when you are able to connect UX value to a high business value. Like every story, it needs to have a beginning, a middle, and an end. The beginning is the setup: here is the problem to be solved/business value to be served – the antagonist of this story. The middle is the narrative: the journey to a strategy that solves or serves that antagonist. And the end is the finale: here is the hero, my solution, and how it uses the strategy on the antagonist.

This works because it frames the relationship between the business value and your solution; it reveals the solid logic underpinning the strategy; and it ties the two together before the "subjective" aspects of the solution are introduced. You can use this preemptively, or as the opening of your defense to ensure everyone understands the purpose of the feature.

## Snap the elastic user

Often when stakeholders speak about their concerns about "the user," they're doing one of two things: they're using reverse empathy to assume the user thinks the same way they do, or they're using overcautious imagination to diminish the user's capabilities. This leads to a perfectly elastic user, who can either be a power user or a novice, depending on what point the stakeholder wants to make. A challenge to a feature aimed at power users, because a newbie won't understand it, is hard to defend against in this frame. Have your personas available and visible in feedback meetings so you can tie your justification back to the correct actor. Better still, use your personas in the introduction of features with narrow target groups. Always remember the space that lies outside the personas. If the challenge is out in this no-man's-land, it may be enough of an edge case that it can be deprioritized completely.

## Letting the client/stakeholder fail

Sometimes, when you have explored all other options of communicating and building evidence for the best path forward but stakeholders still challenge the direction to be taken, consider a well-reasoned approach to letting them fail, one that takes all caveats into account. Explain your concerns and the likely outcomes you expect. Recommend they reconsider their approach and test their idea with user research to validate their assumptions quickly before investing more time and resources in this direction. Recommend a Lean approach to creating an experiment that tests their assumption at a low cost of change. But make it an option that they can choose their preferred path, against your best judgment. You can use the outcome of this learning experience to help them iterate the solution.

## How to remedy a wrongly given-up point

If you've wrongly backed off on something important, often the best course of action is to accept the loss and learn from it for next time. It's not a good idea to reopen every lost discussion for reconsideration, especially not ones that were lost a long time ago. However, there is a spectrum of tone that you can use, from the simple and lightweight soon after the event – "I gave [decision] more thought and I'm not comfortable with where we ended up on it. Can we revisit that discussion?" – all the way up to waiting until the omission becomes painful to the project and reintroducing the idea (without saying "I told you so" as you do).

However, you'll never gain back ground if you've been seen to brood over defeat. So when you do concede or lose, do it with grace and good humor. Explore the winning solution, so that, if it doesn't work, you can demonstrate the problem visually. If you need to have discussions to keep your own solution in play, have them informally and present them as a get-out-of-jail-free card, just in case.

## Tips

Connect socially with other UX professionals when you don't feel confident. Share war stories, successes, and advice to (re)build your confidence and remind yourself of the part you can play.

Find allies within the business and use them as a sounding board for your design decisions. Pre-screening will give you an idea of what may be contentious and keep you prepared for the challenges.

If you ever have to spend goodwill to defend the right thing, check in afterward with the other party to begin the process of refilling the bucket.

## Terminology explained

Sakichi Toyoda

Five Whys

Toyota

Reverse empathy

# CASE STUDY

*Figure 13.3: Richard Wand*

You can't win every design debate, and it's been a while since I regret failing to defend a significant design decision. Still, the last time sticks in my throat. On that occasion, the client applied unrealistic user scenarios to support their misguided design feedback. They weren't considering their solution in the context of real-world scenarios, so their design assertions were naturally flawed.

It's not the first time, and it won't be the last time, that I've allowed a client to push through a decision that I don't agree with. It's not that I don't have any fire in my belly; I'm far from a pushover. It's just that sometimes you have to concede to someone else's opinion because failure to compromise would hinder the progress of a project.

The particular time in question, the client had a product configurator that was leaking customers. I was tasked to identify where their customers were abandoning the product and recommend design enhancements to improve conversion. This didn't seem like a complex challenge, so I agreed to take a Lean approach and skip detailed research activities, other than reviewing their conversion funnel analytics and carrying out a heuristic evaluation of the configurator.

The main finding was that the decision architecture was flawed. Critical information was either missing or presented in a way that would be hard for customers to process. I considered the customers' information needs and recommended enhancements to make their decision-making easier. The client didn't agree.

In fairness, the client was relatively new to the world of experience design and wanted to protect the minimal design of the interface – albeit at the expense of their customers' needs. He argued that their customers would already be well informed on the product before using the configurator and, therefore, didn't need additional information.

In the absence of a more detailed discovery process, I couldn't prove or disprove his hypothesis. Sixteen years as a practitioner meant that I had the necessary expertise, but the lack of an agreed set of customer scenarios rendered this impotent.

What really frustrated me was that all of this stemmed from my own naïve judgment. I assumed the stakeholders and I had the same understanding of what we were trying to achieve, who we were designing the system for, and the context within which this audience would interact with it. After all, this was a brief to improve the conversion for a seemingly straightforward flow. However, I came to realize that everyone saw the brief through his or her own lens, which, unsurprisingly, led to different interpretations and, therefore, different expectations and visions.

What this taught me was simple. No matter how simple the task might seem, never start designing without an agreed-upon experience brief: a document that defines the experiences a customer should enjoy with a product or website. It is this brief that ensures you focus on real people and real-world scenarios, providing the necessary insight to inform, guide, and support any design decisions. No more elastic users or fictitious scenarios. Overnight, the experience brief graduated, for me, from a nice-to-have document to an absolutely-must-have document.

And what's just as important as delivering the experience brief, if not more so, is the process I go through to gather the information for it. For me, nothing tops a collaborative problem-framing workshop for stakeholders to collectively present their knowledge and insights about a problem.

It's this collaborative session, along with supporting research and insight gathered during any discovery activities, that informs the experience brief. It ensures that the internal team and stakeholders share an understanding of the problems they're trying to solve and all its boundaries. It also makes stakeholders feel that, right from the outset, they are part of the solution, giving them a sense of ownership in any design solutions proposed.

This is only the start of the design journey, but the collaborative session and experience brief help to ensure that the journey gets off on the right track. Of course, it doesn't guarantee you won't suffer the odd skid along the way, but setting the project up right from the beginning reduces the chance of design challenges that aren't grounded in genuine insight, in turn making it easier to defend your design decisions.

Thus, the design journey I go on involves telling stories to educate and inform the stakeholders and creating an understanding of the design decisions being made, all tied back to the experience brief.

The greatest source of design friction stems from the lack of articulation of the design challenge. Clearly articulating the design challenge isn't a silver bullet for pain-free design, but establishing a well-defined experience brief and telling stories that tie back to it make defending your design solutions far more palatable.

*Rich Wand is Customer Experience Director at Hugo & Cat, a London-based Customer Engagement Agency that specialises in business transformation through digital. Over the past 20 years, Rich has made it his mission to put the client's customers at the heart of everything their brand does; "After all, brands need their customers more than they need them." With experience at agencies such as EMC Digital, Proximity and POSSIBLE, he has created some truly transformative initiatives for their brands and fantastic experiences for their customers. Ask Rich what he does and he'll tell you, "it's simple, I create meaningful and compelling customer experiences, with just a sprinkling of fairy dust to bring delight to the user."*

## REFERENCES

1. Ohno Taiichi. Toyota production system: beyond large-scale production. Productivity Press; 1 March 1988.
2. Sunk Cost Fallacy. Available from:http://dictionary.cambridge.org/dictionary/business-english/sunk-cost-fallacy [accessed 9.1.15]; http://en.m.wikipedia.org/wiki/Sunk_costs#Loss_aversion_and_the_sunk_cost_fallacy [accessed 11.1.15].

# TAKEAWAYS

1. Consensus is important, but if you're not getting good quality of experience into the product, you're not offering value to your employer.

2. Understanding your colleagues' professional value structure is key to knowing when to defend or concede.

3. The Five Whys is a proven tool for discovering the underlying values behind a colleague's decision or assertion.

4. Remember the bucket of goodwill and take opportunities to fill it so you have more in credit for tougher challenges.

5. Have artifacts on hand that will help you justify your thinking and snap elastic expectations.

6. Whenever possible, tell a great story.

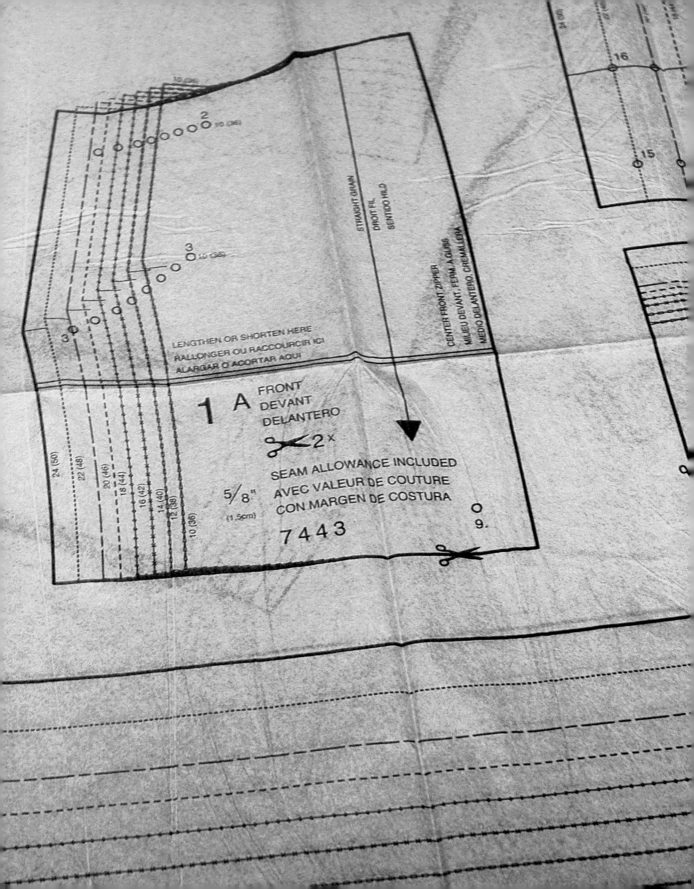

# CHAPTER 14

## Identifying and fixing your own anti-patterns

In the course of the last 13 chapters, we've shown you some of the most common anti-patterns that we encounter in the course of building digital products. Each of those anti-patterns can manifest in a wide variety of different behaviors, and we hope that one of the lessons you've taken away from the book so far is how to map these behaviors to the anti-patterns. But anti-patterns tend to spring up like weeds, so there are many more than we could ever capture in a book. It's time to flex your newfound muscles and discover some anti-patterns for yourself.

## The tip-off

As every anti-pattern essentially manifests itself in the form of one or more behaviors, the first place to look is in those moments when something has gone wrong in communication. This could be a quarrel that blew up; a time you found yourself being shut out of decision-making; or even a time when you conscientiously stayed away from something that came back to bite you later. We're not saying that every such instance is a time when you're at fault or an anti-pattern is at play, but you need to be able to assess these moments objectively to determine which ones you can and should work on.

The easiest place to start is at the points of most disruption in communication, perhaps the loudest, most memorable, or most cringe-worthy. The longer you've carried a moment like this with you, the more obvious a tip-off it will be. The authors still remember being involved in screaming arguments and throwing our hands up in disgust at feedback in the previous century. The first place to look is in these moments of the past, and whether any of the reasoning or behaviors that led you there are things that you still encounter today.

Another place to find tip-offs is, of course, in the way other people perceive you. Many organizations have instituted 360-degree reviews to help people discover the perceptions of their colleagues. You can check for feedback on your own with sympathetic colleagues after meetings: "Did that feel like it went well? Do you think I was a bit hard on *x*?"

It's a little more challenging, but with practice, you can even learn to feel yourself slipping into a behavioral pattern. For example, think about how you change your voice and the cadence of your speech when you give a presentation. This is a form of behavioral pattern that we invoke consciously. There is a sense of intense focus on the moment, with an almost zen-like quality of concentrating on the big stuff – the strategy of the talk, the wealth of insight behind the words – and letting the small stuff – the words themselves – flow. Indeed at the most pronounced end, behavioral patterns are part of what Mihaly Csikszentmihalyi describes as *flow*.[1] Anti-patterns tend to be so tied up with emotion that it can be harder to be self-observing when they appear, but feeling the argument sweep you away or shut you down is generally a sign that a pattern is taking over.

## About flow

Flow is a state that we enter when we focus intently on activities that are complex but that we have skill in. Examples of activities that trigger flow state might be playing a musical instrument, competing in a sport, or writing some complex code. When we enter flow state, the outside world recedes and our perception of time diminishes. We become less aware of individual decisions and actions, or physical motions, and instead perceive ourselves as directly achieving the outcome – a sort of telepathy with our tools.

Flow can make you highly productive, but it also contributes to being in the room but not in the team. You can balance this by learning to recognize both flow itself and the circumstances that help you enter it. Once you can replicate the circumstances effectively, you can enter flow more quickly and more reliably.

## The cool-down

When you do find yourself displaying or acting out an anti-pattern, it can be tempting to try and identify and resolve it as soon as possible. However, this can be a counter-productive approach. An anti-pattern occurs because we tell ourselves a story about the situation and the path to our desired outcome and, in the immediate aftermath, that narrative is still playing in our minds. We felt justified in acting that way at that time; we need time and perspective to get to a place where we can evaluate the situation more dispassionately.

That time may mean more than just leaving the meeting and getting the hot drink of your choice. You need to fully internalize the other party's suggestion so you can empathize with it. If you catch yourself thinking "[This person] is such an idiot, his suggestion is ridiculous," you're probably still not ready. Nine times out of ten, your colleagues aren't idiots. To distance yourself from the initial emotional response, take a break from the work for awhile so you can approach it with a fresh eye, and the alternative suggestion from your team in mind. This will help you identify whether you were caught by the IKEA effect – that is, being a little over-invested in what you made.

## Get an outside perspective

For this activity, it helps to have a feedback session. Find a colleague who can help you look at the situation from the outside. Don't go for the colleague who will automatically back you up or turn this into a pity party. Look for the one who can evaluate the situation objectively and thoroughly. Talk through the situation with as though you were in a retrospective. It may help to repeat the *retrospective prime directive* (see Chapter 3) to frame your conversation neutrally. Try to evaluate your motives and the other party's motives; what you and your colleague know of the other party's previous interactions; what the real intentions were behind any suggestions or complaints made; any unexpected reactions or statements on the other party's half.

Work with your colleague to identify any previous times that this anti-pattern may have occurred in situations they have witnessed, and any causes or resolutions they have observed. This works both ways – for your behaviors, or the ones of your colleague in question. It's important to understand the context of this behavior pattern and whether you're causing it or responding to it.

## Find the common factor

What you're searching for now is the theme that connects the occasions you've identified. Who were the players? What was the challenge you were responding to? Was there anything familiar in the counter-arguments? These are all clues that will help you understand the broader context of your anti-pattern. Once you understand what it is and where it's coming from, it's time to look at turning it around.

## Forgive yourself

If you've had an interaction that resulted in conflict or where you were proved decisively wrong, you're probably feeling pretty bad about it. The first thing to do in coming around to a more positive way of thinking is to let yourself off the hook. We all have anti-patterns and they are *not our fault*. Blame is an unhelpful action in dealing with anti-patterns and will not help you resolve these anti-patterns. Instead, understand that you are on a path of personal growth and learning, and that it's OK to learn by making mistakes as you go.

## Identify some patterns

With the colleague who's helping with your feedback assessment, brainstorm different paths that the conflict could have taken. Try to figure out if the point was ever winnable or whether the smart thing would have been to concede gracefully.

There are lots of patterns in this book that can be repurposed to address anti-patterns other than the ones we've attached them to. Try role playing the scenario again with a few candidate patterns – some of the very broadly applicable ones include Stepping Back, Paraphrased Playback, Yes and ..., and Breaking the Meeting.

If the anti-pattern has a more physiological basis, look at what you could do in the form of a pre-meeting ritual to address it. This can be as simple as a context reset – James has taught himself that snapping the elastic band around the cover of his Moleskine notebook means a change of context, and that acts as a useful reset. If, for example, you become terse when hungry, it could mean getting into the habit of having a handful of peanuts or a banana before late-morning meetings. If you slow down while digesting and the fatigue affects your interactions, try to avoid having a heavy lunch when you've scheduled a 2 p.m. session.

## Make it a habit

Once you've identified the pattern you want to use, you'll need to find a way to make it your natural response. One of the reasons we name all our patterns is so you can use the name to call up a pattern in the heat of the moment, like a mantra. Make the name of your pattern memorable so it's easy to remember and recall as needed. You can use role-play with your helpful colleague to get used to calling up the pattern during challenging moments.

Knowing that you have a toolbox full of patterns to call upon can be helpful all on its own. As you enter interactions, that knowledge lets you take a more strategic view of the conversation and opens up opportunities to guide the conversation in fruitful directions that may not otherwise have been available.

## Keep going

Before the pattern becomes second nature, you'll have to work at it a few times. You might also need to tweak it before it becomes optimally effective. Don't let a lack of success early on discourage you. Test the pattern, learn from the outcome, and refine your implementation, just the same way you would use testing to refine a UX proposition.

REFERENCE

1. Csikszentmihalyi M. Flow: The Psychology of Optimal Experience. New York: Harper Perennial Modern Classics; 2007. ISBN: 978 0061339202.

# CHAPTER 15

## Relaxation techniques at work

Work can be stressful. Many of us thrive in this environment, delivering great results while under pressure. When working collaboratively, however, it is often beneficial to remain calm, focused, and open to new ideas.

As humans, we are hard-wired to respond immediately to perceived threats. When we encounter stressful situations at work, such as a disagreement with a coworker, our body often registers this as a threat to our safety, kicking into gear the "fight or flight" response, which can make it difficult to maintain a calm and open frame of mind. Our sympathetic nervous system, which manages the fight-or-flight response, ensures that energy is directed toward those parts of the body that are vital to fleeing or defending oneself from a potential attack in the face of danger.

If you were about to be attacked by a tiger, for example, your heart would begin beating more quickly, moving blood toward the limbs, and away from your immune system and prefrontal cortex, where you do your analytical thinking. Your hearing and peripheral vision would become impaired. Your body would be doing everything it could to equip you to survive the direct threat in front of you.

Throughout evolution, this response has been an invaluable resource. Without that response, it is unlikely you would be reading these words. Faced with a tiger and potential death, it wouldn't matter that your immune system defended you from a cold, or that your prefrontal cortex allowed you to analyze the situation from the tiger's point of view. However, in our daily life, the sympathetic nervous system can often kick in when it is not welcome or useful.

Every day, we encounter situations that our mind and body may mistakenly label as threats – criticisms of our work, being left out of a loop. While these situations may seem like life or death at times, they generally require a different set of priorities and direction of energy than the sympathetic nervous system provides. Instead of routing your energy to your limbs, you need to lower your heart rate and maintain a calm, clear mind. You certainly want to be aware of the sounds and sights around you. To do this, you need to activate your parasympathetic nervous system – the part of your nervous system that is responsible for stimulating calmer "rest-and-digest" behaviors. Luckily, there are ways to do this and, in time, you'll find it just happens naturally. In the same way that the body can affect your mind when encountering a perceived threat, you can learn to use your body to realign your mind more quickly with your actual environment, allowing you to get on with your work more effectively.

## In the moment

The flight-or-fight response diverts energy from the exact functions that you need for a successful meeting or workshop. You need to listen and see your colleagues, and you have to be able think analytically about the different needs of the multiple stakeholders in the room. This is nearly impossible if your sympathetic nervous system kicks into high gear. What to do if this happens? Here are some tricks.

### Breathe

It sounds simple, but focusing on your breath will help you to stay in the moment and maximize your ability to pause between the stimulus – what your colleague may have just said for example – and your response. Slowing down your breathing and increasing the duration of your exhale will help to kick in your parasympathetic nervous system, enabling you to relax and better handle the situation at hand.

**Best for**

Calming your mind and regaining focus.

*Figure 15.1: Take a moment to breathe. (Photo credit: public domain.)*

### Time

Whatever you've got! Even a few breaths in this manner will help your para-sympathetic nervous system kick in. It works even better if you can excuse yourself and take 5 to 10 minutes to relax and breathe better.

### The exercise

Focus your attention on your breathing. Notice if it is deep or shallow. Pay attention to the length of the inhale and exhale – are they equal, or is one longer than the other? Feel the air moving in and out through your nostrils. Bringing your attention back to the body will help to calm your mind.

Begin to increase the length of your exhale. Breathe in for a count of 4 and out for a count of 6. If it is comfortable for you, you can increase this to a 1:2 ratio, breathing in for a count of 4 and out for 8. Everyone is different, and this should never be uncomfortable, so find what works for you.

## Stay present

Jon Kabat-Zinn[1] defines mindfulness as "the awareness that arises by paying attention on purpose, in the present moment, and non judgmentally." By learning to communicate in this manner consistently, you will be better equipped to take in new ideas and work effectively with other people.

**Best for**

This exercise brings you back into the body and can help stop your mind from running away into potential future conversation.

**Time**

Depends on the length of your meeting.

*Figure 15.2: Stay in the moment. (Photo credit: Martina Hodges-Schell.)*

**The exercise**

Mindful conversation is a technique developed by the legal community, but it can be useful in most situations. It involves three steps: *mindful listening, looping,* and *dipping.*

*Mindful listening* is as simple as it sounds. When someone else is speaking, give them your full attention. If you find your mind has wandered ahead to what you want to say next, or anything else at all, bring your attention back to the speaker. As much as possible, refrain from asking questions or leading the speaker – including through either verbal or facial communication. Give this time completely to the person speaking to allow them to express themselves fully and honestly.

*Looping* is short for "closing the loop of conversation." This step ensures that the listener has fully understood what the speaker has conveyed. All you need to do is repeat back what you believe the other person has said, and allow them to correct any misunderstandings. It's that easy.

*Dipping,* the third and final step in mindful conversation, helps you avoid getting distracted by internal thoughts and feelings. It's just an internal check-in with yourself to see how you are feeling or reacting to what is being said. By doing this preemptively, you can help to prevent your mind from wandering away while the other person is speaking.

## *Fake it till you become it*

Although not necessarily a relaxation technique, your nonverbal communication affects the way others perceive you and, more importantly, the way that you perceive yourself. The way you hold yourself, your postures, and your gestures, directly affect the way you communicate and participate in a group setting.

According to Amy Cuddy, a social psychologist at Harvard University, more-confident body posture has been directly linked to higher participation

*Figure 15.3: Fake it till you become it. (Photo credit: public domain.)*

rates in group environments. People holding confident body postures have higher testosterone levels and lower levels of the stress hormone cortisol. This combination makes you feel more confident, which enables you to participate more authentically. In other words, by changing the way you hold your body, you literally change your mind and therefore your behavior.

Confident postures take up space. The feet will be squarely on the floor, the shoulders back, and the arms wide open. The gestures will be direct and assertive. Conversely, a less-confident posture will take up as little space as possible, and often appear closed off and defensive. The arms and legs may be crossed, and the shoulders may be hunched over. This type of posture will trigger your body to decrease testosterone and increase cortisol – the exact opposite of what you want to happen!

**Best for**

Addressing your physical posture to influence your self-esteem.

**Time**

2 minutes

**The exercise**

Before a big meeting, find a space to yourself – the bathroom often works well. Take an assertive posture: shoulders back, shoulders in line over hips, both feet on ground. Raise your hands in victory position above your head. Think of a champion runner who has just crossed the finish line – that's pretty much what you're going for here.

During the meeting itself, remember to maintain your confident stance (maybe without the "victory" arms). If you find yourself slouching, pull your shoulders back and down. Over time, you will find that you don't need to think about this – you will naturally carry yourself more confidently, which, in turn, will help you communicate more effectively.

## Lifestyle

Although small changes in the moment can lead to great benefits, supportive changes in your lifestyle can make these benefits even more significant and long-lasting.

### *Eat for well-being*

The way you eat affects everything else you do. It can make you feel energized and increase mental facility, or it can make you feel sluggish and confused. There are a million different diets out there, and each person has different needs. There is no perfect diet that will work for everyone. There are, however, a few basic guidelines that can help keep your mind and body functioning more effectively.

**Best for**

Everyone, all the time.

*Figure 15.4: A better diet improves your well-being. (Photo credit: Martina Hodges-Schell.)*

**Get more of**

Fatty fish, such as salmon and sardines, are full of Omega 3, which helps to increase brain function as well as general well being.

Whole grains with a low glycemic index (GI) will give you slow-releasing energy to even out the peak-and-slump effect of consuming sugar.

Fruits and vegetables, blueberries in particular, help protect the brain from oxidative stress and may also help to prevent age-related conditions such as Alzheimer's and dementia. Broccoli and kale are also full of vitamins and nutrients to keep you healthy and focused.

Nuts and seeds are full of vitamin E, which helps protect against cognitive decline.

Water, water, and more water!

**Avoid**

Sugar, caffeine, and processed foods. The motivation is understandable: James used to survive afternoons at a busy agency in London by eating a bag of Gummi bears and drinking black coffee. What happens when you eat these types of food, though, is a shock to the system – it gets a hit of sugar and/or caffeine, followed by a crash... which leaves you craving more sugar and/or caffeine. These peaks and troughs are tough on your body, and they are not great for your work effectiveness, either!

## Meditation

Research has shown that as little as 12 minutes of mediation a day will start to restructure the neural pathways in your brain, helping you maintain focus and stay in the moment. By adding this to your daily routine, you will find that techniques such as "Stay present" and "Breathe" happen without you thinking about it.

*Figure 15.5: Find a quiet corner to meditate. (Photo credit: Martina Hodges-Schell.)*

**Best for**

Increasing your capacity to focus and stay present.

**Time**

12–60 minutes.

**The exercise**

Find a comfortable seated position. This can be sitting cross-legged on a cushion, or in a chair with your feet flat on the ground and your spine straight. Your posture should be comfortable, but alert.

Close your eyes and settle into your body.

Bring your attention to your breathing. Don't try to change it; just follow the inhale and the exhale. From time to time, you may find that your mind has wandered. Bring it back to your breath. The point of this exercise is not to rid your mind of all thoughts; it is to strengthen your ability to focus. Each time you guide your attention back to your breathing, you are doing just that.

It is more important to make this a regular part of your routine than to sit for a prolonged amount of time. Meditating for 12 minutes a day, every day, will have a bigger impact than meditating once a week for an hour.

## Yoga

Yoga means yoke or union. The purpose of yoga, according to its earliest practitioners, is the stilling of the mind. As with meditation, yoga helps the practitioner to remain calm, centered, and focused during their daily lives. Yoga is particularly powerful as it addresses both the mind and the body. By tying breath to movement, it becomes a moving meditation allowing you to calm your mind, while also stretching and strengthening your body.

*Figure 15.6: Yoga. (Photo credit: Ellen Arnold.)*

**Best for**

There are many different styles of yoga. A restorative class is relaxing and a wonderful antidote to a stressful day. A vinyasa class will be faster-paced, more energizing, and invigorating. It's a good idea to explore a number of different classes and styles to find what works for you.

**Time**

A typical yoga class will be between 60–90 minutes.

**The exercise**

It is very important to learn proper alignment of the yoga poses to avoid injury. We highly recommend that you find a teacher near you if you have minimal exposure to yoga.

Here are a few poses you can try to help calm the nervous system.

**Tree pose**

When you are calm, you have better balance. Conversely, practicing balance poses can also help increase calm and lower anxiety.

Stand with your feet the distance of the inner hip distance. Your hips should be directly over your ankles, and your shoulders in line with them both. Roll your shoulders down and back. Your arms should be by your side, with the palms facing forward.

Slowly shift your weight onto your left foot, lifting your right foot off the ground and placing the sole of your foot on either the calf or thigh of your left leg. Avoid placing it on the knee, as this could cause injury.

Inhale and raise your hands above your head, forming a V. If your shoulders have risen during this movement, bring them back down again, while extending out through your arms. To really test your balance, close your eyes. Breathe.

After 10 breaths, exhale and let your hands and foot down. Repeat on the other side.

### Seated forward fold

Forward folds help trigger the parasympathetic nervous system.

Sit on the ground with your legs straight out in front of you. Ensure that both of your sit bones (the parts of your pelvis that your buttocks cover) are firmly grounded into the floor.

Inhale and raise your arms above your head, and exhale to fold forward, over your legs. Allow your hands to rest where they fall – it doesn't matter if they reach your feet; you will feel the benefits of the pose regardless. Ensure that you still have a natural curve in your lower back, and that your upper back is not rounding. This may mean that you are nearly vertical, which is okay! You will still benefit from the pose.

### Child's pose

This is a calming and grounding posture, often used as a resting pose in a yoga sequence.

Kneel on the floor, with your toes touching and your knees as wide as your yoga mat. Sit back on your heels while reaching forward with your arms and resting your forehead on the ground. You may leave your arms stretched out in front of you on the ground, or bring them back alongside your body, reaching toward your feet. Try both to find what feels better for you.

## About the author

Our friend and former colleague Ellen Arnold contributed this chapter. She specializes in relaxation in the workplace and wants us all to be happier and healthier in the office. An integrative yoga instructor and graduate of the University of California, Berkeley, Ellen is based in San Francisco, CA.

## Additional resources

1. Forbes B. Yoga for Emotional Balance: Simple Practices to Help Relieve Anxiety and Depression. Boston: Shambhala Publications, Inc.; 2011.
2. Tan C-M. Search Inside Yourself: The Secret to Unbreakable Concentration, Complete Relaxation and Effortless Self-Control. Australia: HarperCollins; 2013.

## REFERENCE

1. Kabat-Zinn J. Full Catastrophe Living: Using the Wisdom of Your Body and Mind to Face Stress, Pain, and Illness. New York: Bantam Books; 1990, 2013.

# CHAPTER 16

## Group design techniques

To get you started with group design workshop formats, we have collected our most-used techniques for building better products and services with the whole team. There are hundreds of great workshop formats that could easily fill another book, so this is just a small selection of group design formats that we use most often in our day-to-day design practices.

Facilitating a group can be challenging and mentally exhausting. If you are new to facilitation, start small and find a partner who can support you – another member of your creative group can be a great backup or give you the ability to split the group into two for some tasks, so you can concentrate on a smaller number of people.

## How many people to invite?

With all group exercise formats, consider how many people you are inviting and make sure you have adequate space for them to participate.

As a rule of thumb, workshops get more challenging to facilitate as the number of attendees increases. The more voices in the room, the greater chance of one of those voices becoming dominating, vehemently disagreeing with another voice, refusing to engage with the process, or just using up the scheduled time in unfocused debate. When you're starting out with group facilitation, you may want to try to keep the numbers at fewer than ten people, only increasing the numbers when you're more comfortable with your skills.

When you're confident in your facilitation skills, you'll get the best results by inviting your whole project team, or at least key representatives from each area your team covers – development, product ownership, project management, design, etc. If you want fresh minds to contribute, consider opening the invite companywide, or ask your client to select a handful of people to add to the team. In larger organizations, limit the number of seats to fit your comfort level.

If you are breaking a larger group into teams, think about reconfiguring your space to make that grouping easier and explicit. For example, reserving a table per group encourages the attendees to self-organize naturally when the time comes to split the workshop up.

## How much time to budget?

Timebox all design activities quite aggressively – give them a fixed schedule and a fixed team size – and stick to your plan. Left uncontrolled, workshops have a tendency to degrade into circular discussions that suck up time and don't resolve the question. Aggressively timeboxing activities is a way of both retaining control and preventing ungrounded "what-if" scenarios from taking over. Make sure each activity is time-budgeted tightly enough that the participants won't feel they can afford to go off-course. As the workshop facilitator, it's your job to be the timekeeper.

If you are facilitating for a large crowd or leading a noisy format, consider using a fun way to signal that time is up. A whistle, a gong, or whatever cheesy old game show sound you can find on your smartphone is a great way of getting attention.

Signal when the group has 5 minutes and then 1 minute left. Assess the group to see if they are in the middle of a very productive flow, or if they have completed less than 50% of the task, and offer a few extra minutes if this is the case.

How much time you need to run the workshop depends somewhat on how large your group is. How long does it take them to share ideas? If you consider 2 minutes per person for idea sharing and another 3 to 5 minutes for questions or discussion, you can roughly estimate how long the feedback portion of your workshop will be. Remember that many of the formats we discuss work in an iterative fashion, so you need to budget time for idea sharing and questions for each iteration.

## How to facilitate a group

Be a great host!

Manage expectations in advance. Send invites with an explanation of what's going to happen and what's expected/not expected of each participant. Focus on brainstorming and idea generation. It's important to convey that people don't need artistic design skills to take part and that their ideas don't have to be perfect solutions.

Food is usually a great motivator. Provide refreshments.

## In the room

Take the lead by welcoming everyone to the session and outlining what you have planned for the session.

Set the ground rules for the session: All ideas are good ideas; sketching is not about artistic expression but illustrating your point. If doubts arise about "not being able to draw," consider this quick exercise: imagine that you want to explain what a cat is to someone who doesn't speak your language. Can you get your point across with pen and paper?

Set your timeboxes and be the timekeeper, or appoint someone in the room to call time for each part of the exercise.

Explain the context. Introduce your project and any useful information you have already gathered. Perhaps you already have personas, or a gnarly problem to solve. Keep this short and have visual reminders available, if possible (e.g., stick the personas on the wall). For larger groups, it's helpful to put the exercise objective up on a screen to remind everyone of what's asked of them.

If the participants haven't worked together before, break the ice with a quick warmup exercise. For example, ask everyone to go around the table and give their name, job title, and an unusual fact about themselves. Even if only one participant is new, this will help to make them feel they can contribute to the group.

Make sure you give everyone in the room a voice. You can make that inherent to the exercise (everyone gets to write, sketch, vote) or moderate the discussion by asking individuals who are quieter for their input.

If the conversation gets sidetracked, take a note of the issue, create a "parking lot" section on the wall and stash it there. Suggest taking this topic offline since it's detracting too much time away from the task and focus of the session: "That's a really great point, but with one eye on time, can we capture it and take it offline? Otherwise, it'll open up a rabbit-hole that will drag us way off course in this session."

Make sure there's an action point at the end of the session to address the parking lot with whoever is involved. You can also apply this technique when a difficult personality railroads the conversation. Acknowledge their point of view and ask to pick up on that topic outside the session. If the issue overtakes an idea generated in the session, remind everyone of the ground rules that all ideas are good ideas, and that we are not to judge in the idea-generation process.

## Try out new formats

If you are interested in exploring different design exercises, we recommend *Gamestorming* by Dave Gray, Sunni Brown, and James Macanufo[1] as a great starting point.

### *Elevator pitch*

An elevator pitch is a one-sentence statement that captures the unique value proposition of your product or service, designed to give a 30-second introduction to your goal for the product. The idea is to express the concept in the time it would take to talk about it during an elevator ride.

**Best for**

Focusing the proposition of a product/service.

**Participants**

The whole team can participate.

**Time**

45 minutes.

**Resources**

Ways to capture ideas in the room – whiteboard or easel pad.

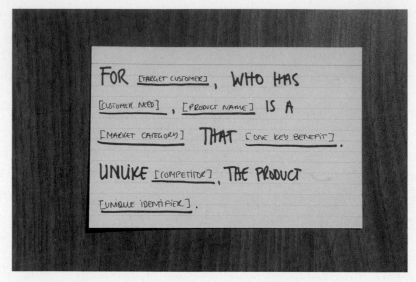

*Figure 16.1: How to construct an elevator pitch. (Photo credit: Martina Hodges–Schell.)*

A room to focus the group, with enough space for lively discussion.

A room with a door to close, to facilitate lively group discussion, and to keep the hustle and bustle of the workplace out to help the team focus.

An outline of an elevator pitch statement would be: "For [*target customer*], who has [*customer need*], [*product name*] is a [*market category*] that [*one key benefit*]. Unlike [*competition*], the product [*unique differentiator*]."

**The exercise**

Explain the elevator pitch concept. Make the outline of an elevator pitch available in the room (projected or on the wall). Go through each blank in the outline and have a group exploration of what words best describe the service. Expect to adjust these several times before the group feels that you've created the right statement together.

**Outcome**

This is your guiding principle throughout design and evaluation of the product or service.

## Business Model Canvas

The Business Model Canvas was developed by Alex Osterwalder[2] to help businesses and startups create better business structures. It structures nine core elements of a business model and their interrelationships on a worksheet. Visualizing how your product creates value for the business and users is a great tool to bring everyone together around a shared view of how you will deliver this value.

**Best for**

Exposing all core elements that deliver a great experience and highlight the relationship between core business and UX elements; this can be an eye-opener for designers and other stakeholders alike. Also best for facilitating a conversation about what is needed to deliver a great experience.

**Participants**

A mix of business, technology, and design people.

*Figure 16.2: Business Model Canvas, ©Alex Osterwalder.[2] (Photo credit: Martina Hodges-Schell.)*

**Time**

90 minutes.

**Resources**

Large printout or sketch on whiteboard of Business Model Canvas

Whiteboard markers

Sticky notes

**The exercise**

Introduce the team to the Business Model Canvas. Walk through each section and explain what information is captured in each.

- Customer segments
- Value proposition
- Channels
- Customer relationship
- Revenue streams
- Key resources
- Key activities
- Key partnerships
- Cost structure

Have the team fill out and together prioritize each section. Does the sum of all parts make sense to the business, to the users? Are we creating value for the business and for users? Does it align with our vision? Where are the blank spots? What hasn't been considered yet?

**Outcomes**

A set of key assumptions to be investigated or tested.

A set of key areas that hadn't been considered yet in delivering this service.

## Design the Box

Sometimes it's hard to make a decision. Designing a notional box for your product to ship in can help focus the team's minds on which direction is the right one.

You can either take all boxes created by individual teams for inspiration, or use this exercise to create consensus and create one version of the box together after each team has explored its version.

**Best for**

Focusing the team on what's important.

**Participants**

At least three or four people.

**Time**

45 minutes.

*Figure 16.3: Creating a box for your product. How will it stand out on the shelf? (Photo credit: Martina Hodges-Schell.)*

**Resources**

Actual plain packaging boxes (These can be bought cheaply in office-supply stores and are the best option. You can use plain paper, or even Sticky notes on old cereal boxes, but it's harder to make your participants recognize the constraints of a real-world package when you use these.)

Marker pens in several different colors

An ice-breaker (This classic YouTube video from 2006 muses about how Microsoft would redesign the iPod packaging and is great for giving everyone a quick intro to packaging design, as well as demonstrating what this exercise is trying to avoid!: http://bit.ly/1f5HHBQ [accessed 18.12.14].)

**The exercise**

Split the group into small teams and give each the task of designing the physical packaging of the product/service you are creating. What is the key message that would make a customer buy this thing? What else would help them make a decision? What reassurance should you give them?

Give each team 15 minutes to create their box. Give each team 3 minutes for to share their creation. If the results are very different, an optional last step is to create one box with everyone's input that brings together priorities.

**Outcome**

A clearer picture of priorities and a core focus for the product you are designing.

## Role-playing a service

### Best for

Whether you are designing a simple user interface or a more complex service proposition – before you start putting pen to paper it can be very insightful to play out the interaction a user may have with this interface or service. You are given the opportunity to explore the natural flow of the conversation between the user and your service, or even evaluate different contextual devices and inputs.

*Figure 16.4: Role play how users experience your service. (Photo credit: James O'Brien.)*

Exploring what an experience should or could be like for users, instilling the team with a human-centered point of view, especially when there are a lot of system-centric thinkers driving decisions.

### Participants

The more, the merrier.

### Time

1 hour.

### Resources

A camera phone available to video the role-play, if possible. Otherwise, document whatever ideas you generate.

### The exercise

Group the participants in pairs or as many actors as the system may have. One person in each or as many actors as the system may have takes the role of a user, while the other takes the role of the system itself – for example, the login flow. The pair acts out how a user experiences an interaction with the system. This can be open or closed. In open role-play, the person acting out the system has freedom in how they respond, allowing the interactions to evolve. This is good early on in system design.

In closed role-play, the person acting out the system can only respond with the messages that already exist in the user's view (e.g., error messages from the form). This is useful for identifying possible usability traps.

**Outcome**

Ideas captured to be explored further.

## Map the experience

**Best for**

Experience mapping is a great exercise for getting an overview of all steps in a user's life cycle with your service, across all touch points. It can help you explore current pain points and future improvements for the whole service from your customers' perspective.

Creating a picture of all the touchpoints in a user's experience of your service. Great for a collective view of what's going on right now, and also to map the future experience you want your users to have.

**Participants**

Three to twelve; can get unwieldy with more than twelve participants.

**Time**

90 minutes.

**Resources**

Brown craft paper by the roll

Plenty of Sticky notes

Marker pens

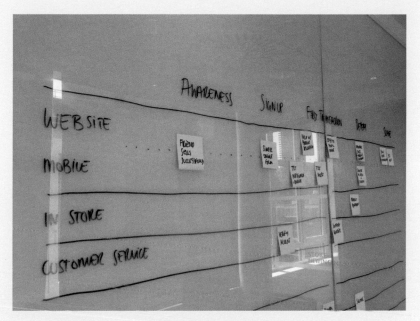

*Figure 16.5: Mapping the experience across customer journey and service touchpoints. (Photo credit: Martina Hodges-Schell.)*

**The exercise**

Divide the paper scroll on the wall into user life-cycle steps along the x axis and different channels on the y axis. Get the team to help you gather the complete picture.

- If the goal is to understand what is happening in the whole ecosystem today, get everyone to map out touchpoints onto Sticky notes and add them to the map.

- If the goal is to ideate a new experience, get the team to map the ideal experience across touchpoints. Encourage them to consider the experience from their users' views, not current business or technology constraints.

**Outcome**

A high level overview for how your customers experience your service. Prioritize high-risk or high-value workflows in the overall system to explore more deeply.

## Storyboard scenarios

### Best for

Storyboards are a visual technique borrowed from film making to explore a narrative for a user scenario. It illustrates the user context and why, where, and how they might interact with a service. Storyboarding helps us indicate what a person might do, and how we can help, to fulfill their goals.

Illustrating how your product fits into the goals your audience is trying to achieve.

Creating a shared understanding of user-centric workflows that can be derived from these scenarios.

Building a design through user journeys, rather than page-by-page.

### Participants

Equally effective with small or larger groups. Divide large groups into smaller teams of three to five.

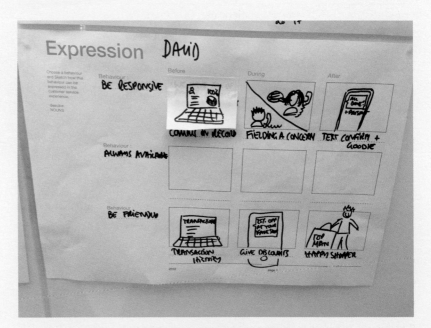

*Figure 16.6: Creating a storyboard for user scenarios. (Photo credit: Martina Hodges-Schell.)*

**Time**

30 minutes (multiply for larger number of scenarios).

**Resources**

Printed-out storyboard templates

Marker pens

Dots for voting (small, round stickers are best, but you can use marker pen dots in a pinch)

Space and means to stick idea sheets up on the wall

Printout or sketch of persona(s)

**The exercise**

Introduce your personas to the group. Highlight challenges and goals. Ask each team to pick a scenario to work through. Give them marker pens and a stack of storyboard templates to sketch out how users achieve their goals and how the idea fits into their lifestyles.

Leave time for each group to share its storyboard. Vote on ideas to take forward and explore further.

**Outcome**

A great starting point for designing out each step in a workflow instead of designing a system page by page.

Instant testable prototype by addressing a whole user journey.

## Design studio

**Best for**

Design studio is a collaborative ideation workshop format devised to explore design challenges and generate many ideas in a short space of time. Small teams sketch, present, critique, and refine their ideas in quick iterations.

Generating lots of ideas. Giving the whole team (and/or users) a voice in the design process. Getting noncreative stakeholders to empathize with design challenges.

*Figure 16.7: Generating ideas in a design studio workshop. (Photo credit: James O'Brien.)*

**Participants**

Minimum of three to four people; if more than six, divide them into groups. Invite your whole team. Also good with groups of users.

**Time**

90 minutes. Add more time for larger groups.

**Resources**

Several 6-up sketch templates per participant

Several 1-up sketch templates per participant

Marker pens

Dots for voting (small round stickers are best, but marker pen dots will do in a pinch)

Space and means to stick up idea sheets on the wall

Printout or sketch of persona(s)

**The exercise**

**Declare goals**

Set the scene with the topic of exploration (this could be a new platform, service, product, or feature). Introduce who this is for (your personas) and what themes you may have already identified (i.e., new search, new workflow).

Alternatively, if you want to capture topics for exploration, ask the group to provide topics (e.g., "We are kicking off an evolution of product X. We'd like to hear from you what your most important issues are.")

**6-up sketching**

Start by getting everyone to pick a theme to work through. Ask them to quickly come up with six ways to solve this problem. You can repeat this exercise with a second or third topic to generate lots of ideas. A strict timebox helps creativity at this stage by forcing participants not to focus too closely on irrelevant details.

Get everyone to quickly introduce their ideas and identify a particularly promising one.

**1-up sketching**

Take that promising idea and make a single-page sketch of it. This sketch can go into more detail to think through the idea some more.

Again, share with the group and put up all ideas on the wall.

**Dot Voting**

Get the group to dot-vote to identify which ideas to explore further.

**Outcome**

A set of ideas to inspire your design process and test out promising ideas with users quickly to validate these early assumptions.

## Moodboarding for personas

Having trouble with the user-centered point of view in your team? Create moodboards of the service for each persona; that is, through their eyes, not the team members' standpoint.

**Best for**

Helping the team adopt a user-centered point of view.

**Participants**

Up to twelve. You need quite a bit of space for each participant to create a moodboard.

**Time**

60–90 minutes.

*Figure 16.8: See the world through your personas' eyes with mood boards. (Photo credit: Martina Hodges-Schell.)*

**Resources**

Large sheets of card or easel pads (participants will create a poster sized mood board for each persona)

Scissors

A broad range of magazines to clip images from

Glue

Printouts of your persona(s)

**The exercise**

Bring your personas to the session and introduce them to the group. Get everyone to pick one persona to work with, or alternatively create a group per persona.

Ask the team to make a moodboard that reflects the persona. Next, ask them to also make a moodboard for what the persona expects from your product or service.

Get everyone together in the last 15 minutes of the session to share their creations and feedback.

**Outcome**

Posters you can display in your team work space to remind the team of the users' expectations.

## Hypotheses testing

**Best for**

Lean startup has taught us to validate our assumptions with users. Our ideas are hypotheses, and to test them means to design experiments that will give us a clear answer as to whether our ideas facilitate the desired user outcome we expected.

Testing ideas. Finding quick and easy ways to evaluate assumptions.

*Figure 16.9: Creating quick prototypes to test your assumptions. (Photo credit: Martina Hodges–Schell.)*

**Participants**

Any group size will work. Divide groups of six or more into teams.

**Time**

Depending on number of ideas, about two hours. This is a hands-on design session, so give it some space.

**Resources**

White wall

Paper

Marker pens

Sticky notes

Optionally, a computer for lo-fi prototyping[3]

**The exercise**

Get each team to come up with ideas for how to test one of the assumptions you have about your product right now.

Ask the group to consider: What's our riskiest assumption? How can we test it with least time and resources? Where do we find participants?

Get the group to be creative. Encourage them to think smaller, with tools that are already available. Do we need to build anything at all?

Happy hacking.

**Outcome**

A set of agreed-upon hypotheses that can be tested with real users to inform product development, iteration, or a pivot.

## Retrospectives

A retrospective is a team meeting that looks back at recent project events and, without blame, tries to discover what lessons can be learned, actions that can be taken, and what worked well to improve the team work for the next iteration.

We recommend that you schedule retrospectives into your workflow in weekly (or once-per-sprint) cycles. Some teams schedule retrospectives only at the end of a project, but, in our experience, these typically take longer or can only focus on fewer points, and learnings can only be applied to the next project.

Rinse and repeat regularly! Retrospectives help you and your team make your working environment even greater. The name might suggest post-project analysis, but is much more effective to be built in on a weekly basis. The issues that arise are easier to tackle and the team has a regular outlet for praise.

*Figure 16.10: Reviewing the good, meh, and ugly. (Photo credit: Martina Hodges-Schell.)*

### Best for

Reviewing the working process and outcome; a feedback session on how the project is going and how everyone is doing, what is working well, and what needs addressing.

### Participants

Everyone who has worked on the project. It is important not to exclude anyone, or allow anyone to exclude themselves – if someone is too busy to attend a retrospective, there's a problem that the retrospective should be dealing with.

### Time

An hour, more or less (if you run retrospectives regularly throughout the project, they take less time and negative sentiments don't have time to build up).

### Resources

Sticky notes for everyone

Marker pens

(Categories on the wall)

**The exercise**

Begin by encouraging everyone to interact positively in the retrospective. Have everyone repeat the Retrospective Prime Directive out loud:

"Regardless of what we discover, we understand and truly believe that everyone did the best job they could, given what they knew at the time, their skills and abilities, the resources available, and the situation at hand."

Saying it out loud really does make a difference – it shifts the tone of the retrospective away from the potential of blame and recrimination to discovery and learning.

Have 10 minutes for everyone to note down their 'great,' 'meh,' and 'not so great' points on a sticky note each.

Get them all on the wall, in categories.

Have a facilitator pick off a point from each category in turn and discuss with the group. (You can use dot voting to prioritise)

Note down any action points that arise, and find an owner for each who will commit to moving them forward for the next retrospective.

**Outcomes**

Action points on key issues that are slowing the team down (These should be checked-in on at the next retrospective, or addressed with the setup of the next project.)

## How to prioritize

It's important to get the group to prioritize ideas generated so you focus maximum energy on the ones with the best likelihood of success. Working through structured processes also helps keep the decision making more objective.

*Figure 16.11: Quick and effective prioritization with dot voting. (Photo credit: Martina Hodges-Schell.)*

## Dot voting

Dot voting is a simple and effective way for small and large groups to cast their votes. Put each item for discussion on an individual Sticky note. Give each participant three votes in the form of small round stickers (dots) and have everyone stick their dots on their preferred item.

Participants can either use one dot per idea they like, or identify the riskiest assumption to call out, or they can use multiples per idea. There is no rule against voting for your own ideas.

If ideas are laid out on the table and not on the wall, individually wrapped chocolates are a fun and efficient way to dot-vote (but take a photo of the table, because the "votes" will disappear at the end of the meeting). If small, round stickers are hard to come by in your organization, marker pen dots will do the job, too.

## Prioritization matrix

You also can get the group to organize ideas on a two-by-two grid. The axes can be specified to reflect your goals, such as how relevant to users and how easy to make. This would result in sectors with *Easy & High User Value, Hard & High User Value, Easy & Low User Value,* and *Hard & Low User Value.*

Expressing priorities in this way helps the business understand more of the implications of the features they are choosing and focus on the most valuable ideas. Pet projects of the person with the loudest voice or the biggest paycheck can be tested and included in the priorities on merit.

## Additional resource

1. Sherwin D. Creative Workshop: 80 Challenges to Sharpen your Design Skills. Cincinnati, OH: HOW Books, F&W Media; 2010.

### REFERENCES

1. Gray D, Brown S, Macanufo J. Gamestorming: A Playbook for Innovators, Rulebreakers, and Changemakers. Sebastopol, CA: O'Reilly Media; 2010.
2. Osterwalder A, Pigneur Y. Business Model Generation: A Handbook for Visionaries, Game Changers, and Challengers. Hoboken, NJ: John Wiley & Sons; 2010.
3. Warfel, TZ. Prototyping: A Practitioner's Guide. Brooklyn: Rosenfeld Media; 2009.

# CONCLUSION

We hope this book has given you the tools to make yourself happier, more productive, and more creative in your work. Researching and writing about anti-patterns has certainly changed the way we look at our own working relationships – we find that using this approach has helped us to encourage our teams to gel and to defuse moments of tension with our colleagues.

## We want to hear from you

We think there is much more to be discovered about behavioral anti-patterns in the workplace. There are more anti-patterns and patterns than we have had space to explore in this book. Our hope is that we will inspire other creative professionals to explore this space. Finding better working patterns is, in our opinion, the key to putting great design into the world more often.

We've created a website to explore and share patterns and anti-patterns. We'd love to hear about your experiences and discoveries with them:

http://www.communicatingtheuxvision.com/

You also can reach us on Twitter at @13antipatterns or use the #13antipatterns hashtag.

## Play the game

To help explain and explore some of the concepts from this book, we've created a fun card game that follows the product design process. We've played this game at conferences and workshops we've hosted and we find it works best with four to six players.

You can download the cards and the rules from http://www.communicating theuxvision.com/. Enjoy!

*Card span. (Photo credit: Chris Rain.)*

## Go and put great design into the world

User experience is the craft of creating happiness. So much of how we feel about our work comes from our relationships with the people we work with. If you use what you've learned from this book to make your users and your colleagues happy, then at the same time, you'll be making yourself happier. The happier you are, the more great work you'll be able to achieve. We can't wait to see what you create.

# GLOSSARY

| Term | Chapter | Definition |
|------|---------|------------|
| $5 word effect | 1 | When people pay more attention to impressive-sounding jargon than its natural-language equivalent |
| **A** | | |
| Active confirmation | 4 | Repeating back what you've heard to clarify or confirm that you understood correctly |
| Active listening | 12 | Nonverbal signs of attention given to a speaker to demonstrate engagement |
| Agency | 1 | A company that provides services to other organizations (e.g., research and design services. See also Consultancy) |
| Agile | 1 | A software development philosophy that promotes self-organizing, cross-functional teams, and working code over documentation combined with continuous improvement and a flexible and rapid response to change |
| Anti-pattern | 1 | A habit or process that seems as if it should achieve a desired outcome, but actually achieves the opposite |
| Architectural patterns | 5 | Common, repeatable solutions to requirements that often or always appear when designing a building |
| **B** | | |
| Balanced team | 5 and 13 | A collaborative, cross-disciplinary team of practitioners that brings together a complete product team skillset |
| Behavior-driven design (BDD) | 7 | A way of specifying software features based on the need they serve and the outcome they provide |
| Brand | 13 | The name and (visual) identity of a company that distinguishes it from other products |
| Business: | | |
| -Business analysis | 1 | Identifies business needs through research and aims to find solutions to business challenges and opportunities |
| -Business dialect | 1 | The discipline - and often organization-specific - vocabulary developed to communicate more efficiently around specialist topics |
| -Business Model Canvas | | A tool first developed by Alex Osterwalder to explore business models beyond writing a business plan |
| -Business theater | 12 | The selective amplification of chosen interpersonal interactions to convey goodwill, shared purpose, and a desire to make the whole team look good |
| -Business value | 1 and 12 | The financial or other benefit that the business gains from the successful implementation of a feature |
| Buzz in the room | 5 | The low-level conversations that occur in an open-plan office space as a natural part of collaborative software development |

*(Continued)*

| Term | Chapter | Definition |
|---|---|---|
| Buzzword Bingo | 6 | A sarcastic game in which players monitor a meeting or presentation for jargon or popular buzzwords |
| C | | |
| Canonical source of why | 3 | The person on a product team who can explain the reason for all the decisions that have been made to date |
| Casting feedback | 4 | Understanding the meaning behind feedback on solutions and rewording it as something actionable |
| Code: | | |
| –Code literacy | 8 | An elementary understanding of and ability to read software code |
| –Code quality | 7 | A measure of the ease with which the code of a product can accommodate change |
| Collaboration | 12 | Teamwork, commonly across disciplines and organizations, toward a common goal |
| Cognitive fatigue | 1 and 11 | Diminished ability or willingness to mentally process new impressions due to stimulus overload |
| Conscious internalization | 3 | Actively listening and taking note to remember important information |
| Consultancy | 1 | A company that specializes in embedding itself into a client organization to assist them with process change and value creation (e.g., product development) |
| Context | 4 | |
| –Design context | 4 | The surrounding influences that affect a design |
| –Context imbalance | 4 | The difference in understanding between someone who works with a design continuously and someone who only sees it intermittently at reviews |
| Continuous availability | 5 | To actively encourage others in the team to seek your input at all times |
| Cost of argument | 1 | The detrimental effect, in time and colleague goodwill, of a disagreement that stems from a clash of business dialects |
| Customers | | |
| –Customer experience | 13 | The summary of all interactions a customer has with a company or product |
| –Customer lifecycle | 4 | The cyclical engagement life cycle a customer follows with a product or company, from initially becoming aware of a product while in search of fulfilling a need, through post-engagement |
| D | | |
| Deliverables | 1 and 7 | Assets created by a UXer in the course of the product design process |
| Design: | 1 | The process of solving problems |
| –Co-design | 8 | Two or more people working together to create a solution |
| –Designer | 1 | Person who solves a problem by defining a product |
| –Design studio | 8 | A design-led ideation workshop that encourages the input of all team members, not just designers |

| Term | Chapter | Definition |
|------|---------|------------|
| Development/ Developer | 1 | Person who implements design in code |
| Downstream | 7 | Processes that take place after the subject process |
| **E** | | |
| Experience principles | 4 | A set of guidelines that define the behaviors of the product at a high level |
| Experience landscape | 6 | The context in which a user is experiencing your product; may include topical competitors and other digital experiences that inform a user's expectations |
| **F** | | |
| Fail early, fail often | 1 | A risk-management strategy that states it is better to fail while the money and time invested in the experiment are low |
| Feature creep | 10 | The natural tendency during development for members of the team to suggest new ideas for inclusion; if not managed carefully, results in uncontained upward expansion of the scope |
| Fidelity | 8 | The amount of effort expended on a deliverable |
| Five Whys | 13 | A method for seeking the root cause of something, developed by Toyota |
| Functional grammar | 10 | In the context of software development, a set of agreed-upon terms that specify groups of features |
| **G** | | |
| Game face | 3 | A facial expression that says you are taking the current situation with the utmost seriousness |
| **I** | | |
| The IKEA effect | 12 | A psychological reaction in which people tend to ascribe more value to things they have created themselves |
| Implementation | 7 | The phase of the product development process that executes on ideas and produces a shippable product |
| Information architecture | 1 | The structure of content across a product to help customers navigate and easily find what they are looking for |
| Interaction design | 1 | The design discipline that focuses on how interactions between users and a product work |
| Iteration | 1 and 14 | The process of refining a solution by repeatedly refining, testing, and adjusting according to feedback |
| **K** | | |
| Kanban board | 10 | A self-organizing workflow tool that offers categories for "needs to be done," "doing," "to be reviewed," and "done"; team participants move jobs they are working on into appropriate categories to visualize what work is being done |
| Key Performance Indicators (KPIs) | 2 | Values and metrics measured by a company to assess how effectively they are achieving important business goals |

*(Continued)*

| Term | Chapter | Definition |
|---|---|---|
| **L** | | |
| Lean | 1 | A production philosophy originated by Toyota that focuses on creating value for their customers by reducing waste (any use of resources not directly related to creating customer value) |
| Lean startup | 5 | A method for developing successful businesses and products based on validating assumptions with customer feedback and iterative enhancement |
| Lorem ipsum | 8 | Filler text, created from a reordered Latin manuscript, often used to simulate copy when the actual words are not yet known |
| **M** | | |
| Maps: | | |
| –Affinity mapping | 1 | Sorting into thematic groups |
| –Empathy map | 1 and 4 | A tool to create empathy for customers that maps what they see, think, say/do, and hear; also captures their pain points and gains |
| –Experience Map | 4 | Similar to a service blueprint; captures the user journey across touchpoints to achieve a set of user goals |
| –Story map | 4 | Structuring of a product's features into thematic user stories and mapped across a number of product development phases |
| –Site map | 4 | Visualisation of the information architecture of a product to show what information can be found where |
| Meetings: | | |
| Kickoff meeting | 1 | At the start of the product development process, the meeting that defines the problem and the approach the organization will take |
| Meeting before the meeting | 1 | The time when attendees are assembling for a meeting but the meeting has not formally begun |
| Meeting after the meeting | 1 | The time when a meeting has formally finished but the attendees still have contact as they disperse |
| Mental Model | 10 | The perceived explanation a user has created to rationalize how something works |
| Minimum viable product (MVP) | 10 | An experiment to discover whether product-market fit exists |
| Mockup | 1 | A guess at how the end product will look, usually created in Photoshop (or similar visual design software) |
| **N** | | |
| Navigation | 1 | The mechanism by which users find their way around a website |
| **P** | | |
| Pairing | 4 | Two people with similar or disjointed skill sets, working at the same desk at the same time on the same thing |
| *Pan narrans* | 4 | The storytelling chimp; a more accurate classification for humans than *Homo sapiens* |
| Paraphrased playback | 11 | Repeating something back, but rewording it to make your interpretation clear |

| Term | Chapter | Definition |
|---|---|---|
| Pattern | 1 | A repeatable solution to a common problem; for example, username and password as a solution for the problem of secure access to a service |
| Personas | 1 | An archetype of a segment of users, to clearly define who the product is aimed at, designed to communicate research insight to the wider team; a user-centered communication and decision-making tool with the team. |
| Planners and Doers | 7 | Two types of team members whose styles of action can cause conflict |
| Polite fiction | 12 | A not-quite-truth that a social group adopts to save the standing of one or more members |
| Prototype | 6 | An quick and simplified experimental strawman for a product to test ideas and validate assumptions ahead of production |
| Q | | |
| Qualitative user research | 8 | Research designed to better understand user behavior, the underlying reason and the context |
| R | | |
| Reflective listening | 11 | Listening to someone in such a way that they know they are being paid attention to |
| Respondent fatigue | 11 | A psychological effect in which people get bored with answering questions and become sullen |
| Retrospective | 16 | A meeting that looks back at recent events and, without blame, tries to discover what lessons can be learned to make better progress in future |
| Retrospective prime directive | 3 | Acceptance that, regardless of what we discover, we understand and truly believe that everyone did the best job they could, given what they knew at the time, their skills and abilities, the resources available, and the situation at hand |
| Return on investment (ROI) | 1 | A ratio of the profit that the business will receive based on the outlay it will spend to get there - for example, if I spend $1 on advertising but make $4 profit from resulting sales, my ROI is 4:1 |
| Roadmap | 10 | A document that lists the future development aims of the product and the timescale in which each of those aims will be fulfilled |
| Ron Jeffries's "3 Cs" | 7 | Card, Conversation, Confirmation - requirements written in the form of user stories on cards; a reminder of the conversation the team had about the requirement; confirmation essential to check that the requirement was met successfully |
| S | | |
| Sakichi Toyoda | 13 | Japanese inventor, industrialist, and the founder of Toyota Industries Co., Ltd. |
| Service blueprint | 6 | An artifact that maps customer goals to touchpoint interactions and supporting services across the customer life cycle |
| Service design | 0 | The practice of creating holistic customer experiences across a broad range of touchpoints, from physical to digital, with a range of personnel and processes |

*(Continued)*

| Term | Chapter | Definition |
|------|---------|------------|
| Silos | 7 | The vertical segmentation in larger organizations that often make collaboration and communication difficult |
| Solutionizing | 4 | Presenting feedback in a form that suggests a replacement feature, rather than addressing the business need that is not being addressed |
| Sore thumb paradox | 3 | Situation in which a stakeholder can be easily appeased by making the solution to their need stand out like a sore thumb, at the expense of the user's experience |
| Specialized dialect | 1 | The specialized vocabulary adopted by different disciplines or businesses to communicate more effectively |
| Sunk Cost Fallacy | 12 | The irrational bias toward putting more money/effort into something that has already been paid for, although it doesn't yield the right results |
| Stakeholders | 1 | Any participant or contributor to a project |
| Stakeholder safari | 1 | Informal contextual research to understand your stakeholders and their goals and needs better |
| Statement of work | 6 | A formal document by which a company and client agree what work needs to be done, in what time frame and at what cost |
| Strapline | 13 | A short sentence that accompanies a logo |
| Sustainable pace | 10 | A work pace and working hours that can be maintained over long periods of time |
| T | | |
| Technical debt | 7 and 10 | A quick and dirty solution used by the development team to get a feature released, that will degrade future development if left in place |
| Toyota | 13 | Japanese car manufacturer who pioneered Lean manufacturing; source of inspiration of Lean startup software development |
| U | | |
| Universal translator | 1 | A device from "Star Trek" that can translate any language into any other language |
| Upstream | 7 | Any process that happens before the subject process |
| Usability | 0 | The ease of use and learnability of a product or service |
| Usability testing | 8 | Testing the usability of a design concept or live digital product to see if people understand it and are able to complete their goals with ease; a form of research usually run in a series of one-on-one qualitative research session with an individual from the (desired) target audience |
| Users: | | People using a product or service |
| –User champion | 13 | The person in an organization who draws attention to user needs and goals and advocates user centric product design |
| –User interface design | 0 | See design |
| –User journeys | 1 | An illustration of the steps a user takes to complete a task |
| –UX life cycle | 7 | See Experience life cycle |

| Term | Chapter | Definition |
|---|---|---|
| -User research | 8 | Research conducted with (intended) users of a product to inform and validate product development, often in one-on-one interviews |
| -User stories | 7 | A software build request broken down into a small chunk and presented from the view of the user of the software with clear indication what the user should be able to accomplish: "As the team manager, I want to be able to approve vacation requests" |
| **UX:** | | |
| -User experience | 0 | The emerging field of digital product and service design that brings together user needs with business goals and technical feasibility to create valuable and useful digital interactions |
| -UX camp | 6 | A UX-specific "unconference" format modeled after the popular BarCamp events where all participants are encouraged to present their ideas in a peer-to-peer forum |
| -UX debt | 10 | A quick and dirty solution to a user need that, if left in place, will degrade the experience in future |
| -UXer | 0 | An umbrella term for any practitioner working on creating great user experiences; can include designers, researchers, architects, content strategists, and any number of job titles that have blossomed in the field of making great digital products and services for people |
| -UX strategy | 1 | The strategic framework that outlines the user experience goals for a product; summarizes insights and goals gleamed from formative research to inform user needs, business goals, and the competitive landscape to create a unique value proposition and decision-making framework |
| -UX value | 13 | The value created through user experience |
| -Agile UX | 5 | User experience design within an Agile environment |
| -Lean UX | 5 | User experience design within a Lean Startup environment |
| V | | |
| Value proposition | 7 | The promise of benefit that a product makes to a user |
| Velocity | 10 | The number of story points a development team can deliver in an Agile development sprint |
| W | | |
| Wireframe | 1 | A visual representation of the information architecture and interaction design of a page or feature |

# INDEX

## A

Acceptance criteria, 41, 127
Active agreement, 44–45
Active listening technique, 211
Adobe Photoshop, 197
Agency model, 151
Aggressively timeboxing activities, 287
Agile, 79
    cyclical iterative process of, 81
    definition of, 79
    project management processes, 80
    projects, 79, 187
    software development, 80
Agreement, 13
    active, 44–45
    ambiguous term of, 6
    gain, 231
        positive, 48
Anti-patterns, identification and fixation, 260
    cool-down, 264
    find common factor, 265
    flow, 263
    forgive yourself, 265
    identify patterns, 265
    keep going, 266
    make it a habit, 266
    outside perspective, 264
    tip-off, 262–263
Argument, cost of, 8, 17
Atlantic magazine, 78

## B

Baeck, Aline, 36, 160
Balanced product team, 242
BDD. *See* Behavior-driven design (BDD)
Behavior-driven design (BDD), 125
Berger, Jonathan, 200
Bikeshedding, 27
Bonding effect, 8
Box, designing of, 176, 293, 294
    best for, 293
    exercise, 294
    outcome, 294
    participants, 293
    resources, 294
    time, 293

Brainstorming sessions, 176, 242
"Bread-and-butter" business, 8
Breakout spaces, 147
Breathing, 271, 272
    best for, 271, 273
    exercise, 272
    stay present, 273
    time, 272, 273
Brown bag sessions, 242
Bucket system, 190
    baseline, 189
    facilitator of, 190
    optimistic buckets, 189
    thinking out loud, 190
    vision, 189
Budding digital entrepreneurs, generation
        of, 194
Business
    creative aspects of, 14
    dialects, 4, 7, 8, 12, 24
    value, 5
        types of, 247
Business model canvas, 291–292
    best for, 291
    exercise, 292
    outcomes, 292
    participants, 291
    resources, 292
    time, 292
Business Theater, 225–227
Buzzword bingo, 101–102
    swear jar, 111

## C

Card span, 311
Caveat, 206
Cereal boxes, 294
Circular conversations, 5
Code quality, 122–124
    outcomes of, 123
Co-design
    sessions, 154
    workshops, 155
Coffee break, 214
Cognitive costs, 77
Cognitive fatigue, 7

Collaboration, 174
  drawbacks of, 240
  technologies, 131
Collaborative design session, 145
Collaborative development models, 86
Collaborative session, 256
Collaborative sketching, 128
Common factor, finding of, 265
Communicate core concepts, 8
Communication, 9, 122, 124, 135
  aspect of, 204
  disruption in, 262
  efficiency in, 4
  efficient, 9
  forms of, 85
  high-bandwidth method of, 17
  in human, 223
  rules for, 217
  styles of, 207
Complex verbal concept, 9
Confident postures, 275
Conflicting sets of requirements, 48
Consistent design language, 98, 104–105
  anti-pattern, 109
  Buzzword bingo, 101–102
    swear jar, 111
  case study, 112–114
  filename elements, 107
  label police, 111
  liked it, or label on it, 105–106
  make a toolkit, 111
  note on labeling files, 106–107
  own the process, 111
  patterns, 110
    mindful of your language, 110
  playback, 111
  present in context, 110–111
  put label on it, 110
  step too far, 108–109
Consultancy-type organization, 5
Contact gap, 55
Context imbalance, 55
Contextualization
  anti-pattern, 64
    breaking of, 65
    infliction of, 68
  case study, 70–72
  common assets for providing, 55–61
  example agenda, 69
    feature-by-feature feedback, 69
    session
      goals for, 69
      structure of, 69
    strategy check, 69
    wrap, 69

good feedback, 63–64
  patterns, 65–68
    actively confirm understanding, 67
    be present to present, 66
    casting feedback, 66–67
    half-silvered mirror, 68
    prepare for presentation, 65
    set scope expectations, 67
  presenting without, 52
  story of UX, 61–62
Conversational spaces, 14
Conversations, 142, 193, 266
Cooperation, 251
Creative space, 147
Cross-functional team, 161
Cultural context permitting, 46
Customer-based key performance indicators
      (KPIs), net promoter score (NPS), 34
Customer life cycle, 59

D

Dead Poets Society, 153
Decision-making, 262
  matrix, 249
Defending
  anti-pattern, 251
  case study, 254–256
  defend user research, 249–250
  everyone's critic, 240–241
  explaining UX, 241–243
  not hard enough, 238
  patterns, 251
    arrive via MoSCoW, 251
    beginning, middle, and end, 252
    letting the client/stakeholder
        fail, 251–253
    snap the elastic user, 252
  remedy wrongly given-up point, 253
  right decision, 243–245
  tips, 253–254
  understand business value, 245–249
    closing the whys, 247–249
    framing of, 245–246
    whys persuasively, 246–247
Defending, too hard, 220
  anti-pattern, 225
  business theater, 225–227
  case study, 232–234
  hidden cost, 225
  objection, 230–231
  patterns, 227–230
    choosing your battles

concede gracefully, 229
don't get attached, 228
embrace and extend, 230
get them to expand, 230
get to the why, 229
let silence speak, 228
tactical retreat, 229
tips, 231–232
type of client, spotting, 223–224
Deliverables, 186
anti-pattern, 153
best-in-show, 140–142
business, getting out of, 148–149
collaborate, 145–146
make space for, 146–147
collect user feedback, 151–152
conversations, not lectures, 142–146
beware the IKEA effect, 143–145
documenting digital experiences,
increasing difficulty of, 143
leaner, meaner... UX, 148
living in, 138
pattern, 153–158
dead poet society pattern, 153
embrace creativity of everyone,
154–155
fast feedback, 156
push the changes upward, 158
spring clean, 156
toolbox bonanza, 157
prototyping, 149–150
types of, 142
work in agency, 151
Deliverables, over the fence, 116
anti-pattern, 132
case study, 136
code quality, 122–124
of fences and obstacles, 119–122
making the case, 124–131
collaborate across the project timeline,
130–131
deliver awesome products, 131
find a shared rhythm, 129–130
pattern, 132–135
battle to the planners, 132
breaking down the fence, 133–134
bring your defense, 135
champion of design, 134
make the value proposition
obvious, 133
meet and greet, 133
sharing a rhythm, 135
track inefficiencies, 135
tearing down the fence, 118–119
Departments, 8, 9, 17, 24, 25, 28, 76

Design assumption, 164
anti-pattern, 174
infliction of, 178
case study, 179–181
design consulting, 179
designers belong inside the team, 180
integrating design into the whole team,
180–181
research is the key, 181
whole team needs to be user-centric, 181
creating design, 166
"creative" isn't noun, 170
easier sharing, not-invented-here
bias, 171
feeding back, 172
get HiPPO on board, 173
hero designer, 168
live in designed world, 169
note from authors, 166
pair design, 171
pattern, 174–177
collaborative workshops, 174
design the box, 176
dot voting, 176
i-invented-this pattern, 177
Kate Rutter's skills map, 177
moodboards, 175
paper mockups, 175
principles to strive for, 177–178
empower the nondesigners, 178
facilitation magic, 178
frame of reference, 178
pairing for design and development, 178
respect, 177
transparency, 177
use everyday language, 177
role-playing, 176
sketching, 175
storyboarding, 175
word association, 176
people view creativity as risk, 173–174
pitchslapped, 168
pretentious little jerks, 167
toothbrush theory, 171
understanding design, 166
well-intended suggestions, 172
Design-based key performance indicators
(KPIs), 35
Design-centric organization, hallmark of, 40
Design-centric working environments, 187
Design project, 194
Design studios, 147, 299–301
best for, 299
exercise, 301
declare goals, 301

Design studios *(cont.)*
    dot voting, 301
    1-up sketching, 301
    6-up sketching, 301
  ideas generation in, 300
  outcome, 301
  participants, 300
  resources, 300
  time, 300
Design Thinking, 31
Design vocabulary, 172
Dialects, 5
Digital business, 173
Dipping, 274
Disagreement, 5, 222
Disco-ball jacket, 46
Discovery process, 187, 255
Documents, 148
Doers, 119
Domain-specific language, 7
Dot voting, 308
Downs, Chris, 70

**E**

EasyWidget website, 71
Eat for well-being, 276, 277
  avoid, 278
  best for, 276
  get more of, 277
Elevator pitches, 32, 289–290
  best for, 289
  concept, 290
  construction of, 290
  crafting, 33
  exercise, 290
  outcome, 290
  participants, 289
  resources, 289
  time, 289
Emotionally draining
    process, 65
Empathy maps, 17, 56, 58
Engineering organizations, 34
Ethnographic research, 35
Etiquette, 12, 13
Exercise, 274
  breathing, 272
  business model canvas, 292
  design studios, 301
  dipping, 274
  elevator pitches, 290
  hypotheses testing, 305

  looping, 274
  meditation, 279
  mindful listening, 274
  storyboard scenarios, 299
  yoga, 280
Experience map, 56, 57, 296–297
  best for, 296
  exercise, 297
  outcome, 297
  participants, 296
  resources, 296
  time, 296
Experience principles, 59

**F**

Facebook, 87
Face-to-face conversation, 205
  trumps, 125
Fake it till you become it, 274, 275
  best for, 275
  exercise, 276
  lifestyle, 276
  time, 276
Feedback, 54, 62, 151, 172
  aspects of, 228
  assessment, 265
  lack of, 222
  loops, 240
  sessions, 55, 230, 231, 264
Fishbone diagram, 246
Flow in anti-patterns, identification and
    fixation, 263
Freiermuth, Sophie, 232
Functional grammar, 187–191
Function-specific key performance indicators
    (KPIs), 36

**G**

Gain agreement, 231
  positive agreement, 48
Gamestorming, 289
Gimmicks, 150
Glycemic index (GI), 277
Goals
  anti-pattern, inflict of, 48–49
  not embracement, 38
    anti-pattern, 43
    onto the right path, 40–42
    patterns, 44–48

active agreement, 44–45
canonical source of, 44
co-design, 46–48
consciously internalize, 45–46
present in context, 46
stakeholders are people, too, 46
sore thumb paradox, 42–43
when, in it, 43–44
Good feedback, 63. *See also* Feedback
Goodwill, 248, 251
Gothelf, Jeff, 148
Grinblo, Evgenia, 112
Group design techniques, 284
business model canvas. *See* Business model canvas
design studio, 299–301. *See also* Design studio
design the box. *See* Box, designing of
dot voting, 308, 308c
elevator pitch. *See* Elevator pitch
facilitate group, 288
hypotheses testing, 303–305. *See also* Hypotheses testing
map the experience. *See* Experience map
moodboarding for personas. *See* Personas, moodboarding for
people to invite, 286–287
prioritization, 307
matrix, 309
retrospective, 305–307
best for, 306
exercise, 307
outcomes, 307
participants, 306
resources, 306
time, 306
role-playing service. *See* Service, role-playing
in the room, 288–289
storyboard. *See* Storyboard scenarios
time to budget, 287
try out new formats, 289
Group design workshop formats, 286
Group exercise formats, 286

Human communication. *See* Communication
Hypotheses testing, 303–305
best for, 303
exercise, 305
outcome, 305
participants, 304
resources, 304
time, 304

**I**

Ideation
process, 171
sessions, 181
IDEO method cards, 111
IKEA effect
beware, 143–145
in tone, 210
Implementation, 119
Incentives
financial, 25
piecemeal provision of, 26
Index cards, 125
Informal social occasions, 209
Information architecture, 40
In-person communication, 87
Instant testable prototype, 299
Interactions, 12
behaviors and business-design links, 124
design, 241, 242, 265
designer, 6, 18, 19
grammar, 137
interpersonal, 86
low-fidelity, 197
social, 6
Internet, 78, 90
Interpretations, 16, 204
Introverts *vs.* extroverts, 78
Ivory towers, pictures of, 167

**J**

Journey map, 10

**H**

Half-silvered mirror, 65, 68
Hero designer, 168
Hierarchy, 205
Highest paid person's opinion (HiPPO), 173
on board, 173
HiPPO. *See* Highest paid person's opinion (HiPPO)

**K**

Kerth, Norm, 45
Key performance indicators (KPIs), 22–37
anti-pattern, 28

Key performance indicators *(cont.)*
 inflict of, 31–33
  handle organizational change
   singlehanded, 31–33
 bikeshedding, 27
 case study, 34–36
 challenges of, 32
 clashes, 26
 customer-based. *See* Customer-based key
  performance indicators (KPIs)
 design-based. *See* Design-based key
  performance indicators (KPIs)
 elevator pitch, construction, 32, 34
 function-specific. *See* Function-specific key
  performance indicators (KPIs)
 gap, 35
 intrinsic motivation, 25
 organizations measurement successfullness,
  24–25
 patterns, 29–31
  diligent discovery, 29–30
  don't butt heads, 30
  tu casa es mi casa, 30
 success, definition, 26
Kick-off session, 105

**L**

Label police, 111
Lean startup, 80
 iterative build–measure–learn loop of, 82
Legal stenographers, 87
Lifestyle, for relaxation technique, 276
Linear waterfall process, 81
Linguistic disarray, 105
Looping, 274
Low-fidelity wireframes, 62

**M**

Maps, 55
Meditation, 278
 best for, 279
 exercise, 279
 time, 279
Meetings, 12–14, 17, 215
Mental model method, 112
Metaphor, 8, 17, 167
Method cards, 111
Mind-body considerations, in tone, 213
Mindful conversation, 274
Mindful listening, 274

Minimum viable product (MVP), 80, 148, 189
Mobile project walls, 106
Motivation, 40, 68, 278
 of design disciplines, 31
 intrinsic, 25
Motivations, 40
Multilingual projects, 19
MVP. *See* Minimum viable product (MVP)

**N**

Natural human communication, 76
Navigational model, 8
Nelson, Sarah, 94
Net promoter score (NPS), 34
New product development (NPD), 76
New York City technology, 200
Nodder, Chris, 179
Nonjudgmental language, 30
Nonverbal communication, 274
Nonverbal conversations, 205
Non-verbal signs, 83
Norwegian Department of Defense, 19
NPD. *See* New product development (NPD)
NPS. *See* Net promoter score (NPS)
Nuclear reactor, design, 27

**O**

Objectivity, definition of, 186–187
Organizational silos, 76
Organizations
 handle, change singlehanded, 31–33
 measurement successfullness,
  24–25
Osterwalder, Alex, 291

**P**

Page hierarchy, 175
Pan narrans, 61
Paper prototype, 152
Paraphrased playback, 211
Parasympathetic nervous system, 271
Parkinson's law, 27
Passionate disagreement, 207
Patterns, 10–16
 concept of, 88
 lowering the wall, 14–16
 meeting after the meeting, 14

meeting before the meeting, 13
    and meeting after the meeting, 12–13
play it back, 16
stakeholder safari, 11–12
step back, 16
Perfection, insisting on, 184
    anti-pattern, 195
        infliction of, 198
    case study, 198–200
        articulating objective and subjective
            design, strategy for, 199
        design types, provisional taxonomy of, 199
        product design, 199
        user experience design, 200
        user interface design, 200
        visual design, 199
    delivering on your vision, 186–187
        defining objectivity, 186–187
    inspiration from start-up entrepreneurs, 194
    introducing functional grammar, 187–190
    knowing when you're done, 193
    launch your idea, 194
    pattern, 195–197
        checking in with yourself, 195–196
        design/UX debt, 196–197
        divide form and function, 197
        pairing with developers, 197
        90% rule, 197
        sketch i code, 197
    setting expectations, 187–188
    sustainable pace, 192–193
    trade-offs, 191
    UX debt, 193
Perfectionism, 187, 192, 195
Permission, 15, 155
Perpetual beta mentality, 194
Personas, 55, 125
    example, 56
    moodboarding for, 302, 303
        best for, 302
        exercise, 303
        outcome, 303
        participants, 302
        resources, 303
        time, 302
Persuasive design techniques, 223, 224
Photography, 140
Photoshop, 179
Physical cards, 128
Pivotal Tracker, 128
Pixel-perfect solution, 168
Planners, 119, 133
Polite fiction, 226
Positive disagreement, 228
    patterns, 146
Power of silence, 212–213

Pratchett, Terry, 61
Pre-project kickoff meetings, 90
Prioritization, 307
    matrix, 309
Process maps, 55
Product
    concept, 141
    creation process, 222
    delivery process, 119
    design, 199
        lifecycle, 132
    development cycle, 148
    development process, 223
Production-ready code, 122
Product owner (PO), 141
Professional designer, 198
Programming community, 171
Project delivery, 159
Project life cycle, 128
Project manager, 26, 83
Public-facing product, 6
PUMA project, 19

Q

Quality assurance (QA), 76
Quality feedback, 63. See also Feedback

R

Reflective listening, 211
Regressions, 123
Relaxation techniques
    breathing, 271, 272
        best for, 271, 273
        exercise, 272
        stay present, 273
        time, 272, 273
    eat for well-being, 276, 277
        avoid, 278
        best for, 276
        get more of, 277
    Stay present, 274
        dipping, 274
        looping, 274
        mindful listening, 274
    fake it till you become it, 274, 275
        best for, 275
        exercise, 276
        lifestyle, 276
        time, 276

Relaxation techniques *(cont.)*
  meditation, 278
    best for, 279
    exercise, 279
    time, 279
  in the moment, 271
  at work, 268
  yoga, 279, 280
Respondent fatigue, 210
Retrospective prime directive, 264
Return on investment (ROI), 5, 43
Review, 54, 59
  control of, 65
  successive rounds of, 64
Roadmap, 190
Root business value, 247
Rule of thumb, 61, 286

## S

*The Science of Discworld II: The Globe*, 61
Scrum, 124
Seiden, Josh, 148
Self-deprecating humor, 15
Self-herding tendency, 45
Self-siloing, 91
Service
  based support system, 35
  blueprint, 109
  role-playing by, 294–296
    best for, 294
    exercise, 295–296
    outcome, 296
    participants, 295
    resources, 295
    time, 295
Sharpie markers, 175
Siloed model, 76
Siloed organizations, 12
Six Sigma quality assurance process, 245
Skype calls, 85
Skype video, 131
Software development, 76, 186
  anti-pattern, 86
  assumptions in, 121
  case study, 92
  collaborating in iterative environments,
    82–83
  focus in an open-plan world, 83–85
  locking out of their silo, 91
  old models of, 78
  patterns, 90
    carve out a space, 88
    life in mono pattern, 88

    mind-body considerations, 89
    push for in-person access, 87
    rear view mirror pattern, 90
    scary face pattern, 89
    sensible scheduling, 90
    simplify your tools, 90
    stenographers' pattern, 87
    turn off the information firehose, 90
  processes, new collaboration models, 78–82
  tips, 91
Solid communication foundation, 110
Sore thumb paradox, 42–43
  situation, 43
Speaking different languages, 9
  anti-pattern, 9
  case study, 18–20
Split high-fidelity visual design, 197
Sprint rhythm, 129
Stakeholders, 6, 10, 11, 17, 26, 41, 48, 62, 65,
    104, 135, 170, 178, 216
  are people, too, 46
  feedback in, 54
  needs of, 43
  nondesigner, 41
  out-of-domain, 66
  performance, 29
  requirements, 42
Stakeholder safaris, 11–12, 17
  round of, 12
Standard banners, 40
Static documents, 143
Stephen Anderson's Mental Notes™ cards, 111
Stickies, 175
Storyboard scenarios, 298, 299
  best for, 298
  exercise, 299
  outcome, 299
  participants, 298
  resources, 299
  time, 299
Story card, 125
Story maps, 56, 58
Subjectivity, 186
Success metrics, 26
Sunk Cost Fallacy, 250
Sustainable pace, 192–193
Sympathetic nervous system, 270

## T

Teams, 130
  members, 180
Technical debt, 123
Third-party service, 121

Toftøy-Andersen, Eli, 18
Tone
    anti-pattern, 211
    confrontational/misunderstanding of tone,
        216–217
    gaps in understanding, 206
    IKEA effect strikes again, 210
    nonverbal, not unimportant, 205
    pattern, 211–216
        break it up, 213
        encountered this anti-pattern, 216
        encourage feedback at natural
            breaks, 215
        meeting before the meeting and meeting
            after the meeting, 215
        mind-body considerations, 213
        mirror, mirror pattern, 214–215
        paraphrased playback pattern, 211
        power of silence, 212–213
        set expectations, 211
        subvert the script, 216
        yes, and... pattern, 212
    respondent fatigue, 210
    responding to, not content, 202
    tips, 217–218
    tone varies with culture, 206
        caveat, 206
    who you are and who you're perceived to be,
        208–209
Toothbrush theory, 171
Trade-offs, 191
Traditional static deliverables, 143
Translator, role as, 9
Trivial, 6, 7
Trust, 27, 41, 42

U

UCD. *See* User-centric design (UCD)
UID. *See* User interface design (UID)
User-centered designer, 100
User-centric design (UCD), 76
    product design, 206
User-centric workflows, 298
User experience (UX), 241, 311
    cardinal rule of, 216
    debt, 193, 196
    design, 200, 225, 242
        role of, 77
    designers, 5, 25
    discovery, 55
    jargon, 8
    key performance indicators (KPIs), 25
    lifecycle, 118

    practitioner, 83, 113
    process, 135, 169
    requirements, 229
    staff, 191
    title generator, 108
    value, 30, 248
    viewpoint, 124
    vision, 80
    vocabulary, 100
User feedback, 156
User interface design (UID), 200, 241
User journeys, 100, 109
User-tested prototype, 181
UXers, 77, 100, 120, 131, 140
    opportunities for, 151

V

Validating hypotheses, 159
Verbal commitment, 45
Verbal stress, 205
Version control system, 7
Virtuous cycle, 41
Visual design, 199
Vocabulary, 6, 102, 109, 204

W

Wacom tablet, 88
Walking meetings, 89
Wand, Richard, 254, 256
Waterfall-based delivery process, 119
Waterfall method, 79
Waterfall model, 79
Wireframes, 8, 77, 241
"$5 word" effect, 7
Workshop projects, 93
Wrap, 69

Y

Yoga, 280
    best for, 280
    child's pose, 281–282
    exercise, 280
    seated forward fold, 281
    styles of, 280
    time, 280
    tree pose, 280–281